Mixing in Pro Tools®: Skill Pack

Second Edition

Brian Smithers

Course Technology PTR

A part of Cengage Learning

COURSE TECHNOLOGY
CENGAGE Learning™

Australia • Brazil • Japan • Korea • Mexico • Singapore • Spain • United Kingdom • United States

COURSE TECHNOLOGY
CENGAGE Learning

**Mixing in Pro Tools®: Skill Pack,
Second Edition**
Brian Smithers

**Publisher and General Manager, Course
Technology PTR:** Stacy L. Hiquet

Associate Director of Marketing: Sarah
Panella

Manager of Editorial Services: Heather
Talbot

Marketing Manager: Mark Hughes

Acquisitions Editor: Orren Merton

Project Editor and Copy Editor:
Kim Benbow

Technical Reviewer: Colin MacQueen

Editorial Services Coordinator:
Jen Blaney

Interior Layout: MPS Limited,
A Macmillan Company

Cover Designer: Mike Tanamachi

CD-ROM Producer: Brandon Penticuff

Indexer: Sharon Shock

Proofreader: Laura Gabler

For product information and technology assistance, contact us at
Cengage Learning Customer & Sales Support, 1-800-354-9706

For permission to use material from this text or product, submit all requests online at **www.cengage.com/permissions**
Further permissions questions can be emailed to
permissionrequest@cengage.com

Library of Congress Control Number: 2009933320

ISBN-13: 978-1-59863-972-8

ISBN-10: 1-59863-972-2

Course Technology, a part of Cengage Learning
20 Channel Center Street
Boston, MA 02210
USA

Cengage Learning is a leading provider of customized learning solutions with office locations around the globe, including Singapore, the United Kingdom, Australia, Mexico, Brazil, and Japan. Locate your local office at: **international. cengage.com/region**

Cengage Learning products are represented in Canada by Nelson Education, Ltd.

For your lifelong learning solutions, visit **courseptr.com**

Visit our corporate website at **cengage.com**

Printed in the United States of America
1 2 3 4 5 6 7 11 10 09

To Wesley R. Smithers, Jr.: "Junior" to his folks (despite his objections), "Smitty" to his school and Navy pals, "Wes" to our Mom, "Dad" to the four of us—and a hero to me. I miss you, Dad.

Acknowledgments

Thanks to the team at Cengage Learning, especially Orren Merton and Kim Benbow, for helping shape this book and bring it to life. I am deeply indebted to my brain trust at Digidesign, especially Andrew Hagerman, for patiently helping me track down even the tweakiest tidbits. Thanks also to Colin MacQueen for being my technical reviewer and making sure I got it right.

I am continually challenged and inspired by my colleagues at Full Sail University, whose appetite for learning is second only to their commitment to teaching. Thanks to Jeremy Burnum for keeping me on my toes, Ryan Summers for putting everything in perspective, Lee Riley for helping make sense of it all, Mike Orlowski for always assuming I know what he's talking about even when he's talking way over my head, Atom Troy for his relentless enthusiasm, John Berry for having a big heart and a probing mind, Eric Abraham for being the devil on my shoulder when necessary, and to the rest of our Audio Workstations team for bringing their incredibly diverse perspectives to bear for the betterment of all.

I would have never put virtual pen to virtual paper without the encouragement of my great friend Tony Hill, who prodded me to pick up the phone and call editor David Battino. David gave me my first writing opportunity—he is a gifted editor who always makes me a better writer. I am grateful for the inspiration and encouragement of my friend and mentor Tom Macklin, the greatest undiscovered author of our time. The fantastic crew at *Electronic Musician*, past and present—Steve Oppenheimer, Dennis Miller, Gino Robair, Len Sasso, Geary Yelton, and company—continually challenge and inspire me, and I am grateful to be part of the *EM* extended family. Thanks also to Paul Pettingale at *Music Tech Magazine* for giving me an ongoing outlet for software tutorials.

I thank God for myriad blessings, most especially the love and support of my family and friends. Thanks to my beloved wife Barb for her encouragement, support, and comfort. Thanks to my parents for helping me believe in a world where anything is possible. Finally, I would not have retained an ounce of sanity through this process without the feline wisdom of Nermal, Hillary, and Leopold, who regularly reminded me that nothing else matters but their happiness.

About the Author

Brian Smithers is a musician, conductor, composer, and educator who has been performing and teaching music for more than three decades. His extraordinarily diverse professional and artistic life has taken him from the concert hall to the nightclub, from the recording studio to the classroom. Equally at home performing in jazz combos and symphony orchestras, he is also in demand as an arranger and recording engineer. For several years, while he conducted the world-famous Walt Disney World Band by day, he led a double life as a music technology writer for *Electronic Musician*, *Music & Computers*, and *Keyboard*, a calling he pursues to this day. Mr. Smithers was at the vanguard of the movement to use notebook computers for live remote recording, performance, and production. As Department Chair of Workstations at Full Sail University in Winter Park, Florida, Mr. Smithers coordinates and guides the curriculum of what is arguably the largest digital audio workstation lab environment in the world.

Contents

Chapter 8
Bouncing Your Mix
155

Chapter 9
Doubling Parts
179

Chapter 10
Stems and Submixes
189

Chapter 11
Advanced Dynamics   199

Chapter 12
Stereo Enhancement   211

Chapter 13
External Effects   225

Chapter 14
Managing Mix Resources   233

Index. 245

Introduction

Mixing in Pro Tools: Skill Pack, Second Edition is designed to help you boost your understanding of the art and craft of creating great-sounding mixes in Digidesign's industry-standard DAW Pro Tools. Starting with the basics of essential processors and working up to advanced signal routing and sophisticated sonic manipulation, this book will boost your confidence in your ability to produce polished professional-sounding mixes. As you work with the sample sessions on the included CD-ROM, you will develop your ears as you expand your knowledge.

I have aimed this book squarely at Pro Tools LE and M-Powered users, because there are so many of us out there, and because a fair percentage of Pro Tools HD users are already well-versed in the subject. However, it's important to understand that virtually everything in this book applies to the high-end Pro Tools HD software as well. To be sure, many readers will find themselves soon enough sitting in front of an expensive Pro Tools rig applying the skills they learned on a Digi 003 or Mbox 2.

Although this book was written on version 8.0 of the Pro Tools software, it is sure to be valid through several subsequent software revisions. The fundamental signal flow of the Pro Tools mixer, the operation of EQs and compressors, and the essence of time-based routing are not going to be thrown out any time soon. Perhaps a new automation behavior or enhancements to mix grouping will be added, but these can easily be absorbed by anyone who reads this book in its current version.

Who Are You?

You are someone interested in learning more about mixing. You know how to get good-sounding basic tracks, but you want to know how to polish and tweak them as well as how to make them fit together better. You see mixing as part of the creative process, an extension of playing the right part on the right instrument into the right microphone.

You have a working knowledge of Pro Tools LE or M-Powered. You needn't be an expert, but I will not guide you step by step through basic functions, such as file management, track creation, switching views, controlling playback, and so forth. In Chapter 7, "Automation," you will need to know basic editing tools and techniques to edit automation graphically. (For a really good introduction to Pro Tools, read *Pro Tools LE 8 Ignite!* by Andrew Hagerman, also from Cengage Learning.)

You want a practical, hands-on approach. Although I'll walk you through the essentials, I won't delve deeply into theory in these pages. Instead, you'll use your hands and, more importantly, your *ears* to work your way through a series of tutorials, exploring important mixing concepts from the fundamentals to cool advanced tricks. I do, however, encourage you to find out as much as you can about the theory behind it all. Although your ears should always guide your mixing efforts, your knowledge can get you out of a jam one day and inspire your creativity the next.

You own or have access to a system running Pro Tools LE or Pro Tools M-Powered. It doesn't matter which, as they are virtually identical. Unless I specify otherwise, every time I refer to Pro Tools LE it applies equally to Pro Tools M-Powered. If you own Pro Tools Essential, you will find that all of the basics apply to you, as well. PT Essential has a more limited feature set, but it's fundamentally the same as LE and M-Powered. Furthermore, everything in this book works in high-powered Pro Tools HD systems, so your experience will serve you well if you find yourself sitting in front of the "heavy hardware." (For many users, that's a key attraction of owning a Pro Tools LE system.)

You are running a Mac or a PC—it doesn't make any difference at all. Pro Tools LE and M-Powered run identically on the two platforms, so use whichever makes you most comfortable. I've used screen shots from both to illustrate the chapters, so you'll get used to seeing that the only differences are cosmetic.

Who Wrote That Song?

Everything on the CD was written and recorded by me in my modest home studio with some help from Ryan Summers, who contributed the brilliant example of vocal sibilance in Chapter 4, "Special Effects." The majority of the sounds were created within the computer using commonly available software instruments. All saxophone and flute parts were played by yours truly. Virtually all mixing was done within Pro Tools M-Powered using the included plug-ins. (Of course, I left most of the mixing for you!)

We retain all rights to these works, and include them here expressly for your use in the context of this book. You are free to use the material in the book's exercises and in your personal private pursuit of mixing prowess. Any other use, including copying, sharing, interpolation, sampling, modification, and the like is prohibited. See the enclosed license statement for complete information.

Who Am I?

First and foremost, I am a musician. Everything I have done in my career stems from that simple truth. I grew up playing the saxophone, and for most of my career I have made my living as a performer. Early on, however, my brother Mike explained to me some of the ways in which a recording studio influences a band's music. Although I had no plans to become an engineer, words such as overdub, mix, EQ, reverb, and delay worked their way into my vocabulary. Most significantly, I started listening to recorded music differently, noticing the efforts of more than musicians on each record.

I learned basic synthesis and recording in Dr. Kellermeyer's electronic music class in high school. A friend worked as a jazz disc jockey at the tiny local radio station, and he shared his budding knowledge of broadcast engineering with me. Other friends gave freely of their time and wisdom along the way, most notably Tony Hill, my "wiring expert."

Then my long-lost twin brother (in every sense other than genetics), Andy Hagerman, showed me the wonders of MIDI, digital audio, and computers, changing my world for good. We wrote and recorded music together, absorbed everything we could about the technology, and wound up teaching it to others together at one of the country's most prominent schools of recording arts. There I have the privilege of "paying it forward" to aspiring engineers and musician/engineers whose paths to and from Full Sail are as unique as their footprints.

No matter where you are on your path, you are the product of your dreams, your efforts, and your influences. You've had friends and teachers along the way to guide and inspire you. You've had creative successes that motivated you and technical setbacks that schooled you. I'm honored that you have chosen this book to help you grow to the next level, and I hope it serves you well.

How Does This Work?

Each chapter is accompanied by a Pro Tools session. Drag the entire session folder from the book's CD to your hard drive, open the session, and follow along. Note that you cannot simply run the session from the CD, as Pro Tools won't allow it. You can drag the entire contents of the CD to your hard drive if you have room, but each session is self-contained, so this isn't necessary.

If you are using any version of Pro Tools 7, you may see a warning when you open the session that it was created using a later version. Certain aspects of the Pro Tools 8 session format will be lost. Most of these will have no effect within the context of the book's exercises, so you can safely ignore the warning.

Each chapter's session has been divided into *memory locations*. If you are unfamiliar with Pro Tools memory locations, you will learn about them in Chapter 5, "The Rough Mix." Until you get there, suffice it to say that each time the text tells you to advance to a particular memory location, you need only click its name in the Memory Locations window to rearrange the session for the relevant exercise. This window is open by default in every session, but if it should ever disappear on you, just recall it from the Windows menu.

Most of the memory locations are designed to loop a section while you make adjustments and listen to the results. It's essential that you listen carefully as you change parameters so you can get the sound of each scenario and each processor in your ears—mixing is *nothing* without critical listening! If the section doesn't loop, be sure Loop Playback is enabled. If the selection is lost when you stop playback, press Start+N (Ctrl+N on a

Mac) to disable the Timeline Insertion/Play Start Marker Follows Playback setting (also found under Operation Preferences).

Wherever appropriate, I have included my own effects settings in the form of *plug-in settings*. These are equivalent to the presets on a hardware effects processor and will allow you to compare your results to mine. Just call up my preset from the Settings menu on the plug-in in question.

Everything in this book can be done using only the plug-ins that are included with every Pro Tools LE or M-Powered system. If you are using Pro Tools 7.x, you will not have the Creative Collection plug-ins that were introduced in Pro Tools 8, so you will need to substitute the EQ III or Dynamics III where appropriate. Of course, there are plenty of fancy third-party plug-ins on the market, and you may own some of them already. Feel free to use them—the principles of operation are the same, even though the sound will be different.

To be an efficient Pro Tools user, you should learn as many of its keyboard shortcuts as possible. There is a complete list of these in the Help menu—print them, study them, and use them regularly. Whenever possible, I will include relevant keyboard shortcuts throughout these chapters, using Windows modifier keys with Macintosh modifiers in parentheses. Typically, the Mac Control (Ctrl) key is substituted for the Windows Start key, the Mac Option (Opt) key for the Alt key, and the Apple, or Command (Cmd), key for Control (Ctrl). The Shift key needs no substitution.

Although the PC keyboard has two Enter keys, the Mac has a Return key on the alphanumeric keyboard and an Enter key on the numeric keypad. Since Pro Tools started life as a Macintosh application, it views these two keys differently. To avoid confusion, I will always specify "Enter on the numeric keypad" when I mean the Mac Enter key. Otherwise, I am always referring to the alphanumeric Enter (Return) key.

Basic Mixing Concepts

Although I will necessarily touch on many aspects of the theory, philosophy, and practice of mixing, they are not the real focus of this book. This is a book on mixing in Pro Tools. There are excellent books available on the art and science of mixing, and I encourage you to read several of them as you develop your mixing skills. (I highly recommend *The Mixing Engineer's Handbook* by Bobby Owsinski, also from Cengage Learning.)

Some fundamental mixing concepts you should keep in mind as you work your way through this book are as follows:

- **Use good studio monitors.** The more accurate your monitoring system, the more accurate your judgments while mixing. Headphones are a poor substitute for good monitors.

- **Mind your room's acoustics.** The shape, size, configuration, and contents of your mixing room affect its sonics and can have a profound effect on your mixing. There are numerous books and products available to help you optimize your monitoring environment.

- **Monitor at a reasonable volume.** Although listening at high volume may be exciting, it is not very accurate. Our ears are more accurate at moderate volumes—not too soft and not too loud.

- **Protect your hearing.** A mix engineer can't afford hearing damage. In addition to monitoring at a reasonable volume, you should wear high-quality musicians' earplugs when you go to clubs, concerts, or theme parks, when you mow the lawn, and whenever your ears are likely to be exposed to potentially damaging volumes.

- **Listen to great mixes.** In addition to listening critically to as many great mixes as you can find, you should deliberately compare your current mix to your favorite examples within the same genre.

- **Document thoroughly.** Name your tracks, sessions, regions, and files in such a way that you will be able to tell what's what a year from now. Keep a log of what works and why so you can build on your success.

- **Have a plan.** When you first listen to a song, figure out what makes it tick and how you can capitalize on that. Devise a strategy to enhance the song's strengths and overcome its weaknesses.

- **Go somewhere.** Just as the musical arrangement changes and grows during the course of the song, so should your mix. Process the vocal differently in the chorus than in the verse. Make a background part more prominent in the second half of the song. Have a direction.

- **Serve the music.** Don't simply try to impose your will on a song. Your mix should serve the artist's vision, not rework it in your image.

Now it's time to put the CD in your drive, copy the Chapter 01 session folder to your audio drive, and start mixing!

Companion Website Downloads

You may download the companion website files from www.courseptr.com/downloads.

CD-ROM Downloads

If you purchased an ebook version of this book, and the book had a companion CD-ROM, you may download the files from www.courseptr.com/downloads.

1 Equalization

M ixing is the penultimate step in music production, followed only by mastering. All the performances have been captured—the mix engineer doesn't get to ask for another take or a different instrument. Still, the mix engineer has the daunting task of ensuring that everything fits together in a cohesive sonic landscape.

The mix engineer employs a variety of powerful tools to sculpt both individual sounds and groups of sounds. These tools can alter the timbre, dynamics, temporal character, balance, and relative position of the musical parts. We'll explore each of these tools in turn, and we'll start with equalization.

Equalization is the manipulation of *timbre*, or tonal color. More specifically, an equalizer is a processor that enhances or reduces specific portions of a sound's frequency spectrum. For example, if a snare drum has a nasty ring to it, you can use an equalizer to zero in on the offending frequency and reduce it, making the snare sound more palatable. If the singer got too close to the microphone and ended up sounding a bit too boomy, you can roll off some low end to clean up the sound.

Equalization is also used to change the apparent balance of competing parts. By emphasizing a guitar's high frequencies, for example, you can make it sound brighter. This draws the listener's attention to the guitar without actually making the part louder. Conversely, if you turn down the low frequencies of a kick drum, you can stop it from interfering with the bass solo.

Like most equalizers, the DigiRack EQ III (see Figure 1.1) offers several *bands* of processing. Each band affects a different user-definable frequency range. A band ordinarily has three controls: frequency, gain, and bandwidth. Frequency determines the focal point, or center frequency, of the band's effect, while gain determines the degree of the band's effect. Bandwidth defines how far from the center frequency the effect will be applied, allowing you to boost or cut a very narrow or very wide range of frequencies. In EQ III, bandwidth is labeled *Q*, which is sometimes said to stand for "quality factor" because it determines the character, or quality, of the effect.

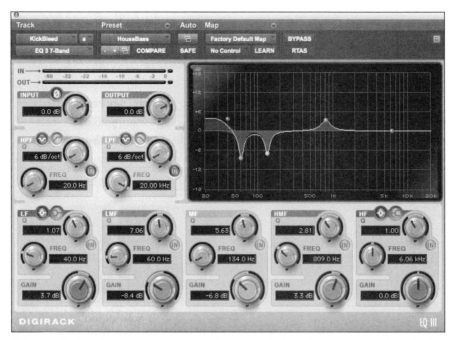

Figure 1.1 The DigiRack EQ III provides multiple bands of equalization. Each band includes controls for frequency, gain, and bandwidth (Q), and some bands offer a choice of filter type.

Note: Digidesign uses the Roman numeral III everywhere but in the plug-in list, where it uses the Arabic numeral 3. To avoid confusion, I'll stick with "EQ III," so when you open the plug-in list, you'll know what I mean, right?

High-Pass and Low-Pass Filters

Sometimes the job of an equalizer is quite simple—to get rid of all sound above or below a certain frequency. This is taken care of by a high-pass filter or a low-pass filter. They do exactly what their names suggest. A *high-pass filter* allows all sounds higher than a certain frequency to pass unaffected while removing all sounds lower than that frequency, and a *low-pass filter* does the opposite. (If you think they should have been called "low cut" and "high cut," respectively, you're not alone!) I'll demonstrate by using high-pass and low-pass filters to remove unwanted sounds.

1.   Start Pro Tools and open the session called Chapter 01.ptf.

2.   In the Memory Locations window, found in the lower-right corner of your screen, click memory location number 1, which is called Low-Pass.

Note: The shortcut key for recalling a memory location is to type a period, the number of the memory location on the numeric keypad, and another period. To recall memory location number 5, for example, type the three characters between these brackets: [.**5**.]. You can get the Memory Location window out of the way by pressing Ctrl+5 (Cmd+5) on the numeric keypad. When you need it again, use the same key combination to show it. Note, however, that it is not necessary for the Memory Location window to be open to recall memory locations with the shortcut.

3. If necessary, Start-click (Control-click) the Play button to enable Loop Playback.

4. Press the spacebar to begin playback, and you'll hear a kick drum with a lot of snare and hi-hat bleeding in. Ideally, you'd like to hear only the kick drum without a trace of the snare or hi-hat. The only way to accomplish that would be to record each drum in a different room, but the drummer's arms probably aren't that long. You can, however, use a low-pass filter to reduce the amount of bleed without affecting the kick drum significantly.

5. On any insert of the Kick track, call up the 1-Band EQ III (mono). Note that you don't need to stop playback to insert a plug-in. You could get the same results with the 4-Band or 7-Band EQ III, but the 1-Band EQ III makes less of a demand on your CPU.

6. Click the Low-Pass filter Type button and see how the frequency graph changes. The graph now shows a flat line at 0 dB from 20 Hz to 1 kHz, indicating that no change is being made to the lower part of the frequency spectrum. Starting at 1 kHz, the line goes gradually down to show that the volume is being reduced progressively for higher frequencies.

7. Turn the Q knob to see how the slope of this graph changes. As you can see in Figure 1.2, the most gradual rate of change is 6 dB/oct (decibels per octave), and the most abrupt rate of change the EQ III offers is 24 dB/oct. You want to draw a sharp line between the kick and the bleed-through, so set the slope to 24 dB/oct.

Note: Because a low-pass filter's Frequency knob determines the point above which sound is more or less cut off, it is commonly called the *cutoff frequency*. Note that with a low-pass filter, the Gain knob is disabled: All frequencies below 1 kHz pass unchanged, and all frequencies above that are gradually attenuated.

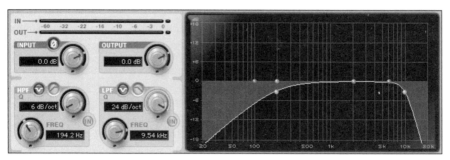

Figure 1.2 The slope (Q) of a low-pass or high-pass filter determines how quickly the equalizer changes from allowing frequencies to pass to blocking frequencies completely. On the left of the graph is a high-pass filter with a gradual 6 dB/oct slope. On the right is a high-pass filter with a sharp 24 dB/oct slope.

8. Turn the Frequency knob all the way up (to 20.0 kHz) and hit Play (that's the spacebar, right?) if you stopped to insert the EQ.

9. Slowly and steadily turn the Frequency knob down, listening carefully for any change in the sound. As the cutoff frequency moves from 20 kHz to 10 kHz, you'll hear a bit of a change in the hi-hat, but not much else because neither the snare nor the kick has much energy up there. Moving down from 10 kHz, you'll hear the hi-hat start to wane and the snare start to lose some sparkle. Starting at around 5 kHz, you'll hear the kick starting to be affected, too. By the time you get to 3 kHz, the hi-hat will be mostly gone. Most likely, though, you'll start to think that the kick has lost too much character, so find a spot between 3 and 5 kHz that gives you the best compromise of snare reduction and kick character.

10. Before you despair at still having to put up with some snare bleed-through, toggle the Bypass button on and off to hear how much better it sounds. Big improvement, isn't it?

11. Next, with the effect un-bypassed (the button will be gray), listen to the effect of changing the filter's slope. Turn the Q all the way down to 6 dB/oct and hear how much more snare is audible. Turn it back up to 24 dB/oct, and you'll hear the snare change significantly while the kick hardly changes at all. The steep slope lets you draw the sharpest distinction between the low frequencies that pass and the high frequencies that are reduced.

Note: Many of the examples, such as the one you just used, are intended to loop a section of audio so you can take as much time as you want to hear the changes you're making. This is a useful technique when you're trying to find the right settings for a short segment of audio. Should you find that the section is not looping, simply recall the memory location to re-establish the loop.

12.   Press the spacebar to stop playback, and close the plug-in window.

13.   Bring up memory location 2, called High-Pass, either by clicking it in the Memory Locations window or by using its shortcut key (.2.).

14.   Listen to this drum loop and imagine using just the snare, hi-hat, and clap parts with a different kick-drum part. You're going to do exactly the opposite of what you just did with the low-pass filter, filtering out as much of the kick as possible while retaining the character of the treble instruments.

15.   Because this is a stereo track, you get a choice of multi-channel plug-ins or multi-mono plug-ins. Later, you'll explore the difference between the two types, but for this exercise you can call up either version of the 1-Band EQ III.

16.   Using the same technique you used earlier—its mirror image, actually, because you're cutting out low frequencies this time—gradually reduce the kick drum to taste. Choose the high-pass filter, set its Q to 24 dB/oct, and pull its frequency all the way down to 20 Hz.

17.   Start playback and slowly raise the cutoff frequency, listening carefully to the effect of the filter. Between 20 and 100 Hz, you'll hear the boom of the kick drum fade away while very little else changes. From 100 to 300 Hz, you'll hear the kick continue to thin out as the snare loses a bit of low end. In some applications, this could be as far as you need to go. As you approach 500 Hz, the snare changes character quite a bit, but it still has enough presence to be useful; the kick, however, is now pretty insignificant. By 800 Hz, the snare is pretty lo-fi, and as you approach 2–3 kHz, it almost sounds like part of the hi-hat pattern.

Note: Instead of dragging the Frequency knob, you can simply grab the little gray dot on the EQ graph and drag it left and right.

By using a single band of EQ, you have changed a simple drum loop into a variety of different but complementary sounds. You could use the lo-fi setting for the song's intro, bypass the EQ to hear the full loop for the verse, use a moderate setting to get the kick out of the way of your alternate kick pattern during the chorus, and use the extreme setting for the break-down section in the middle of the song. There's an important lesson here: It's not the price, prestige, or complexity of your tools that determines the success of your mix—it's the imagination with which they're applied!

High and Low Shelving Filters

Often it's desirable to affect a range of frequencies without cutting them off altogether. For this purpose, a *shelving* (or *shelf*) filter is the tool of choice. A low shelving filter can boost or cut frequencies below the cutoff so that all low frequencies are treated equally. In other words, if the cutoff is 200 Hz and the gain is −4.5 dB, then 150 Hz will be reduced by 4.5 dB, 100 Hz will be reduced by 4.5 dB, 50 Hz will be reduced by 4.5 dB, and so forth. As shown in Figure 1.3, the graph of all these low frequencies being reduced by the same amount produces a level line below the cutoff—thus the "shelf" reference.

Figure 1.3 A shelving filter boosts or attenuates an entire band of frequencies (the "shelf") by the same amount.

The most familiar examples of shelving filters are the tone controls on a typical stereo. The bass control lets you boost or cut all low frequencies, and the treble control lets you boost or cut all high frequencies. EQ III adds variable cutoff and Q, as you would expect of a professional tool. Variable Q lets you choose the filter's slope—how quickly the transition from the unaffected band to the processed band is.

1. Using the same session as before (Chapter 01.ptf), go to memory location 3, Low Shelf. Listen to the loop and note that it's pretty bottom heavy. If you were to use it alone, that might be fine; but if you want it to blend with other elements—especially if you want to write a bass line or complementary kick-drum part—you'll need to reduce its low end a bit.

2. Insert the 1-Band EQ III on the track. It doesn't matter which insert you use or whether you use the multichannel or multi-mono version.

3. Click the Low-Shelf filter Type button.

4. Set the Gain value to −12 dB.

5. Click the Q value and type **0.8**, then press Enter.

6. Start playback and listen to how the low end has been reduced. With the gain turned down this far, the effect is almost like a high-pass filter, except that you can still hear a fair amount of the low end.

7. Slowly sweep the Frequency knob down, listening to how the sound changes. As you approach 350 Hz, you'll start to hear the most active synth bass become prominent. As you move below 200 Hz, you'll start to hear the slap bass kick in. Below about 80 Hz the simple synth bass dominates, and the lower you go the more it takes over.

8. Raise the cutoff back up to around 200 Hz and find the spot where you feel the appropriate frequency range is being affected.

9. Now raise the gain until you reach the proper amount of reduction. Once you've reached the proper gain reduction, you may want to tweak the cutoff a bit because, by changing the gain, you've also just changed the slope of the transition band.

Note: What's the "proper amount"? Well, that's for your ears to decide! It depends on several factors. First, what kind of sound are you after? If this loop is supposed to sit behind dialog, giving a subliminal feeling of agitation, you may want to reduce the bass frequencies substantially. If it's intended to work with a complementary kick drum, the proper amount of attenuation depends on the timbre of the kick. For now, your choice is arbitrary. (My choice is −6.4 dB at 290 Hz, for what it's worth!) Of course, if you really want to feel like you're out on the dance floor, why not turn up that bass? Just for sport, turn the gain up to between +2 and +4 dB. This accentuates the basses compared to the rest of the loop and points up another difference between a low-shelf filter and a high-pass filter: A shelving filter can ordinarily cut or boost the selected frequency band.

Note: In addition to dragging the dot on the EQ graph horizontally to change frequency (as you did previously), you can drag it vertically to change gain.

Controlling Clipping

You may also notice that something else about the sound changed when you boosted the gain: There's a sort of harsh, crunchy edge on all of the attacks now. That's the sound of *clipping*, the distortion that occurs when you turn a digital sound up too far. Note that the red light at the top of the meter on the track, called the clipping indicator, is illuminated (see Figure 1.4). The best way to avoid digital overload distortion is to avoid setting off the clipping indicator. The solution in this case is to turn down the Input knob on the EQ. That way, the signal is lowered as it enters the plug-in, so when you add gain to the low end it doesn't reach the level of clipping.

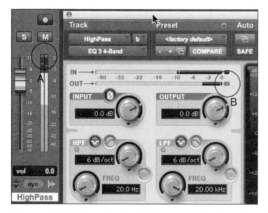

Figure 1.4 Clipping indicators on the track meter (A) and plug-in output meter (B) show that the level has distorted. Adjust the plug-in's input level to eliminate the clipping, and click the clipping indicators to reset them.

By default, the clipping indicators in Pro Tools stay red until you reset them, so you won't see the results of your input gain reduction right away. Turn the input down a few decibels, then click the track's clipping indicator to reset it. (On a stereo track, clicking either channel's clipping indicator resets both.) Wait for the loop to play through a complete cycle; if the clipping indicator goes off again, repeat the process. When you have arrived at a level that doesn't trip the red light, you're okay.

Before you leave this loop alone, let's try one more thing just for kicks. Turn the Q all the way up to 2.00 and turn the gain down quite a bit. Notice that now the graph shows a peak at the upper corner and a dip at the lower corner of the transition, as in Figure 1.5. This means that the frequencies close to the cutoff will be accentuated, and those close to the lower "elbow" will be de-emphasized. This characteristic is called *resonance*, and it is used to call attention to the filter. Sweep the filter's frequency up and down, and listen to the squirrelly sort of whooshing sound that moves with the cutoff. This would be an interesting effect to automate; you'll learn about this in Chapter 7, "Automation."

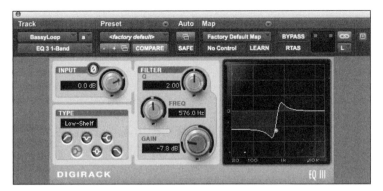

Figure 1.5 Setting the shelving filter's bandwidth (Q) to its maximum value creates an unusual sonic effect, known on a synthesizer as *resonance*, in which the cutoff frequency is accentuated.

Emphasizing Higher Frequencies

Go to memory location 4, High Shelf, and give it a listen. This string passage would sound perfectly fine for a classical recording, but it lacks the sizzle necessary to cut through a pop song. A bit of high-frequency emphasis courtesy of a high-shelf filter should do the trick.

1. Insert your trusty 1-Band EQ III on the track and set it up as a high-shelf filter. This time, start with a maximum boost in gain and a frequency of 20 kHz. Set the Q to 0.8 as before for a natural-sounding transition.

2. Gradually lower the frequency, listening carefully as always. At first, you won't hear much difference, as our ears are not very sensitive in the extreme high and low ranges. As you near 10 kHz, though, you'll hear the upper harmonics of the strings come to life. As you continue to lower the cutoff, you'll find a point at which the filter is starting to change the heart of the string timbre. This is too drastic—the goal is to give the sound some air without changing its essence. Roll the cutoff back up to around 8 kHz and lower the gain to 3 or 4 dB.

3. You've seen what happens when you increase the shelving filter's Q—let's see what happens when you lower it. As you pull the knob down, you'll see the curve flatten. The transition band becomes wider (remember, Q means bandwidth), making the change more gradual. Find a setting that lets the airiness of the shelf feel like a natural extension of the strings' core timbre.

Peak Filters

A *peak filter*, sometimes loosely referred to as a *band-pass filter*, is one that affects the sound only within a certain range of frequencies. Technically, the thing that distinguishes a peak filter from a band-pass filter is that a band-pass filter is passive, only attenuating frequencies outside its bandwidth, whereas a peak filter can also amplify whatever falls within its passband. Also, because the peak filter in EQ III can both increase and decrease the level within that band, it's probably more accurate to call it a *peak/notch filter.*

In the DigiRack EQ III, peak filters are fully parametric. The name *parametric* comes from the notion that all aspects (parameters) of the EQ are fully adjustable. As you've seen, you can adjust both relevant parameters of the high-/low-pass filters and all three relevant parameters of the shelving filters, but in common practice when we say parametric, we normally mean peak/notch filters.

In a peak EQ band, the Q (bandwidth) setting literally corresponds to the width of the band of frequencies being boosted or cut. Frequencies above or below the passband are not affected. Because there are cutoff frequencies at both the low and high ends of the passband, the Frequency setting actually refers to the *center frequency*, a point halfway between the two.

When you look at the actual Q values, it may seem backward to you that a large Q means a very narrow band and a small Q means a very wide band. This is because Q is the ratio of the center frequency to the range of frequencies being affected. So, for a center frequency of 1,000 Hz, affecting a range of 2,000 Hz means a Q of 0.5 ($1,000 \div 2,000$), while affecting a smaller range of 500 Hz means a Q of 2.0 ($1,000 \div 500$). The smaller bandwidth yields a larger Q value. If the math gives you a headache, just watch the width of the EQ curve change as you turn the knob (see Figure 1.6).

Removing Hum Using the Peak Filter

Go to memory location 5, Peak 1, and listen to the selection. You are listening to the air-conditioning hum in a concert hall, albeit turned up a bit for emphasis. This is the infamous electrical hum that engineers regularly encounter in various guises. In this case, the air conditioning threatens to distract listeners from the beautiful subtleties of the upcoming flute solo. You must reduce, if not eliminate, the distracting noise.

1. Insert a 1-Band EQ III on the track and set it to Peak mode.

2. Crank the gain all the way up—you're going to find the offending frequency by emphasizing it, and then you'll eliminate it by turning the gain down.

3. Set the Q to maximum, which of course means minimum bandwidth. A narrow band will help you zero in on the precise center frequency.

4. Sweep the filter and listen to the pitch of the boosted frequency. When you get to the right spot, you'll hear the hum jump out at you.

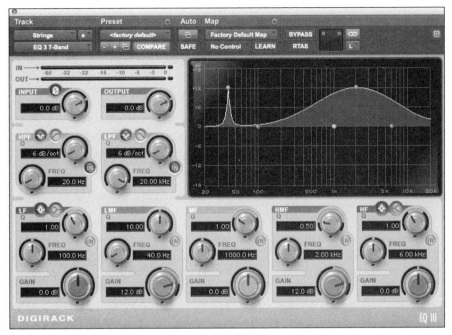

Figure 1.6   A high Q value, such as the low-mid filter's 10.00 (left), means a narrow bandwidth; a low Q, such as the high-mid filter's 0.50 (right) means a wide bandwidth.

5.   Carefully adjust the frequency until you've achieved the maximum boost.

6.   Now simply lower the gain to eliminate the offending hum. You can do this instantly by Shift-clicking on either the Gain knob or the appropriate control dot on the EQ graph. The curve will invert itself.

Note: When you're trying to pinpoint the hum's frequency, hold the Ctrl (Cmd) key to adjust the Frequency knob with greater precision. Ctrl-dragging (Cmd-dragging) to achieve finer parameter resolution is a technique that works on virtually all controls in Pro Tools, including third-party plug-ins.

You should have landed very close to 120 Hz. Because North American electrical systems run at 60 Hz, whenever electrical noise creeps in where it's not wanted, it occurs at this frequency or a multiple (harmonic) thereof. You'll need to listen carefully to be sure you haven't done more harm than good. Keeping the Q very high, as shown in Figure 1.7, helps ensure you're affecting as little of the musical spectrum as possible.

Figure 1.7 The EQ III in Peak mode notching out the drone of a rogue air conditioner.

In fact, you may find it preferable to put the EQ in Notch mode. The notch filter features an ultra-narrow bandwidth and automatically drops the gain as much as possible. For maximum rejection of a very specific frequency, the notch filter can be very useful. Just be sure it's not robbing you of any important musical material. Because this hum is at 120 Hz, where a great deal of musical activity occurs, I prefer to have the gain flexibility of the peak filter.

Basic Kick Drum EQ

Let's try working with some musical material. Recall memory location 6, Peak 2. This is a simple drum part, limited to kick, snare, and hi-hat for simplicity.

1. Click the name of the Kick track to select that track, then Shift-click the name of the Hi-Hat track to extend the selection to all three tracks.

2. Hold the Shift and Alt (Opt) keys while you insert a 7-Band EQ III on any one of the three tracks. An EQ will open on each track.

Note: Pro Tools follows the standard Windows and OS X techniques for making multiple selections. Shift-clicking selects all contiguous items within a range, and Ctrl-clicking (Cmd-clicking) selects multiple discontiguous items.

Note: Any time you want an operation to apply to all *selected* tracks in Pro Tools, hold the Shift and Alt (Opt) keys while performing the operation. Holding just the Alt (Opt) key applies the action to *all* tracks, whether selected or not.

---

3. Click the Solo (S) button on the Kick track so you can focus completely on its sound.

4. Before you start adjusting the kick's EQ, be sure the EQ window you're viewing is the right one. In the upper-left corner of the EQ window is the current track name, as shown in Figure 1.8. If it doesn't say Kick, click whatever it does say and choose Kick from the drop-down menu.

Figure 1.8 The top-left field in the plug-in window shows the current track. Clicking that field opens the Track selector, from which a different track may be chosen.

5. The 7-Band EQ III (see Figure 1.9) has five bands that can work as peak filters. Each has a limited frequency range, and they are arranged in the lower half of the plug-in window from left to right in order of ascending frequency range: low (LF), low-mid (LMF), mid (MF), high-mid (HMF), and high (HF). Low and high can also operate in Shelving mode, and in fact by default, they start in that mode when you insert the plug-in. Note also that you can enable each of the seven bands independently by clicking its IN button. Use the low band in Peak mode, crank up the gain, narrow the Q, and start sweeping the frequency.

6. Start from either the top or bottom of the frequency range and as you listen take note of the fact that different frequencies emphasize different aspects of the kick's character. You won't hear much below 30 Hz, regardless of how good your speakers are. There simply isn't that much energy in the drum that low. From 30 to 50 Hz you'll hear increasing amounts of the kick's dominant *boom*; near 80–150 Hz you'll note the *thud* that gives it drive, and in the vicinity of 300–500 Hz you'll hear a hollow character that you may not find very flattering. (Then again, you might love it!) Make mental (or physical) note of these frequencies, as you'll be using a different band to affect each one independently of the others.

7. Now turn this technique on its head and pull the gain *down* all the way. Sweep again, listening for any frequencies that make the overall sound better or worse by their absence. When you find one, disengage the band by clicking its IN button to make a quick sonic comparison. This will probably help you zero in on the exact hollow frequency and convince you of the value of those low boom and thud frequencies.

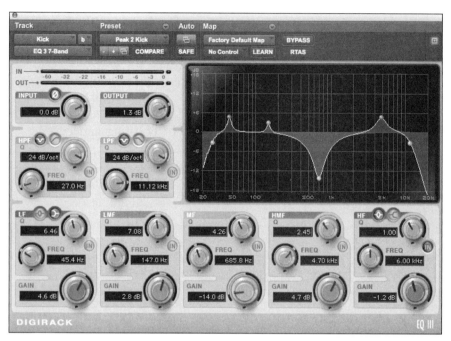

Figure 1.9 The 7-Band EQ III.

8. Next, sweep the high-mid band to see if there's anything useful above 500 Hz. Some engineers like to roll off all the high frequencies on a kick drum using the low-pass filter starting as low as 2 kHz, but you may find the *snap* of the beater on the head to be useful in helping the kick cut through a dense mix. You'll find that somewhere between 4 and 5 kHz on this drum.

Note: Notice that I'm not giving you exact frequencies. That's by design, and not just because I'm cruel! Mixing is all about the *sound*, and that means you must use your ears. After about a zillion hours of experimentation with mixing, you'll eventually develop the skills to know just by listening that you want to cut at 1.5 kHz and boost at 65 Hz, but to get there you need to listen carefully to the sound as you fiddle with the knobs. This is ear training, and it's a life-long pursuit for all of us.

Now that you're intimately familiar with the sound of this kick drum, it's time to reshape it according to your needs and desires. Remember that each band has only a limited frequency range, so you need to plan your attack. Use the low band to boost your favorite boom frequency and the low-mid to boost your favorite thud. You may find that boosting the low-mid at twice the frequency of the low yields a powerful sound. Pull out the hollowness with the mid band, and find the snap with either the mid-high or high. For those bands you're boosting, add the minimum amount that you can get away with, as it's easy to get boost happy and end up with a mutant kick drum. (Not that that's necessarily a bad thing!) It's also useful to note that, although boosting is often necessary, cutting (subtractive EQ) is usually more natural sounding due to the phase shift inherent in equalization. Most sounds benefit from a combination of boosting and cutting, as shown in Figure 1.10.

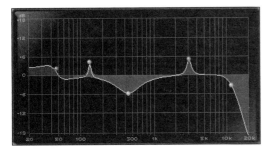

Figure 1.10   Good use of EQ includes both cutting and boosting bands as well as carefully controlling bandwidth.

As you tweak each band, don't forget that the Q is adjustable. Just as a painter chooses a fine or broad brush for different tasks, a mix engineer adjusts bandwidth as carefully as frequency and gain depending on the desired sonic result. As always, you must use your ears to determine what is best, but you may find that relatively narrow bands are useful for the boom, thud, and snap bands while a wider band helps take out the hollowness in the middle. You must also keep in mind that boosting bands can cause clipping, so adjust the input gain as necessary.

Note: If you hold the Start (Control) key while dragging the dot on the EQ graph, you can adjust the band's Q (bandwidth). You hardly need the knobs at all!

As a finishing touch, use the high-pass and low-pass bands (be sure they're not in Shelving mode) to roll off those unused frequencies at the far ends of the spectrum. This may not have a large effect on the sound, but if you add these to the unimportant ranges of dozens of tracks, you end up with sonic clutter that can make a mix sound muddy. Set the slope (Q) to 24 dB/oct. Try bringing the low-pass filter down to 1.5 kHz and see what you think.

Basic Snare Drum EQ

Now turn your attention to the Snare track. Un-solo the Kick track, and solo the snare. (Click the Track selector in the plug-in window and choose Snare.) Use the same techniques you used on the kick to familiarize yourself with the interesting and/or problematic frequencies of the snare part. Note that there's virtually nothing happening below about 100 Hz—this is a job for your high-pass filter, right? The snare has a *ping* around 800–1,000 Hz that you may want to accentuate or de-emphasize. Its meat is somewhere below 250 Hz, and its sizzle is in the 3–6 kHz range.

Note: Dragging the control dot on the EQ graph while holding Shift and Start (Control) makes the band function as a true band-pass filter, rejecting all frequencies above and below (see Figure 1.11). This can help you zero in on an important frequency more quickly by allowing you to focus entirely on what frequencies are passing through the band. Simply release Shift and Start (Control) to return to normal mode.

Figure 1.11   Band-pass mode eliminates all frequencies above and below the specified band.

The hi-hat has no energy below about 150–200 Hz. The sound of the stick hitting the cymbal is in the 200–350 Hz range, and the presence of the instrument is at 4–8 kHz. You may even find that you like the sound of the high band in Shelf mode to boost the *air* of the hi-hat.

Auditioning All Your EQs

Now un-solo the Hi-Hat track and listen to all three parts. Do they fit together well? The advantage of soloing tracks to EQ them is that you can hear them clearly without distractions. The disadvantage is that you don't hear them in context. This is another important function of EQ—to help parts blend well in the mix. You may find that you need to adjust some settings now that you're listening to the big picture.

This will be easier if you can see all three EQs at the same time. Click the hi-hat's EQ's Target button, found in the upper right corner of the plug-in window (see Figure 1.12). It's ordinarily red, but when you click it once it turns gray. This is called *anchoring* the plug-in window, and it means that the window will remain open when you open another plug-in window. Click the snare's EQ insert and you'll see that you now have both EQs open. Click the snare EQ's Target button, and then open the kick's EQ window. Now you can see all three EQs together and tweak them without having to open and close windows.

Figure 1.12   When the Target button is red, a newly selected or inserted plug-in will use the same window. When it is gray, the plug-in window is anchored, and the new plug-in will open in a new window.

Note: Another way to open multiple plug-in windows is to Shift-click another active insert. This causes the new plug-in window to be opened already anchored. The original plug-in window is still *targeted*, meaning that if you open another plug-in window without Shift-clicking it will replace the original.

Now that you've listened and considered and tweaked and fussed and stewed and listened some more and tweaked even more, it's time to save your EQ settings for posterity. Of course, you *have* been saving your session regularly, haven't you? You should get to the point that you save reflexively every few minutes so you never lose more than a few minutes of work due to a crash or power failure. Your session file saves all mix parameters, including the settings of every knob and widget in a plug-in, so the next time you open your session it will recall your mix exactly.

However, in order to re-use these settings in another session or to recall them if you should re-work all your drum EQs and then ultimately decide you were better off before, you need to save your plug-in settings. Click the Settings menu drop-down arrow (to the right of the word Preset) and choose Save Settings. The shortcut is Ctrl+Shift+S (Cmd+Shift+S) for the targeted plug-in. Type a name for your preset in the dialog box, and press Enter. Go ahead and do this for each of the three drum tracks.

Note: Once you have saved or recalled a plug-in setting, pressing Ctrl+Shift+S (Cmd+Shift+S) will save new parameters over the previous parameters. Saving new parameters as a new preset requires that you use Save Settings As. There is no shortcut key for this function.

With your plug-in settings safely stored, feel free to give a listen to my choices, which are stored as Peak 2 Kick, Peak 2 Snare, and Peak 2 Hat, respectively. You may find them to be a bit aggressive, but hopefully they make a point about the power of EQ to reshape a drum kit.

Instant Stereo

Here's a way to take a mono part and make it stereo quickly and easily.

1. Go to memory location 7, Instant Stereo.

2. Listen to the loop—it sounds fine, but it's too flat in mono. It would be great to re-record it in stereo, but that's not an option. You could add a stereo chorus or reverb, but that might make it sound muddy, so maybe that's not a great idea. Instead, you'll use a multi-mono EQ to send the low frequencies to the left and the high frequencies to the right.

Note: A multi-mono plug-in is essentially an independent mono processor on each channel of the stereo track. It's as though you plugged the left channel into one EQ and plugged the right channel into a different EQ.

---

3. Before you insert the EQ, first insert a Short Delay II (mono/stereo). A mono-to-stereo effect takes a mono signal in and spits out a stereo signal. In the case of a delay, this allows a mono sound to bounce around the left and right speakers independently. Notice that once the plug-in is inserted, the mono audio track sprouts another meter channel. This is the only time, by the way, that the number of meters on a track doesn't reflect the number of input channels.

4. Click once on the Short Delay II insert to close the plug-in window. You're not really interested in using the delay anyway.

5. While pressing both Ctrl and Start (Cmd and Control), click the Short Delay II insert again. This makes the plug-in *inactive*, meaning that it has no effect on the sound and uses no resources. Why not just bypass the plug-in, you ask? That would prevent the plug-in from affecting the sound, but it would not stop the plug-in from using processor cycles. Now the only thing the delay is doing is taking a mono signal and splitting it into left and right signals.

6. Now choose the 1-Band EQ III from the multi-mono plug-in list on the insert following the delay.

7. By default, the two mono processors are linked so the settings on each processor are identical, but you're going to unlink them by clicking the white-on-blue Master Link button, shown in Figure 1.13. You can now assign different settings for the left and right EQs. While holding the Alt (Opt) key, click the Channel selector (the uppercase L beneath the Master Link button). This opens the plug-in window for the right channel, so you can adjust both channels side by side.

Figure 1.13 The Channel Selector (L), Master Link (illuminated), and Link Enable buttons in a multi-mono plug-in.

8. Set the left EQ to Low-Pass mode and the right EQ to High-Pass mode. Set each to a 6 dB/oct slope so the transition from left to right will be as gradual as possible.

9. Click the two Link Enable buttons to temporarily link the controls of the two processors. Drag the Frequency knob on either, and the other will move with it in lockstep. Find a setting that seems to divide the spectrum of the part evenly between left and right. You are free to deselect the Link Enable buttons and experiment with overlapping the two frequencies or leaving a gap. Each will have a different sound, with identical settings being the most natural.

10. To hear the difference you've made, Ctrl-click (Cmd-click) on the EQ III's insert to bypass both left and right processors, then Ctrl-click (Cmd-click) again to hear the effect. *Voilà!* Stereo! Once again, I've stored my settings for your reference. They are called StereoLeft and StereoRight.

United Nations of EQ

Can't we all just get along? With the help of some diplomatic equalization, we certainly can! It's the job of every musician to get the biggest, fattest, most complete sound possible, but it's often the job of the mix engineer to chisel away a little of that block of fatness here and there to make room for other sounds.

The most common conflict is between kick drum and bass. Regardless of whether they're acoustic or synthesized, bass and kick occupy the same frequency range. This frequency range also happens to be a part of the spectrum where our ears are somewhat less sensitive. It's essential, then, to resolve any basement conflicts early in the mix.

1. Go to memory location 8, Kickin' Bass, and take a quick listen. It sounds pretty good, but there's no real clarity to the kick and bass parts. They may coexist, but they hardly cooperate. Insert a 4-Band EQ III on each, and open both windows as you did earlier.

2. Start by soloing each and using Band-Pass mode to search out the most interesting frequencies on each. When you've found their respective characteristic tones, boost each as needed. It's important not to boost the same frequencies on each, however, as that will only exacerbate the problem. You may need to make a hard choice here!

3. Give a listen to all three parts.

4. You'll find that boosting each at non-conflicting frequencies is a good start. Still, there's more you can do to make room at the bottom. This may require more than four bands, so click the Plug-In selector (see Figure 1.14) and choose the 7-Band EQ III. Note that all your settings carry over from the 4-Band EQ III, so you don't need to waste any time reinventing your sounds. Were you to switch the other direction, all settings would still be retained, but all bands would be bypassed. You would choose which four bands to use by clicking their IN buttons.

Figure 1.14 The Plug-In selector always shows the name of the current plug-in. Clicking it opens the same menu of plug-ins that appears when you click a track insert.

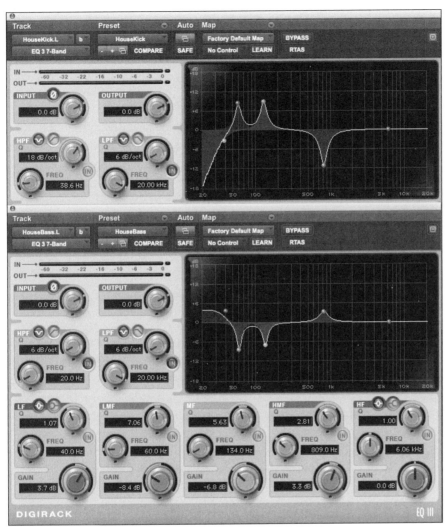

Figure 1.15 Complementary EQ curves each cut the frequencies where the other is boosted.

5. Go back and cut a little kick at the frequencies you boosted in the bass, and vice versa. This quite literally carves out sonic space for the boosted frequencies, making the whole sound fit together like a jigsaw puzzle (see Figure 1.15).

6. As you listen, Ctrl-click (Cmd-click) the two inserts to bypass the EQs to hear the difference you've made. With the EQs engaged, you should hear each part come through with more clarity along with a greater sense of space in the low

end. Note that you've accomplished this without touching a volume fader! Check out my settings for comparison: HouseKick and HouseBass.

This brings us back to where we started this discussion of equalization, doesn't it? EQ is a way to shape the timbre of a sound, often either to make it stand out or to make it blend in. Sometimes it's a bit more like posing people for a photograph, making sure everyone has a spot in the picture without being blocked by someone else's big hat. Musicians shape and reshape their tones constantly during an ensemble performance to be sure they stick out or blend in as the music demands. Once they've packed up and left the studio, such decisions are ultimately in the mix engineer's hands, and EQ is the tool for the job.

2 Dynamics

This chapter explores the mysteries of dynamics processing. Sometimes turning the volumes of specific parts up or down is not enough to balance the volume of many different layers of music, so sharper tools must be applied. We'll look at compressors, expanders, limiters, and gates and see how to apply them all. As usual, most memory locations in this chapter's session have corresponding plug-in settings so you can compare your results with mine.

I hardly need to point out that dynamics are an important part of music. A singer accents important words and makes you listen really hard for subtle nuances. The saxophonist starts a solo with a couple of gentle notes and then builds to a screaming climax. Beethoven starts with those four famous notes really loud and then develops them *sotto voce*. These dynamic contrasts are like the alternate contraction and relaxation of your heart, pumping the music through your veins.

By contrast, when you listen to some modern metal bands, the effect is more like a fire hose, with no letup in the barrage of raw energy. The music is written, performed, recorded, and mixed in a concerted effort to keep the volume at "11" all the time. *Dynamics processing* is a key element in achieving that effect.

If you read music, you're familiar with the countless terms composers use to express dynamics: *forte*, *piano*, *crescendo*, *diminuendo*, and many more. This chapter introduces you to the terms and concepts of dynamics processing and shows you how to apply them.

Compression

I remember (many years ago) listening to the radio and noticing that every time the lead vocal entered the song, the rhythm section got quieter. As a budding musician, I knew this was the appropriate thing for accompanists to do, but it didn't sound as though they were *playing* softer. It sounded as though some third party was turning its volume down to make room for the singer, and then turning it back up when the singer paused. When I pointed this out to my brother the rock star, he explained that this was accomplished by a device called a *compressor*.

The job of a compressor, such as the DigiRack Compressor/Limiter III shown in Figure 2.1, is simple: When the volume gets too loud, turn it down; when it gets soft, turn it back up. This effectively compresses the dynamic range of the audio (thus the name!), reducing the contrast between the quiet parts and the loud parts.

Figure 2.1 The DigiRack Compressor/Limiter III plug-in.

If you've ever tried to listen to classical music in the car, you know why this would be desirable. Unless you've got an extraordinarily quiet car, you have to turn the radio up to hear the oboe solo over the road noise, and then turn it back down when the brass section kicks in to keep from blowing out your speakers (and your ears!). There simply isn't enough room between what you can hear over the car's noise floor and what's uncomfortably loud to fit the entire dynamic range of an orchestra. Your hand on the radio's volume knob is doing the job of a compressor.

Popular music is meant to be heard in noisy environments—clubs, cars, malls, and parties—so it has to fit effectively within a limited dynamic range. Compressors are used at various stages in the mixing process to squash everything within this narrow window.

> **Note:** The use of dynamics processing varies greatly according to musical genre. In classical music and acoustic jazz, dynamics processors are used very sparingly, if at all. The idea is to reproduce the original performance (or an idealized version thereof) as accurately as possible. In rock, hip-hop, country, and other more commercial styles, a recording without a significant amount of compression would stick out immediately.

Threshold

Open the session Chapter 02.ptf and call up the first memory location, Threshold. This acoustic bass part sounds pretty good by itself, and it would be perfectly appropriate in a jazz combo. Un-mute the AcouBassLoop track, though, and you'll hear that the notes on the off beats get completely lost. Turn the volume of the bass part up enough so that you can hear the quiet notes, and the loud parts simply stick out too much. If this sounds to you like a job for a compressor, you're right on target.

1. Leave the Bass track turned up for now, and press the spacebar to stop playback.

2. We'll use the DigiRack Dynamics III compressor for this track. Click any insert of the Bass track, and from the Dynamics menu choose Compressor/Limiter Dyn III (mono).

Note: As with the EQ III, Digidesign uses the Roman numeral III everywhere *except* in the plug-in list, so I'll stick with III.

---

3. Click once in the Knee field, and type the number **10**.

4. Press Tab, and you'll see that the Attack field is now highlighted, as shown in Figure 2.2.

Figure 2.2 Specific values can be typed directly into a plug-in's numeric displays. The Tab key advances the cursor to the next field.

5. Type **7** and tab twice to bypass the Gain field and go to the Ratio field.

6. Type **4**, tab to the Release field, and type **100**.

7. Press the Enter key on the alphanumeric portion of the keyboard. I'll get to what each of those parameters means, but for now let's focus on threshold.

Note: The PC keyboard has two Enter keys—one on the numeric keypad and one with the alphanumeric keys. On a Mac, the alphanumeric Enter is labeled

Return. Pro Tools often treats these two keys differently—for example, using Enter to confirm data entry and Return as a navigation key. Ordinarily, the PC's alphanumeric Enter is equivalent to the Mac's Return. However, when you enter numeric values in plug-in parameter fields, you must use the *alphanumeric* Enter to confirm the entry. Using the Enter key on the numeric keypad will leave the last field highlighted for further data entry.

8.   The compressor's *threshold* is the volume at which compression begins. When the audio going through the compressor is below this level, the signal passes unchanged. Once the signal rises above the threshold, however, the gain is turned down progressively. The more the signal exceeds the threshold, the more it is turned down, so really loud notes get turned down more than moderately loud notes. Thus the difference between the softest notes and the loudest notes is reduced. Turn the Threshold (Thresh) knob all the way up to 0.0 dB, and then click Play.

9.   Listening carefully, start gradually pulling the Thresh knob down. You'll hear the notes that stick out the most start to stick out less and less, while the softest notes continue to come through unaffected. Eventually, you'll reach the point at which all the notes fit together nicely and can still be heard along with the loop. This is one of the fundamental uses of a compressor—to help even out a part's volume so it sits in the mix properly.

10. It's actually a little unusual to compress a part and then raise its track fader to make up for the lost volume, which is effectively what you've just done. The fader is there to balance parts, not to compensate for processing, so let's remedy this. Look at the track's volume (vol) display, just above the track name in the Mix view, and make a note of the number there. Alt-click (Opt-click) the track fader to set it to nominal level (0 dB), and then raise the compressor's Gain control by the same amount you just lowered the track fader. This is often called *make-up gain* because it makes up for the volume reduction caused by compression.

Note: It might seem paradoxical, but a compressor only makes loud things softer—it never makes soft things louder. It's only by using make-up gain, when you raise the now-less-loud signals back up to their pre-compression levels, that you bring the softer parts up with them. With the part's dynamic range now reduced, the overall sound of the track is louder than it was to begin with.

Ratio

The threshold, then, answers the first question of compression: "What gets compressed?" The second question is, "How much does it get compressed?" The *ratio* provides the answer to that question. When the ratio is 2:1, a signal that rises two decibels above the threshold will be reduced by one decibel. A signal that rises six decibels above the threshold will be reduced by three decibels. In other words, every two decibels in equals one decibel out. With a 4:1 ratio, a signal eight decibels above the threshold would be reduced by six decibels, yielding a signal that exceeds the threshold by only two decibels (8:2 = 4:1). Figure 2.3 illustrates how higher ratios compress the signal more aggressively.

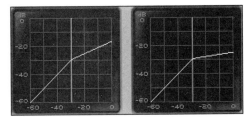

Figure 2.3   Ratio determines how rapidly output gain will be attenuated compared to input gain. A higher ratio (right) means more aggressive compression.

1.   Click Play and turn the Ratio knob all the way down to 1:1. You're right back where you started before you lowered the threshold, because at a 1:1 ratio nothing is compressed.

2.   Raise the knob gradually, and listen to how the sound changes. The louder notes will start to get softer, as they did before, but this time you're changing the *amount* of compression instead of how many notes are getting compressed.

3.   Stop at 2:1 and lower the gain so the bass part blends with the loop. The louder notes will still fit pretty well, but you'll have to strain a little more to hear the softer notes.

4.   Raise the knob to 8:1 and adjust the gain to compensate. Now there's very little contrast between the loudest and softest notes, and the part never gets lost in the shuffle. Theoretically, you could lower the threshold all the way so everything is compressed, raise the ratio all the way so everything is squashed as much as possible, and raise the gain so the part sits on top of everything else. Of course, that would completely eliminate all dynamic variation from the part. If you did that to every part, they would all be the same volume all the time, and listeners would never be able to distinguish foreground from background!

This is the compromise of compression. You need to balance what is gained—keeping soft notes from getting lost while keeping loud notes from sticking out—with what is lost—dynamic contrast. Even in aggressive music, dynamic contrast is what allows parts to take turns grabbing the listener's attention. Compression is a powerful tool with a sharp blade, and it must be treated with respect.

Note: Compare the mixer's job to that of the musical arranger. The arranger has to decide which instrument plays the lead role at any given time and which instruments must be subordinate. The mixer must also decide which sounds are most important and which are least important at different points in the song. Heavily compressed tracks are very easy to make sit "on top" of an arrangement, but when you turn their volume down they get lost very easily. Keeping good dynamic range makes it easier to allow parts to interact with each other, rather than turning music into a win/lose proposition.

Knee

The compressor's *knee* determines how abruptly compression will begin as signal reaches the threshold. A "hard" knee treats the threshold as an absolute—below the threshold, there is no compression, while above the threshold compression kicks in immediately. A "soft" knee eases into the compression as signal approaches the threshold, so it's less clear when compression begins. Figure 2.4 shows the compression curves of both a hard and soft knee.

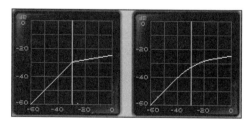

Figure 2.4   A hard knee (left) and a soft knee (right).

While some compressors simply offer a choice of hard knee or soft knee, the Compressor/Limiter III allows continuous variation from a hard knee to one that eases into compression over a range of 30 dB. You can hear exactly how this variable knee affects the compression.

1. Go to memory location 2, Knee, and take a quick listen. It's the classic machine-gun snare, stolen straight from the dance floor at your local club. (Okay, the

tempo is a bit slow for dancing, but it's perfect for this demonstration!) Its crescendo is exaggerated to demonstrate the effect of the compressor's variable knee.

2. Insert the Compressor/Limiter III on the track and call up the Knee preset. You'll find it in the session's Plug-In Settings folder.

3. Listen to the compressed sound, and note that the compressor kicks in at about the beginning of the 32nd notes. With the 4:1 ratio compressing the 32nd notes, most of the crescendo now happens in the first three beats, doesn't it? Note that the Gain Reduction (GR) meter (see Figure 2.5) shows no activity until the level at the Input meter reaches the Threshold arrow, after which it shows progressively more compression with each note.

Figure 2.5   The Compressor/Limiter III's meters show input and output levels as well as gain reduction. The orange triangle at the left of the Input meter shows the current threshold.

4. As the track loops, slowly raise the Knee control and, as always, listen carefully to the resulting change. Compression begins earlier and earlier as you go. By the time the knee reads 8–10 dB, you'll see the Gain Reduction meter registering activity while the Input meter's level is clearly below the Threshold arrow. By the time you reach the maximum knee of 30 dB, compression begins by about the second beat of the bar. You have completely reshaped the crescendo with the compressor.

With a soft knee, the Gain Reduction meter shows two different colors. The light orange indicates that the signal is still below the threshold but within the range specified by the knee. The signal is being compressed, but by an amount less than the specified ratio. The dark orange indicates that the signal is completely above the knee's transition and is being compressed at the full ratio. Note also that in the Dynamics Graph display from Figure 2.4, the shape of the curve changes to reflect the Knee setting. A hard knee is shown as a sharp angle in the graph. A soft knee is shown as a gradual curve from uncompressed to compressed. Simply put, a soft knee starts compressing at a lower level, making the transition from uncompressed signal to compressed signal more gradual. Use a soft knee when you want to make the effect as transparent as possible.

Attack and Release

Let's spend a few minutes making the compressor misbehave. Memory location 3, Pumping, is another acoustic bass part; but this time it's completely solo so you can focus on its sound. Fire up the Compressor/Limiter III again, bypass it, and listen closely to the natural sound of the bass. Hear how it has a percussive attack and a smooth, gradual decay? The compressor can reshape those, and that can have a huge impact on the character of the instrument.

1.   Un-bypass the compressor, and call up the Pumping Bass preset. Notice that the notes decay differently now. The compressor lets the first 80 milliseconds of attack pass through unaffected and then clamps down on the signal by a 6:1 ratio until it drops below −19 dBFS. Then it gradually releases the sound to decay naturally. Watch the Gain Reduction meter to see how much the compressor is turning the signal down from one moment to the next.

2.   Turn the Attack knob all the way down. It should read 10.0 us, which means 10 microseconds. A *microsecond* is a thousandth of a millisecond, and technically the "u" should be μ, a lower-case Greek *mu*. This effectively makes the compressor kick in immediately when a signal rises above the threshold. Listen to what it has done to the bass's attack—it has squashed it like a bug! The attack is flat, with none of the characteristic *thwack* of the original. Figure 2.6 shows the effect of slower and faster attack times. Note also that the sound is duller than the original. This is another important point about dynamics processors—in the process of changing dynamics, they change timbre, too. The attack is made up mostly of high frequencies, so when the compressor flattens the attack, you hear less of the high frequencies, making the sound duller.

3.   Let's see what kind of mischief you can get into with the Release control. First, bump up the ratio to about 8:1 so the effect will be more pronounced. Now lower the release to 350 milliseconds and listen closely to the half notes. They seem to swell in volume as the compressor loosens its grip, don't they? This is called *pumping*. If you watch the Output meter, you'll see that the level catches for a moment at around −12 to −14 dB while the input level is still dropping.

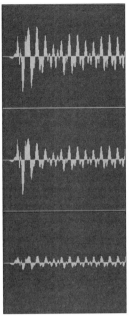

Figure 2.6 The effect of different attack times on compression. At the top is about 200 milliseconds of the original waveform. The waveform in the middle has been compressed with an attack time of 100 milliseconds. The bottom waveform has been compressed with an attack time of 100 microseconds, so virtually none of the original attack gets through uncompressed.

The volume never actually swells, but the interruption of the expected decay draws your attention as though it were a crescendo.

4.   Pumping is not a very natural effect, but it can be cool under the right circumstances. This particular bass, however, wants a more moderate attack and release, so back off on both until you get a more natural sound. Let 10–50 milliseconds of the attack through, and let it decay for a second or more before it releases. Use a soft knee, like 10 dB or more, and a ratio between 3:1 and 6:1, depending on how much you want it to sustain. Set the threshold and make-up gain to taste.

Bus Compression

The term *bus compression* refers to the practice of compressing an entire mix. On a typical mixing console, this compressor would either be integrated into or inserted on the master stereo bus, thus the name. The term is used to contrast the practice with that of compressing individual tracks.

Note: Sometimes you'll see *buss* instead of *bus*, but Digidesign uses only one *s*, so I'll stick with that spelling. Besides, *buss* is an old-school term for "kiss," and that's a completely different type of dynamics!

Mixes are compressed for a variety of reasons. Radio stations compress everything before transmission to be heard above traffic noise without exceeding the bandwidth the FCC allows them. Songs are compressed before being printed to vinyl to keep the signal well above the medium's noise floor without actually bouncing the needle out of the groove. Digital media (such as CDs and DVDs) don't require compression to overcome any such technical limitations, but record labels (and some producers and artists) expect your mix to sound like it's already on the radio, so most mix engineers apply at least some compression at the master bus.

Note: The principles and terminology of track and bus compression are the same. Bus compression simply provides one last opportunity to make the mix a little louder without clipping.

Go to memory location 4, called Bus Comp, and listen to the mix. Insert the multi-channel Bomb Factory BF76 (stereo) on an insert. The BF76 (see Figure 2.7) is a digital re-creation of one of the most famous compressors of all time, the Universal Audio 1176. It is designed to model the behavior of the particular attributes that gave the original its sought-after character, so it will sound different from the DigiRack Compressor/Limiter III even when the two are set with comparable parameters.

Figure 2.7 The Bomb Factory BF76 compressor is modeled after the famous Universal Audio 1176.

The BF76's controls work a bit differently from those of the DigiRack unit. The Input knob controls the level of the signal being sent to what is essentially a fixed threshold. It might seem upside down at first, but turning the knob all the way counterclockwise is like setting the DigiRack compressor's threshold to 0. You've turned the input gain so low that it never rises to the threshold. Push the input gain up, and progressively more of the signal exceeds the threshold. The Output knob is straightforwardly used to set make-up gain.

The Attack and Release knobs control what you would expect, but the short times are fully clockwise and long times are fully counterclockwise. That's right, a setting of 7 is the shortest attack or release time. Be aware, too, that the entire range of times is on the very short end of what the DigiRack unit can do.

Instead of continuously variable ratios, the BF76 gives you four buttons from which to choose within a range of 4:1 to 20:1. Only one meter is provided, but it can be switched from displaying gain reduction (GR) to displaying output levels at either of two different calibration levels. Leave it set on GR and watch the track meter for output level. Because the plug-in's meter does not show any indication of clipping, you will need to watch the track's clip indicator (and listen carefully!) anyway.

Punch the 12:1 Ratio button and turn the Attack and Release controls all the way to 7. Adjust the Input setting to achieve around 5 dB of gain reduction, then adjust the attack and release times to taste. You want the attack to be as short as you can get it without flattening the transients, and you want the release to be short enough for a natural release but not so short that it causes pumping. Now raise the Output knob to bring the track level as high as possible without clipping.

Listen carefully while repeatedly clicking the Bypass button to engage and disengage the compressor. Hopefully, the mix has a bit more punch with the compressor engaged. This is because the loud and soft parts of the mix are closer together, making the mix more cohesive. There's also a palpable change in the mix's overall color because, as you know, the BF76 is modeled after a classic unit with a unique character. These are the basic reasons engineers use bus compression—to make the mix punchier and more cohesive, and sometimes to add a final splash of color.

Limiting

What would happen if you could turn a compressor's ratio all the way up to infinity? If the signal exceeded the threshold by 2 dB, the compressor would turn the signal down 2 dB, wouldn't it? If the signal exceeded the threshold by 10 dB, the compressor would turn it down 10 dB, and so on. The signal would never be allowed to exceed the threshold. It would be *limited* to an unyielding maximum level.

Limiting is compression without compromise. The point at which compression becomes limiting is not sharply defined, but most engineers regard anything over a 10:1 ratio as limiting. Of course, that means there can be "soft" and "hard" limiting because, as an example, the Compressor/Limiter III offers ratios as high as 100:1 (see Figure 2.8). Ultimately, though, that's akin to asking how many times your high school crush refused to go out with you. Whether it was 10 times or 100 times, you were, well, crushed, and so is your signal.

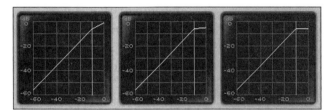

Figure 2.8 Compression (2:0 ratio), gentle limiting (10:1), and hard limiting (100:1).

Now ask yourself what would happen if you turned your hypothetical compressor's ratio all the way up to infinity and then turned its threshold down lower and lower. Gradually, all dynamic variation would be obliterated. It would be like holding your hand at the front of a speaker cone and stopping it from moving out very far. Eventually the very voltage fluctuations that create distinct sounds would be flattened and distorted. In most cases, that would be bad, wouldn't it?

By contrast, it would be perfectly legitimate to lower the threshold drastically with a 1.5:1 compression ratio. The entire signal would be gently squeezed into a one-third narrower dynamic range, which would in fact make it much easier to listen to classical music in the car.

Limiting, then, is clearly to be reserved for detail work like reining in those momentary peaks that jump out from the mix. Such peaks could cause clipping if the overall level is too high. Conversely, if you limit those peaks, you can turn the mix up without risk of clipping. This is in fact the primary modern application of limiting—lopping off the heads of stray dynamic peaks so the mix can be made louder without distortion.

Note: The use of compression and limiting to maximize the volume of recordings so they stand out on the radio has led to a *de facto* competition to be the loudest song on the air. The dynamic range of what we hear on CDs and radio has thus shrunk remarkably over the past two decades, with the pace of change accelerating since the widespread use of DAWs. Many engineers decry this loss of dynamic range, while others accept it as a fact of doing business. Some even embrace it as the core of a new sound. Before you blindly crush the heck out of your mixes because someone said you're supposed to, listen critically to the use of dynamics in recordings you admire (especially older recordings) and then let your ears decide how your mixes should sound.

For more on the negative aspects of this trend, visit www.turnmeup.org or search "loudness war" on Wikipedia.

Maximizing Volume

Go to memory location 5, More Louder, and listen to the mix. It sounds fine, but the label's representative wants it to be competitively loud when it gets played on the radio. You're going to use a limiter to make that happen.

1. Insert the Compressor/Limiter III on the track. (There are plug-ins that function only as limiters, but Digidesign simply built a compressor with extreme-enough settings that it can work as a limiter.)

2. Set a hard knee, minimum attack and release, 100:1 ratio, no make-up gain, and a threshold of 0.0 dB.

3. Your limiter is loaded and cocked, but you haven't yet pulled the trigger. Click Play and gradually pull the threshold down, listening carefully and watching the meters. The maximum levels on the Output meter follow the Threshold arrow almost perfectly, as in Figure 2.9—this is the essence of limiting.

Figure 2.9 Limiting: Regardless of the input level, the output level never exceeds the threshold.

4. At first you probably won't hear the effect of the limiter because it's only working on the briefest transient peaks in the waveform. Gradually, though, you'll start to hear the sound distorting a bit as crunchy artifacts that resemble clipping start to creep in. The reason it sounds like clipping is that the limiter is flattening the tops of the transients just as though they were hitting the 0 dBFS ceiling. Keep lowering that threshold, and you'll hear the sound deteriorate more and more as you bring a once-vital signal to its knees. Did you just hear someone holler "Uncle"?

5. Set the threshold to −10 dB. Ignore the distortion on the bass's attack for now— you'll fix that in a minute.

6. Now add 10 dB of make-up gain and use bypass to compare the processed track with the original. It sounds significantly louder, doesn't it? That's the basic idea behind limiting.

7. That bass attack shows the limitation of limiting, however. It's very difficult to flatten the peaks enough to raise the overall level without distorting transients. A compromise is in order. Reset the gain to 0.0 dB by Alt-clicking (Opt-click-ing) that control. Raise the attack slowly until the bass sounds clean. You're now letting some of the transient through the limiter, so you won't be able to add as much make-up gain but you will still be able to raise the volume of the mix by a few decibels without changing the sound significantly.

Note: Limiting allows you to change the apparent *loudness* of a mix without exceeding the maximum *peak* level of 0 dBFS. Because of the unforgiving nature of digital clipping, digital levels are ordinarily judged by their peak amplitude. By limiting peaks and adding gain, you have just demonstrated that peak levels are not a good indicator of what we call loudness. A full discussion of this relationship is a book in itself, but often a more useful indicator of loudness is a signal's *average* level. Analog-style VU meters ordinarily show average level instead of peak.

Limiters are sometimes used on individual tracks, especially those with lots of transi-ents. More extreme settings that add that clip-like crunch to the sound are used by some engineers as a different sort of distortion effect. In addition to regulating the track's dynamics, limiting to the point of distortion adds a character to the sound that makes it stand out from more natural timbres. Zoom in and analyze the waveform of many contemporary mixes, and you'll see waveforms with remarkably flat tops due to heavy limiting.

Expansion

So compression actually reduces dynamic range, bringing the output volume of the loud parts closer to that of the soft parts, right? Could it be that *expansion* increases dynamic range, making a bigger difference between loud and soft? That's it exactly!

Before you start taking all those hyper-compressed CDs off your shelf and trying to restore some dynamic range to them, consider the following. First, the sonic signature of the compressor will most likely remain after dynamic range has been expanded, so it will be only a partial success. Second, the expander's threshold works in the opposite direction to that of the compressor—it designates signals *below* a certain level as being subject to expansion. You will most likely end up expanding the part of the mix that was below the compressor's threshold and therefore didn't get compressed.

Yes, in some cases a mastering engineer will in fact "un-compress" a mix with an expander, but it's really not an Undo button for a compressor gone mad. The more typical use of an expander is what you might call *downward expansion*, in which softer parts of the signal are turned down even more to create greater contrast with the stronger parts. Figure 2.10 shows the DigiRack Expander/Gate III.

Figure 2.10 The DigiRack Expander/Gate III.

In a live recording, for example, the crowd noise gets recorded by every microphone on stage, so the singer's gentle moment with an acoustic guitar pits those two microphones of subtle music against dozens of tracks of open-mic crowd noise. To level the playing field, expanders turn down the open mics to quiet the background din when the musicians aren't playing and then allow the full signal to pass as soon as they start playing again.

Enhancing Dynamics

To see an expander in action, go to memory location 6, Expansion, and give it a quick listen. Sound familiar? It's the machine-gun snare from the compressor example. This time, instead of reducing the amount of crescendo, you're going to increase it.

1. Insert the Expander/Gate III plug-in on any insert. Most of its controls will look familiar from the preceding discussion of the Compressor/Expander III.

2. Set the ratio to 4:1 and the threshold to −60 dB. This is almost tantamount to bypassing the expander, as only the very softest signals are affected.

3. Click Play and slowly raise the threshold, listening carefully for any change in the rate of the crescendo. As the threshold rises, the first notes of the crescendo get progressively softer. By the time the threshold reaches about −30 dB, the first two beats start noticeably more softly and catch up by beat three, resulting in a wider but faster crescendo. Somewhere around −20 dB, it becomes difficult to hear the first note of the figure, and the rate of crescendo is significantly faster over the first three beats and then slows for the fourth beat.

4. Watch the meters to confirm what you're hearing. As Figure 2.11 illustrates, the Gain Reduction meter shows that the softer the signal, the more it is being turned down—exactly the opposite of what a compressor does. The Input and Output meters have a veritable race to the top, with the Input always having an early lead. The Output meter catches up as the signal reaches the threshold.

Figure 2.11 The meters of the expander show that maximum gain reduction occurs at the lowest signal levels. As the signal rises, the gain reduction gradually decreases until the threshold is reached.

5.   Actually, it doesn't seem to catch up until several decibels *above* the threshold, does it? Try this: Set the attack and release to their minimum values, and set the threshold to about −10 dB. Now the Output meter catches up to the Input meter exactly at the threshold, but it sounds awful! What happened?

With the slower attack and release, the expander was staying closed through the short snare notes, so even though the threshold was −10 dB and the peaks were −8 dB, the silence between peaks was below the threshold, causing the expander to reduce the volume of both the silence and the snare notes. When you shortened the attack and release times, the expander still lowered the volume briefly during the silence, but it responded quickly to the beginning of each snare note, returning the signal to its normal level. This extremely rapid opening and closing of the expander is unnatural, and that's why it sounds so bad.

Note that although *attack* and *release* on a compressor refer to the beginning and end of the volume reduction, the opposite is true on an expander. The expander's attack time defines how quickly the signal returns to normal (no gain reduction) after it rises above the threshold. The release time defines how quickly the signal takes to reach full attenuation after it drops below the threshold. Figure 2.12 shows this in action.

This definition is easier to remember if you consider the most common use of an expander—to duck background noise in a channel until more important musical material passes through. The expander is by default in full attenuation, keeping the unwanted noise quiet. When the saxophonist plays the first note of his solo and the input signal to the microphone rises above the threshold, the attack of that note triggers the attack time of the expander. The start of the note is the end of the attenuation, but both are called "attack." When the saxophonist releases his last note and the input level to the microphone drops below the threshold, it triggers the release time of the expander, which gradually attenuates the signal until it reaches the designated ratio.

Reducing Noise

Go to memory location 7, called Noise, and listen to the example. When the flute is resting, you can hear all sorts of distracting noises in the background, including a computer fan and the flutist nervously clacking keys. The flutist's breaths are a bit too prominent, too. An expander will help minimize the distractions without losing all the ambience.

1.   Insert the Expander/Gate III on the Flute track.

2.   The default settings actually do a pretty good job of eliminating the background noise, but it sounds unnatural for the flutist's breaths to be completely silenced. Start with a ratio of 3:1 and set the attack time as short as you can.

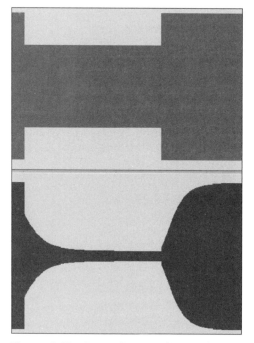

Figure 2.12 Expansion—making soft sounds softer. When the quieter part begins, the signal is turned down gradually over the release time until it reaches the full ratio. When the louder part returns, the signal is turned back up gradually over the attack time until it reaches its original level.

3.   Start with a release time of about a second, and you'll hear that it actually calls attention to the expansion by attenuating the noise so slowly. Shorten the release to 200 milliseconds or so, and the attenuation will seem much more appropriate.

4.   The effect is still a bit too pronounced, so start raising the Range control until the quietest parts are audible. As the shape of the Dynamics Graph suggests, the expander's range determines the point at which no more attenuation will be applied (see Figure 2.13). This brings the ambience back into the picture while still keeping it quiet enough not to distract. Now the room's background noise is a bit more apparent, but if you bypass the plug-in, you'll see that it sounds much better than it did to begin with.

5.   One last tweak will help the flutist a bit. Try raising the attack time very slightly and listen to the sound of the flute attacks. You can gently soften the attacks, making them a bit cleaner and less aggressive. Go too far, though, and it will sound more like a synth than a real alto flute.

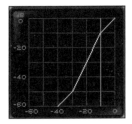

Figure 2.13 The Range control defines the point at which expansion no longer occurs. In this example expansion will be applied only to signals between −10 dB (the threshold) and −30 dB.

Gating

What does a regular old non-audio gate do? You know, the kind of gate that you find in a picket fence? It opens and closes—it's as simple as that. When the gate is open, ducks and geese and cows and neighbors can wander through the gate freely and get into all kinds of mischief. Close the gate, and nobody passes through. No mischief ensues.

Gating, then, is expansion without compromise. Or, if you prefer a formal analogy, gating is to expansion as limiting is to compression. It's the extreme case, where signals below the threshold are not simply attenuated, they are silenced. In a combined expander/gate, as you find in Dynamics III, gating is achieved by setting the ratio and range to their maximum values—in this case 100:1 and −80 dB, respectively, as you can see in Figure 2.14. Gating cuts out all noise from between musical passages; all headphone bleed is eliminated.

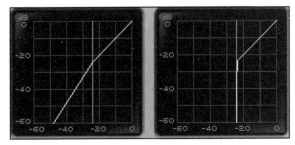

Figure 2.14 Expansion (1.5:1 ratio) and gating (100:1).

Gating can sound unnatural, though, if it is used in the wrong context. In nature, you never hear silence when someone pauses between sentences; there is always traffic, air conditioning, television, or some other conversation to fill the gap, however subtly. A gate, especially a digital gate, can create an artificial and complete silence in the gap.

Silencing Bleed-Through

Listen to memory location 8, Snare Bleed, and you'll hear a snare track with hi-hat and toms bleeding through. You don't want any special processing you apply to the snare to affect those sounds, so you need to get rid of them as much as possible.

Note: The practice of gating drum tracks aggressively like this goes in and out of favor. The most natural-sounding drum kit generally includes a degree of bleed-through among tracks, so minimal gating—or better yet, gentle expansion—should be applied. When applying dramatic effects to individual tracks, however, gating is essential to separate those effects.

---

1. Insert the Expander/Gate III, and immediately set its ratio and range to gate values. The bleed-through goes away easily enough, but it will take some finesse to ensure that the gate doesn't adversely affect the snare.

2. Set the attack time to about 30 milliseconds, and you'll see the worst-case scenario. The snare's attack gets rounded off in a most unusual way. Make note of this sound—someday you'll find a circumstance for which this would be perfect! Today, however, is not that day.

3. Try the shortest possible attack time. Listen carefully to be sure such a short attack doesn't cause any clicks or distortion. With this track, you can probably get away with the shortest setting. If you encounter problems with short attack times, be sure the Look Ahead button is engaged. This actually starts the attack two milliseconds *before* the signal crosses the threshold, so the sound's attack is afforded extra protection.

4. Now turn your attention to the end of the snare notes. Set the hold time to minimum—I'll get to that momentarily. Set the release time to minimum, and listen to what happens to the end of each note. It's as though the note passed too close to a black hole and got its tail torn off!

5. Raise the release time and listen for a change. It gets better as you get to a few hundred milliseconds, but the snare's ring is still chopped off. You need more than a second of release time before you can really hear the snare ring properly. Let's try this another way.

6. Lower the release time back down to about 250 milliseconds, then start raising the hold time. The hold time keeps the gate open a little while before the release

kicks in. In this case, it's allowing the snare to ring out a bit before the gate closes. You should be able to get a good complete snare hit with very little bleed with less than half a second of release and hold times combined. Figure 2.15 shows the effect of hold on the gate.

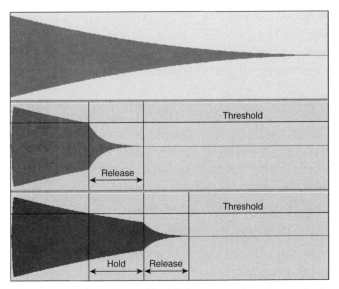

Figure 2.15   The effect of hold time on gating. At top is the original sound. The middle example is gated without hold time. The bottom example is gated with hold time. Hold time prevents the gate from closing for a period of time after the signal has dropped below the threshold.

Big '80s Snare

A classic gate effect from the 1980s, the era of the really big drum set, is to insert a gate *after* the snare's reverb. This allows the use of a great deal of reverb to make the snare sound like a cannon shot without having the reverb's tail cluttering up the next two bars.

1.   Go to memory location 9, Big 80s Snare, and listen once through. Doesn't this just cry out for that classic sound?

2.   Un-mute the Snare Verb track, and suddenly you're swimming in reverb.

3.   Insert the Expander/Gate III after the D-Verb plug-in on the Snare Verb track so you can clean this up.

4.   Set the range and release to gate values as before.

5.   Set the attack to between eight and 10 milliseconds, so the snare's attack gets a chance to be heard dry before the reverb kicks in.

6.   Now turn your attention to the end of the reverb. You need to choose the right combination of settings for threshold, hold, and release to get the desired effect. Set the threshold fairly high, as you're more concerned with timing than with level here. Think of the hold time as being primarily responsible for the length of the reverb and the release time as being responsible for the shape of the reverb tail. The proper timing for the whole effect is longer than an eighth note but no longer than a quarter note. When you find the right sound (or get frustrated searching for it), you can compare your work with my plug-in setting called Big Snare Gate.

Note: You may have noticed that the one parameter I haven't discussed is the Side-Chain parameter. Chapter 11, "Advanced Dynamics," covers that function in detail. I've also ignored the third effect in the Dynamics III suite, the De-Esser. That will be covered in Chapter 4, "Special Effects."

Dynamics processing boils down to having an imaginary hand on the volume knob. This imaginary hand is extraordinary, though, in that it can respond to a change in level in a matter of microseconds. Heck, with Look Ahead engaged, it can effectively go back in time and open a gate prior to the point at which the signal crossed the threshold! It is also precise, flexible, and able to read dynamic changes of a tenth of a decibel. Like any processor, it can be used correctively or creatively, allowing the mix engineer to crush a sound or caress it, as desired.

3 Time-Based Effects

So far you've manipulated the timbre of sounds using EQ and modified the dynamics of sounds using compression and expansion. In this chapter, you will explore the modification of a sound's *ambience*. As before, I've saved presets of my settings for several of the memory locations.

In nature, all sounds occur in some sort of ambient context. In addition to the direct sound that reaches our ears in a straight line from the source, we also hear the sound via indirect paths as it bounces off walls, floors, trees, cars, people, and various other obstacles. If you liken the direct sound to a billiard ball hitting you in a straight shot, then there are also many copies of the sound reaching your ears via every bank shot imaginable. Because those copies travel greater distances than the direct sound, they arrive later and quieter, and our ears thereby recognize them as the ambience of the direct sound rather than independent sounds.

To hear nothing but direct sound without ambient reflections would seem startling and unnatural, as we depend on the reflections to figure out where a sound is coming from. Although not as finely tuned as a bat's echolocation, our ears are nevertheless able to synthesize the direct and ambient sound to determine the position and distance of a sound source to a high degree of accuracy.

The ambience of a concert hall is carefully designed and tuned, and recording techniques for classical music are designed to capture that natural sound. In the recording studio, however, sounds are more often captured with minimal natural ambience so that each sound's apparent position in space can be manipulated artificially in the mixing process. *Time-based processors* are used to create those "bank shots" in the right combination to achieve the desired effect.

Sometimes, of course, those bank shots take on a life of their own and become discrete echoes. This effect can also be put to good musical use, as when imitating the sound of a singer's voice slapping back off the gymnasium walls at a high school dance. At other times, these echoes can be used to enhance a song's rhythm, subtly or otherwise. I'll start with such obvious echoes and work our way through the more subtle applications.

Delay

Few can resist the temptation when standing at the edge of a canyon or gorge to shout "Hello!" and wait for some distant rock formation to return the greeting. Many of us also note the time it takes for the reflection to arrive, estimating the distance to the far wall at a tenth of a mile for every second. This delay between the direct sound and the reflected sound gives us a specific notion of an object's position. In the studio, *delay effects* are used to add this location information to a sound recorded without much ambience of its own.

Open the session called Chapter 03.ptf and go to memory location 1, Simple Delay. The audio region highlighted there is a deliberately simple phrase constructed to help make the results of your first delay experiments clearly evident.

Routing a Time-Based Effect

After all we've been through together, you would think that I'd be about to tell you to insert a delay plug-in on the audio track, but you would be wrong. Although it's possible to do exactly that, the experience of countless engineers over many years of mixing suggests that what follows is a much better way to treat a time-based effect.

1. Click the name of the audio track so it is highlighted.

2. Go to the Track menu and click New.

3. In the New Tracks dialog box shown in Figure 3.1, click the Track Type drop-down arrow and choose Aux Input.

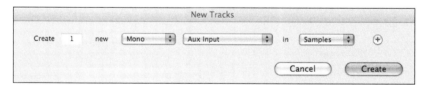

Figure 3.1 The New Tracks dialog box.

4. Leave the other parameters at their defaults, and click Create to create one new mono aux input.

5. Double-click the aux input's name and name it Delay Aux.

6. Solo-safe the aux input by Ctrl-clicking (Cmd-clicking) its Solo button, which will gray out.

Note: Solo-safing the aux input prevents it from muting when a track is soloed. If you didn't do this, the delay aux would be silenced every time you soloed the dry track.

---

7. Click a Send selector on the audio track and choose Bus 1 from the Bus submenu. A copy of the signal from this track is now going through a bus, a sort of virtual patch cable. Where will it end up?

8. Click the Input selector of the aux input and choose Bus 1 from the Bus submenu. The copied signal from the audio track now ends up passing through the aux. You're going to delay this copy.

Note: Standard engineering practice dictates that time-based effects (such as delay and reverb) are inserted on an aux input, with signal from one or more audio tracks being routed to the aux via a send and a bus, as you have just seen. There are many reasons for this, but the most compelling is that it allows one effects processor to be used by multiple source tracks. This is both more efficient in its use of system resources and often more natural sounding than inserting a delay or reverb on each audio track to be processed, as is done with dynamic processors and EQs. As with most rules, there are exceptions, but this is a widespread norm.

---

9. Click any insert of the aux input and choose Long Delay II (mono) from the Delay submenu.

10. Click Play and see whether your ears are sharp enough to hear any difference. Well...? It's okay to say no, because there is no difference! The signal is not getting to the aux input yet.

11. Locate the send output window (shown in Figure 3.2) that opened when you created the send in step 7. If it's not visible, click the name of the send (it should say "Bus 1"). As you've seen, clicking an insert shows and hides the plug-in window; similarly clicking a send shows and hides the send output window. Notice that the send's fader is all the way down—this is the way sends are created in Pro Tools LE by default. Alt-click (Opt-click) on the fader, and it will jump to 0 dB.

12. Now you should be able to hear the delay. Each time a note sounds in the audio track, it is echoed a little more than a half second later in the aux input. Because the send and the aux input are both set to unity gain, the echo is the same volume as the original, which makes it sound more like a repeated note than an

Figure 3.2 The send output window.

echo. Turn the volume of the aux input down 6–12 dB so that the delayed copy sounds like an echo of the original.

As you can see in Figure 3.3, the Long Delay II plug-in has its own Gain control, which could also be used to turn down the volume of the delayed copy. Ordinarily, however, this control in a mono delay is only used to keep the plug-in's output from clipping, as you did with EQ III and Dynamics III. Using the aux input's fader to control the delay allows you to tweak the balance directly from the Mix or Edit window without having to open a plug-in window.

The delay plug-in also has a Mix control, which blends the delayed signal with the original. Standard practice dictates that this should always be set to 100 percent, which means no unprocessed signal passes through the plug-in. After all, the source audio track is already playing the unprocessed signal.

Note: When dealing with time-based effects, the terms *wet* and *dry* are used to refer to the (processed) aux input and the (unprocessed) source audio tracks, respectively. Some time-based processors use wet/dry in place of mix to control the balance of processed signal to original signal. Either way, the control should be set to allow no dry signal to pass.

Figure 3.3 The Long Delay II plug-in.

Delay Time and Feedback

Let the region loop for a little while and experiment with different Delay settings. This control ranges from no delay at all (0.0 milliseconds) to more than two-thirds of a second (678.0 milliseconds). You may be alarmed at the distortion you hear when you are moving the Delay slider. This is caused by the plug-in trying to recalculate the playback of the delayed signal on the fly. It's like someone telling you to arrive at 5:30 for dinner, and then calling you when you're already on the way and asking you to arrive at 5:15 or 6:00. How are you going to adjust when you've already left?

The good news is that you're not likely to adjust a delay time in the middle of a mix. It would be better to set up more than one delay, each with a different delay time, and mute one while you're using the other. If you should find yourself needing to automate a change in delay time, be sure you do it when there's no signal being sent to the delay aux.

Notice that below about 50 milliseconds, it's increasingly difficult to hear the delayed signal as a separate event, even with the aux turned up. It starts to blend in with the original, becoming more of a timbral effect than an ambience effect. This is because our ears have trouble distinguishing two sounds that are very close in time, so we hear them as a blended sound.

Note: Because very short delay times are perceived more as timbral than time-based effects, I will deal with them separately in later chapters. This chapter focuses on delays that are clearly distinguishable from the original.

Click the Long Delay's plug-in selector and choose Extra Long Delay II (mono) from the Delay submenu (see Figure 3.4). You won't see much difference between the two versions until you raise the Delay slider all the way to the top. Extra Long Delay gives you up to 2,726 milliseconds of delay—almost three seconds. There are in fact five versions of what Digidesign collectively calls the Mod Delay plug-in—Short, Slap, Medium, Long, and Extra Long—that are distinguished primarily by their maximum delay times.

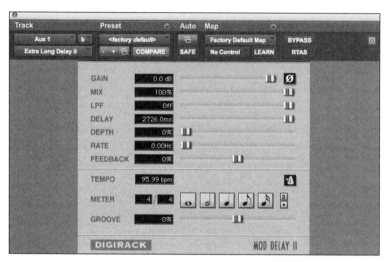

Figure 3.4 The Extra Long Delay II plug-in.

You might be tempted, then, to use the Extra Long Delay all the time, because its shortest delay time is the same as the rest, but it has a longer maximum delay time. There are two disadvantages to that. First, the resolution of the Delay slider at its low end is not as precise on Extra Long Delay as it is on Short Delay. Second, the longer the delay, the more DSP the plug-in consumes. On a reasonably fast computer, the additional hit on system resources is very small, but when every CPU cycle counts you'll be glad you used the shortest delay for the effect you're after.

Set the delay time to 500 milliseconds and turn your attention to the number of delays. This is controlled by the Feedback slider. Feedback controls the amount of the delay's output signal that gets "fed back" into the delay's own input, resulting in a delayed copy of the delayed copy. Yes, this is the same principle as guitar feedback, and at a feedback setting of 100 percent the sound will sustain itself forever. Unless you're doing some unusual sound design, the most useful settings are below 95 percent.

Slowly raise the feedback amount, listening carefully to the number of repetitions as you go. First there's only one iteration, or *tap*, then another, then more and more. If you're having trouble keeping track, raise the delay time so you have more time to sort them out. Once you've explored the outer reaches of delay sanity, reset the delay time to 620 milliseconds and tweak the feedback so you hear three taps of the delay. You've just created a four-note repeating pattern that starts again with each original note and stays in time with itself.

Note: Before you navigate away from this memory location, be aware that when you come back you will no longer see the aux input you created. You've certainly noticed that each memory location shows only certain tracks—this is one of the useful traits of a memory location. When you return to this memory location, it will recall only the Simple Delay track. You can then tell Pro Tools to show the Delay Aux track by clicking its name in the Tracks list.

Artificial Gymnasium

So if a delay is an ambient effect, you should be able to re-create the sound of a real environment, right? Let's start with a sound everyone can recognize—your high-school gym. The thing about a gym is that it's a big box, with hard, flat, parallel walls and a hard floor. It's an acoustician's worst nightmare precisely because of the obvious echoes it creates.

1.   Go to memory location 2, In the Gym, and create a new mono aux input called Gym Delay.

2.   Solo-safe the Gym Delay aux input.

3.   Route a send from the Gym Bass track to the input of Gym Delay. Note that Bus 1 is highlighted in the Bus submenu, indicating that it is already in use. Use a different bus for this send, and select that bus as the input for the aux in track.

4.   Insert a Medium Delay II (mono) on the Gym Delay track. The proper signal flow is illustrated in Figure 3.5.

5.   If a gym is about 130–150 feet long, it should take 260–300 milliseconds for a bass player warming up for the homecoming dance at one end to hear his sound bounce off the far wall. (Sound travels at about one foot per millisecond, so 150 feet down plus 150 feet back equals 300 feet equals 300 milliseconds, more or less.) Set the delay time to around 280 milliseconds, and then boost the feedback to about 55 percent. This should sound like a bit more of an echo than you might think is appropriate, but it will sound better in a minute.

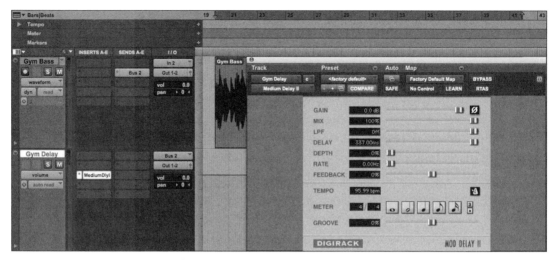

Figure 3.5 The proper routing for a delay. A send carries the signal from an audio track via a bus to the input of an aux input. The delay is inserted on the aux input.

6. Notice that when the send, the aux, and the plug-in are all set to 0.0 dB, the first tap of the delay is the same volume as the original. This never happens in nature, of course, so reducing the level of the delay by lowering the aux input's fader will help the illusion. You'll probably find that more than 6 dB of gain reduction is necessary to make the echoes sound authentic, and then you'll be glad you started with more feedback than you thought was necessary.

7. From the Options menu, enable Pre-Fader Metering. Although we ordinarily leave this off during mixing, right now you need to see the signal level as it leaves the plug-in. Some plug-ins, such as the EQ III, have meters, but this delay does not.

Note: Pre-Fader Metering, as its name suggests, causes the track meters to show the level *before* the fader has a chance to increase or decrease it. If no plug-ins are present, this means the level at the track input or the level of the audio streaming from disk. When plug-ins or hardware I/O inserts are active on a track, Pre-Fader Metering shows the level at the output of the last insert.

---

8. Notice that now the Gym Delay's clip indicator is lit. Although you haven't deliberately turned up the gain at any point, the delays reinforce each other, boosting the signal enough to clip the plug-in's output. Turn the plug-in's Gain control down a half a decibel and click the clip indicator to clear it. If this isn't enough to stop the clipping, keep adjusting in half-decibel increments until the

indicator no longer lights up. When you've stopped the clipping, you may need to adjust the aux input's volume to make up for the gain you've lost.

9. One more thing is missing. If you're trying to re-create the sensation of hearing the bass in a real physical space, you need to think in more than one dimension. Right now the echoes are all coming from the same place as the bass player—dead center. Drag the Gym Delay track's Pan fader to one side or the other, and the gym starts to take shape. You'll probably find the best results toward the extreme left or right. Tweak the pan, track volume, and delay time until it sounds like your high-school gym.

10. Disable Pre-Fader Metering.

Mono-to-Stereo Delay

The limitation of a mono delay aux is that if you pan it to one side, the other side is left completely dry. A *mono-to-stereo* plug-in splits a mono input signal into a stereo signal so each channel can be processed separately. It's as though you were to run the sound through two independent effects and then route one to the left and the other to the right.

1. Click the Plug-in selector and choose Medium Delay II (mono/stereo). You'll see what almost amounts to a clone of the mono plug-in pop up to the right, as in Figure 3.6. Note that the settings of both sides are the same as the mono processor with which you started.

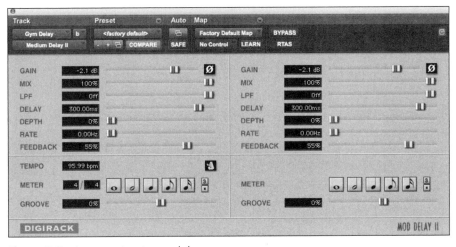

Figure 3.6 A mono-to-stereo delay.

2. Play the region, and you'll note that it sounds exactly the same as it did with the mono delay panned center. This is because two identical sounds panned equally

left and right appear to our ears as one sound panned center. Change *anything* about one side, and suddenly the delays move from the center to the left and right. Try changing the delay of one side by a couple of milliseconds, and you'll hear this effect. As you learned in Chapter 1, "Equalization," hold the Ctrl (Cmd) key down to make the smallest adjustment possible (probably a fraction of a millisecond), and you'll hear the difference. As you increase the amount of change, the delay image will move farther and farther away from center, up to a few milliseconds. Beyond a few milliseconds, the image no longer changes, but the left and right delays start to sound less like a single entity. By the time you reach a difference of 20 milliseconds or so between the left and right delay times, they start to sound like what they are—different delay times.

3. Getting back to the gymnasium idea, consider that a gym is maybe 80–100 feet wide, so the sound would take 160–200 milliseconds to bounce a round trip from bass to wall to wall and back. Set one delay time to 180 milliseconds, raise its feedback just a little, and see if that doesn't sound a lot more realistic. Keep an eye on the clip indicator, and adjust the plug-in gain if necessary.

4. There's still one more variable to be considered here. The farther a sound travels, the quieter it gets, so the echo from the length of the gym (the 280-millisecond delay) should be softer than the short echo. Pull the Gain control on the longer delay about 3 dB below the shorter side for an even more convincing sound. Note that although you left the gain at maximum on a mono delay, the Gain control allows you to balance the two processors of a mono-to-stereo delay.

Hitting the Wall(s)

Let's make more subtle use of this delay by giving a sound a sense of space without a sensation of echo. Go to memory location 3, Hitting the Wall, and listen once through. The sound is nice, but it was recorded dry and has no sense of space at all.

1. Fire up a mono delay aux and a Medium Delay II (mono/stereo), using the same routing as before. Don't forget to name the aux input something informative, solo-safe it, and use a new bus.

2. Holding down the Shift key in order to move both sliders simultaneously, drag either Delay slider to a value of 50 milliseconds or so. This is short enough that it doesn't sound so much like an echo, yet long enough that it's not too close to the original.

3. Crank up the feedback on both sides, again to a little more obvious than you think will be appropriate.

Note: Holding the Shift key while adjusting one control of a mono-to-stereo or stereo plug-in causes its matching control to move to the same value.

4. Now differentiate one channel's delay time by a few milliseconds and listen to how the effect moves out of the center to the walls.

5. Lower the gain of one side by a few decibels to further differentiate the two channels.

6. Pull the volume of the delay aux down by 8–10 dB, or perhaps more, so that the delays end up giving a subtle sensation of the sound interacting with the walls of the room.

7. Tweak the settings, especially the feedback and aux level, until you're satisfied with the results. To give the sensation of a larger room, use longer delay times.

Stereo Delay

Before moving on to the next memory location, try one last thing to see the limitation of a mono-to-stereo delay. While playing the region, drag the audio track's Pan slider back and forth slowly. Notice that although the original signal does indeed move left to right, the delay doesn't change at all. Shouldn't the delay from a sound at the left side of a room be more prominent on the left, too? The plug-in isn't receiving signal from the panned output of the audio track—it's being fed by the send, which, being a mono send, has no Pan control (see Figure 3.7). Because there is only one channel of input to a mono-to-stereo plug-in, the plug-in cannot recognize panning. What's needed is a true stereo plug-in, one with a stereo input as well as a stereo output. That way the input signal can be panned before it hits the delays.

1. Go to memory location 4, Stereo Delay, and you'll do just that.

2. Click the Send selector of the Stereo Delay track and, from the Bus submenu, choose Bus 5-6.

3. Alt-click (Opt-click) the send's fader to bring it to unity gain (0 dB).

Note: Please don't get the idea that sends and auxes should *always* be raised to unity gain! In the exercises so far, it has been a convenient shortcut that guarantees you will hear the desired effect, but when you have sends from multiple tracks feeding the same bus you will use send volume to balance those tracks within the bus. You've already seen that aux input volume is used to control the overall wet mix.

Figure 3.7 Two sends from a mono track, first to a mono bus (left) and then to a stereo bus (right). Note the lack of a Pan control on the send with a mono output.

4. Create a new *stereo* aux input and name it appropriately. Set its input to Bus 5-6 and bring its fader up to −6 dB or so.

5. Click any Insert selector on the aux input and assign a multichannel Medium Delay II (stereo) plug-in. Its controls are identical to those of the mono-to-stereo Medium Delay II, so you should have no trouble dialing in a "hitting the walls" delay along the lines of the one you just did. Take a moment to do that before you proceed.

6. Once you've got the delay set up, you're ready to experiment with panning. Pan the Stereo Delay track back and forth and listen to what happens. What's that? You don't hear any difference between this and the mono-to-stereo version? That's right! There's no difference yet because the pan of the source track has no effect on the aux. In Pro Tools, even if a send is post-fader, like the ones you've created so far, it is still pre-pan. See the Pan control on the Send Output window? That's the one that will affect what's hitting the delay.

7. Set the Stereo Delay track's pan to 70 left, and then set the send's pan to match. Now you're hearing the pan reflected in the delay. Try other pan settings,

including hard left or right, always matching the send to the track. The delay's behavior will change accordingly.

8. Just for sport, try setting the send's pan exactly opposite to that of the Stereo Delay track. It won't sound as natural, but it sounds different—and sometimes different is just what's needed.

Note: To link a send's pan to its track panning, click on its Follow Main Pan button, conveniently labeled FMP. The send's pan control will be grayed out, and it will follow the panning of the track automatically.

Rhythmic Delay 1

So far I've focused on delays as ambient effects, but music often makes creative use of delays obviously timed to the music. Pro Tools makes this easy by featuring tempo synchronization in the Medium, Long, and Extra Long Delays (see Figure 3.8).

Figure 3.8 The Medium, Long, and Extra Long Delays can sync to the current session tempo.

1. Go to memory location 5, Rhythmic Delay 1, and take a quick listen. If you weren't working in a DAW with tempo sync, you'd have to break out your watch and a calculator to find the correct delay times for a passage like this. You'd start by counting the number of beats in 15 seconds and multiplying it by four to get the tempo in beats per minute. Then you'd divide 60,000 by that number to get the number of milliseconds in a beat. If you wanted an eighth-note delay, you would divide that number in half, and so on for other note values.

2. Fortunately, you've got Pro Tools to do the work for you. Watch the main counter tick off the beats as you listen to the music, and confirm that Pro Tools is counting the tempo correctly. If it weren't, then using tempo sync wouldn't do you any good! You would need to use the Identify Beat feature to set the session tempo to the audio's tempo.

3. Following what by now is a familiar procedure, create a new stereo aux input, name it, and route a send from the Synth track to it. Insert the multichannel Medium Delay II (stereo) on the aux.

4. By default, the Tempo Sync button, a tiny metronome icon, is enabled. Click it to disable it, and you will see a slider that allows you to set a tempo independent of the session tempo. Click to re-enable tempo sync.

5. The musical figure is based on 16th notes, so click the left and right 16th-note buttons to set the delay times. Ctrl-drag (Cmd-drag) the right Delay slider a few milliseconds higher or lower to move the effect "out" as you did previously. Notice that the right 16th-note button is no longer highlighted as a result.

6. Click Play and raise the feedback amount, holding down the Shift key so you change both together. Aim for 5–6 taps.

7. Now drop the volume of the aux input so the effect is heard as a decoration on the original synth figure. Experiment with panning the original, panning the send to the same position (or not!).

Rhythmic Delay 2

There's no law that says both sides of the stereo delay must have the same rhythm—that's why there are two sets of note values on the plug-in (see Figure 3.9). Go to memory location 6, Rhythmic Delay 2. Listen for the solo synth part that you're going to delay.

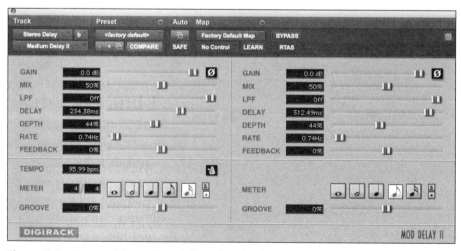

Figure 3.9 Stereo delays allow left and right channels to have independent rhythms.

1. Create a mono aux input, name it, and create a mono send from the Solo track.

2. Insert a mono-to-stereo Long Delay II on the aux.

3. Set the levels of the aux and send to unity. You should be getting pretty comfortable with this procedure, and if you've been practicing your shortcut for creating tracks (Ctrl/Cmd+Shift+N) you're getting pretty quick, too. That's good, because you'll be doing this every time you set up a delay or reverb!

4. Make the following adjustments while the selection loops so you can hear the results immediately. Set the left delay to a quarter note. Set the right to a quarter-note triplet by clicking the quarter-note icon and then the 3 button at the right of the 16th note. Adjust the feedback and aux input level to taste. (This one can afford to be very wet!) As always, watch for clipping and adjust as necessary.

5. If you don't like the triplet feel, you can get a similar result from a dotted rhythm. Set the right side to an eighth-note value, and set the left side to a dotted eighth by clicking the eighth note and then the dot symbol just below the triplet 3. Now you have the same 3:2 relationship between left and right, but the feel is all even subdivisions of the beat.

Note: You may have noticed that I've ignored the delays listed in the multi-mono list. That's because they're virtually identical to the "multichannel" versions. In fact, they are both dual-mono processors with completely independent left and right channels. The only distinction is that the multi-mono version allows each channel to have its own tempo.

Reverb

The echo of a canyon and the slapback of a gymnasium are a far cry from the smooth reverberation of a concert hall or cathedral. Creating fluid reverb electronically is a bigger challenge than simply adding a few delays to the original sound; doing it in the digital domain is more difficult still.

Early recording studios used a clever combination of acoustics and electronics to create artificial reverb, running a speaker into a reverberant room or dedicated chamber where the sound bounced around until it was picked up by a microphone and blended to taste with the direct (dry) signal. Other techniques involved exciting a spring or metal plate and picking up its vibrations with a contact microphone, again blending the signal with the original. Although a great deal of modern reverb (all reverb within a DAW, of course) is created digitally, the names of these classic techniques remain in the parameters and presets of digital reverbs that emulate their sounds (see Figure 3.10).

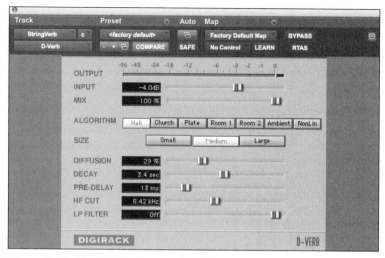

Figure 3.10 The DigiRack D-Verb includes reverb algorithms, such as Room and Plate, that emulate classic studio reverb techniques.

Note: Notice how the interfaces of the Delay II and D-Verb look a little, well, older than those of Dynamics III and EQ III? They are a generation earlier and less sophisticated, although each is worthy of professional-caliber use. Recognizing that they are somewhat behind the curve compared to the stock delays and reverbs bundled with competing DAWs, Digidesign included three new reverb plug-ins created by their AIR (Advanced Instrument Research) group in Pro Tools 8.

The "law" of time-based routing is adhered to more strictly with reverbs than with delays. Historically, because reverbs took up entire rooms and later required extraordinarily expensive devices, studios didn't have separate reverbs for each track, so bussing to a common reverb was the only option. Within a DAW, the price of a reverb plug-in is its drain on the CPU, which is greater than for most other effects. Putting a separate reverb on each track is a quick way to choke your computer, so bussing to one or two common reverbs is still standard practice.

Natural Reverb

Returning to the billiard-ball analogy, the difference between delay and reverb is that in a delay, the bank shots (reflections of the source sound) are distinct and finite in number, while in a reverb, they blur together and are innumerable if not exactly infinite.

Computers like to put numbers on things, which is why it's much easier and less resource-intensive to program a good delay than a good reverb.

A natural-sounding reverb must not only die away smoothly, it must also include reflections on both sides of the stereo field. In a concert hall, a soloist's sound bounces off each wall to a listener's ears and also bounces from one wall to the other and then to the listener's ears. A mono or multi-mono reverb cannot re-create this left/right interaction, so a stereo reverb is preferred when a natural sound is desired.

1. Go to memory location 7, Natural Reverb, and listen to the dry saxophone. It's a good, clean sound, but it sounds more like you're sitting next to the player in your living room than listening to him in concert. Some well-chosen reverb will change the mood.

2. Using the same signal flow you used for delays (see Figure 3.11), send the saxophone to a mono-to-stereo D-Verb. (Are you remembering to name your aux and solo-safe it?) Note that the D-Verb has only one set of parameters rather than separate L/R parameters like the Mod Delay. This is because the D-Verb is a true stereo processor, and it treats the two channels as a single broad soundstage.

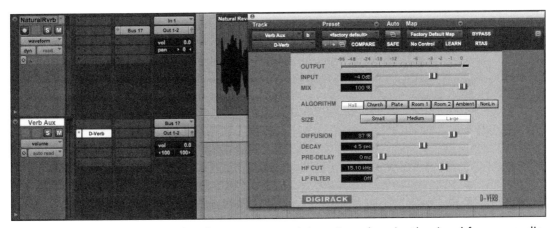

Figure 3.11 Reverbs are routed in the same way as delays. A send carries the signal from an audio track via a bus to the input of an aux input. The reverb is inserted on the aux input.

3. Leave the algorithm on Hall and play a game of Goldilocks with the room size choices. Is Large too big? Is Small too, well, small? Is Mama, I mean Medium, just right? Play with the aux input's level, too, as it controls the ratio of wet to dry. In an uncluttered arrangement like this, the reverb can afford to be relatively big. For a more contemporary sound, though, small reverbs are in vogue.

Note: Keep in mind that although the default decay time changes with the room size, the two parameters can be adjusted independently. The *decay time* is the length of time it takes the reverberation to die away after the original signal stops, whereas the *room size* reflects how far away the virtual walls are. In reality, too, the two are related but not inexorably linked. A large rehearsal hall and a small recital hall are nearly the same size, but the rehearsal hall has more sound-absorbing materials so a large ensemble doesn't get too loud or too muddy. The recital hall is designed and built for a more reflective, reverberant sound to enhance the performance of a chamber group or soloist.

4. Set the room size to Small, then set the decay time to four seconds, and listen critically.

5. Now set the size to Medium and decay time to four seconds, and you will hear the difference room size makes when decay time remains constant.

6. Try it with Large at four seconds decay time.

Saving Plug-In Settings

Wait a minute, there has got to be an easier way to do this comparison, hasn't there? Let's create three presets so you can switch more quickly and focus on the sound rather than the process of changing parameters. You've already recalled several of my presets for comparison—creating your own is just as easy.

1. Start by telling Pro Tools where to save your presets. Click the Plug-In Settings arrow, as shown in Figure 3.12, and point to Settings Preferences, Save Plug-In Settings To, and click Session Folder. This forces Pro Tools to save the presets you're about to create to a folder within your current session folder. If you wanted a setting to be available for recall from *any* session you create, you would change this option to Root Settings Folder.

2. Now to create the presets. First, tweak the plug-in the way you want it: Small Hall with four-second decay.

3. Click the Plug-In Settings arrow and choose Save Settings As from the menu.

4. In the dialog box that appears, type a name for your preset, such as **Small Hall 4 Seconds**. (Although you can create presets with very long file names, doing so is inadvisable for several reasons, the most obvious being that the Plug-In Librarian field can only display 20 or so characters.)

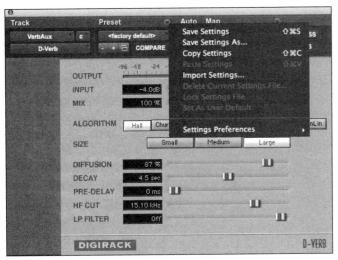

Figure 3.12   Clicking the arrow to the right of the word Preset brings up the Plug-In Settings menu.

Note: Never save! Well, never *just* save. If you choose Save Settings from the Plug-In Settings menu, you overwrite the current preset. Most of the time you will want to save your current settings as a new preset, and that requires the Save Settings As command.

---

5.   Create another preset with a medium hall and four-second decay and a third with a large hall and four-second decay. You can now switch among them using the Plug-In Librarian menu.

Pre-Delay

Pre-delay is the amount of time that passes between hearing the direct sound and hearing the reverberation. Think about this—if you're standing right next to someone on stage in a concert hall, the direct (dry) sound hits your ears immediately, but the first reflected path from any wall takes 80–100 milliseconds (because the nearest such surface is 40–50 feet away). By contrast, if you walk to the back of the hall, you will hear the direct and reverberant sound at virtually the same time because the path from source to side wall to you is not that much longer than the direct path. Your ears use this difference to determine how close you are to a source, and the closer the reverberation is to the original sound, the farther away you seem to be from the source.

Choose one of your presets and experiment with the Pre-Delay value. For any combination of algorithm and size, the Pre-Delay setting can be adjusted between 0 and 300 milliseconds.

The higher settings can make the reverb seem almost disembodied, but if you want an intimate lead vocal with a long reverb, that can be a good thing. With that much pre-delay, the reverb gives the vocal plenty of window dressing, but it doesn't cling to it.

Algorithm, Size, and Decay

Before going on, it's worth your time to dig deeply into the various reverb algorithms and the effect of size and decay on them. Using a very familiar sound is helpful, so you might want to close this session, create a new one, and record 20–30 seconds of yourself speaking, singing, or playing if you are an instrumentalist. Route the track to a reverb as you have done several times now in this chapter and experiment freely. Using a sound you know well allows you to focus on the differences between the parameters. Although your ears are the ultimate judge, consider the following generalizations about the seven algorithms.

- Hall is designed to emulate a typical concert or recital hall. The ambience of a hall is smooth and controlled, and even a small hall is capable of seating a couple of hundred people. Halls are designed to give a sound plenty of space to breathe, and the artist is not very close to the audience. I use halls with 2–3 second decays to enhance classical recordings made in a local venue that is too dry for the style.

- Church is not a mysterious name, is it? Churches are quite reverberant, with countless reflective surfaces and nooks and crannies for the sound to explore on its way to the listener. It's easy for a sound to get muddy with this algorithm, so I often pull the wet mix (the aux input's volume, remember?) back several decibels to let the dry sound dominate.

Note: The Density parameter determines how thick the reverb is in its early stages. Dense reverbs can be dramatic, but sparser reverbs are more transparent.

- Room 1 and Room 2 are more intimate settings, suggesting less square footage than a hall or a church even at Large size. The virtual materials of Room 2 make for a somewhat brighter sound than Room 1, and Room 2 is conceived as a smaller space. Rooms give a sound body without too much clutter. This is a sound that dominates post-millennial popular music, helping create that "in your face" vibe. In video projects, rooms are invaluable for trying to match dialog replacement to production dialog and for creating interior ambiences.

- Plate emulates the sound of a plate reverb as described earlier. Its character is immediately recognizable as artificial, but it is familiar to any listener over the age of

10 because plates have been used so much. The sound is rich and dense and can be used to fatten a sound. Certain classic snare and vocal sounds depend on plates.

- Even at a Large setting, Ambient allows a maximum decay of only one second (see Figure 3.13). It is designed to give a concise, lean sense of space without adding very much to the overall sound. Smaller still, Non Linear has a maximum decay of 500 milliseconds at a Large setting. It has an unnaturally abrupt release, making it a good alternative to the gated reverb you created in Chapter 2, "Dynamics."

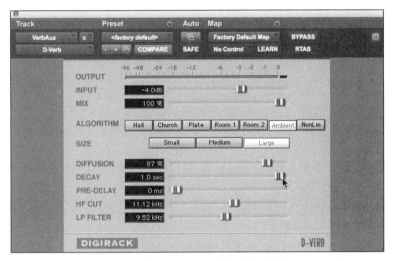

Figure 3.13 Each algorithm/size combination influences the range of decay times available. A Large Ambient setting has a maximum one-second decay.

Mono Reverb 1

If you wanted to sound natural all the time, you would record in concert halls and clubs with nothing more than a stereo pair of mics to capture the real event. Recording in a studio, however, gives you control over every aspect of the sound, along with the ability to create sounds that don't occur in nature. Sometimes you use this power to create an idealized version of a natural sound, while other times you throw reality to the wind. This next technique is one short step down that road—not jarringly unreal, but not exactly true to life either.

Reverb can quickly fill in all the spaces in the mix, so it's customary to pick and choose what gets reverb, how much reverb anything gets, and where that reverb will appear in the mix. Placing a mono reverb in line with the original sound gives the sound a feeling of depth without making it wide enough to interfere with other parts.

1. If you used your own session for the previous section, re-open the Chapter 03.ptf session. Go to memory location 8, Mono Verb 1. As always, listen carefully to the dry sound before you start applying any processing. Create a mono aux and route a send from the Flute track to it. Insert a mono AIR Reverb on the aux.

2. The AIR Reverb's default setting will sound too big at first. Choose the Small Room preset.

3. Tweak the Reverb Time and aux input volume until you are pleased with the sound. Notice how the reverb complements the dry sound without getting in the way of the far left or right sides of the mix.

4. Now pan the source track about halfway to the right, and pan the aux input to match, as in Figure 3.14. As long as the reverb follows the source, our ears are happy to marry them and keep them independent of the other sounds.

5. As a variation, switch the preset to Cathedral. Set its reverb time to 1.2 seconds, and pull the aux's volume back until the wet/dry mix is comparable to what it was with the Small Room. Listen to the difference in the sound. It's warmer and bigger, and yet because it is panned with the dry sound, it doesn't seem to take up much more space in the mix.

Mono Reverb 2

Panning a mono reverb with the dry sound is useful for lead sounds that tend to live near the center of the stereo image, but rhythm sounds are often pulled out to the sides to keep them out of the lead's way, and subtler techniques are required. This next method definitely doesn't happen in nature, but it doesn't draw attention to itself.

1. Go to memory location 9, Mono Verb 2, and set up a mono D-Verb on a mono aux as before, with a send to the aux from the EPiano track. Choose a small Hall setting and leave the decay time at its default for now.

2. Pan the EPiano track hard right, and pan the reverb aux hard left. You should get the sensation that there's a richer sound, but that the sound is not cluttering the center of the mix.

3. Now do the exact opposite to the Clav track, creating a mono reverb aux and panning it hard right with the dry track hard left. The two keyboard parts complement each other in this way, each playing off the other's reverb.

Figure 3.14 A mono reverb setup in the Mix view. When the reverb is panned to the same spot as the dry sound, it gives the sound more depth without taking up more horizontal space.

4. Lower each reverb's HF Cut setting to about 10 kHz. This causes more of the high frequencies in the reverb to die away more quickly. The reverb's initial sound remains the same, but it darkens as it decays, making the effect somewhat subtler.

5. Tweak out the aux volumes and decay times to fine-tune the effect.

6. Replace the D-Verbs with the AIR Reverb and tune the settings to achieve the same effect. Its High Frequencies Cut setting is equivalent to the D-Verb's HF Cut.

Dual-Mono Reverb

This last approach exemplifies the "better than reality" approach to mixing. A realistic reverb covers the entire stereo image, lending both depth and breadth to a sound. Its downside is that it takes up a lot of sonic space, often getting in the way of other instruments. It would be great to have the width without the clutter, wouldn't it?

1. Go to memory location 10, Dual-Mono Verb, and listen. This time you're going to create a stereo aux rather than a mono aux and insert a *multi-mono* D-Verb on it.

2. Create a stereo send on the Sax track and use a stereo bus to route it to the aux. You may recognize this principle, as it's similar to the way you moved the delay out of the center of the mix.

3. Before you unlink the left and right reverbs, however, get the common settings together so you don't have to redo them. Use a medium Church setting with a decay time of around five seconds. Set the pre-delay to 80 milliseconds. Raise the HF Cut and LP Filter all the way to the top (Off) so the reverb retains plenty of high end.

4. Now disable the Master Link button and Alt-click (Opt-click) the Channel selector so both channels are showing, as in Figure 3.15. Change the right processor to a Large Church and reset its decay time to around five seconds. Adjust its pre-delay to 120 milliseconds. It will now decay similarly to the left channel, but it will have a slightly different character.

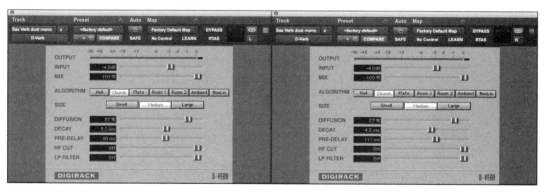

Figure 3.15 The dual-mono D-Verb, with each channel set to slightly different values.

5. To accentuate the effect, let's add some EQ. On the next insert after the D-Verb, insert a multi-mono 4-Band EQ 3. Click the LF band's IN button to disable it, and then enable the MF band. Set the HF band to a shelving filter with a 5 dB

boost at 6 kHz. Set the MF and HMF bands to a 3 dB boost at 1 kHz and 4 kHz, respectively. Shift-click the HMF band's Gain control to invert its curve to a 3 dB cut.

6. Now disable the Master Link button and use the Channel selector to switch to the right channel. Shift-click the Gain knobs of the MF and HMF bands. You have created equal-but-opposite curves on the left and right channels, with both adding shimmer on the HF band. This will make the effect seem particularly far to the sides, so even though the reverb time is long it will not interfere with the intimacy of the dry sax in the center.

7. If you try this exercise with the AIR Reverb, you'll note that it is not available in a multi-mono configuration, which prevents you from differentiating the left and right channels. However, once you follow it with the differentiated multi-mono EQ, the reverb's image will move to the sides as desired.

Whether it's natural or artificial, ambience is critical to our listening experience. Although the current trend is toward drier mixes, don't assume that time-based effects are not present. Many of the techniques you've used in this chapter are present in current mixes, although they may be used in very small amounts. They may also be employed differently in different sections of the arrangement, so in Chapter 7, "Automation," I'll discuss automating mix parameters. Styles change, but our ears' need for ambient context doesn't.

4 Special Effects

This chapter deals with a handful of effects that don't fit neatly into any other category, including chorus, flange, and de-essing. These processes can be used for both creative and corrective purposes. The category could be extended to include distortion, automatic pitch correction, amp modeling, microphone modeling, and other effects. Pro Tools LE 8 includes a variety of such effects—I'll cover a few essentials, but you'll want to devote some serious time to exploring the entire AIR Creative Collection, which are all new in Pro Tools 8.

These special effects are routed like dynamics and EQ, not like time-based processors. That is, they are inserted directly on the track that is to be processed. This is because they are ordinarily intended to affect a single part (or an entire mix) in a unique way, as opposed to the communal spirit of a reverb or delay.

Chorus

Chorus is one of those technical terms that means exactly what it says. It's an effect designed to make one voice (or instrument) sound like a chorus of voices. If you imagine the sound of a singer recording a multitude of takes and combining them all into one big self-choir (think early Enya), you've got the idea.

Chorus is in fact achieved by electronically copying a solo track several times, delaying the copies slightly, and varying the delay times dynamically. If this sounds to you like a glorified delay plug-in, you're exactly right. We're going to use the Mod Delay plug-in to create a chorus effect.

Note: If you've been wondering why Digidesign dubbed this the Mod Delay family, wonder no more. The amount of delay can be modulated, or varied dynamically during playback, to achieve the characteristic chorusing effect. (Modulation is change over time, and it is a technique that occurs repeatedly in audio processing, especially synthesis. The depth of modulation is the amount of change, and in most cases this amount is symmetrically positive and negative. The rate of modulation is

---

the speed of the variation, which is most often a simple cyclic pattern of rise and fall.) This adds a subtle change in pitch to the delays, raising the pitch slightly as the delay is shortened and lowering it slightly when the delay is lengthened. Like a real chorus, the effect depends on slight and variable differences of both timing and pitch to create a thicker sound. A chorus effect is more regular than a real chorus, though, so while the sound is appropriately richer than the unprocessed original, it is nonetheless clearly electronic in origin, a fact which has done nothing to diminish its popularity across all genres of contemporary popular music.

Chorus 1

You're going to apply a chorus effect to the Sax track, but don't go creating an aux input! In this case, you'll break the time-based rule because you're using the Mod Delay in a different way than you did in Chapter 3. Here's what to do:

1.   Open the Chapter 04.ptf session and go to memory location 1, Chorus 1.

2.   Go ahead and be naughty—insert the Short Delay II (mono/stereo) on the Sax track, as shown in Figure 4.1.

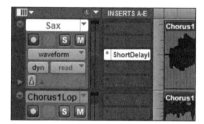

Figure 4.1 Although a chorus is related to a delay, it is routed more like a dynamic effect than a time-based effect.

3.   Set the delay time to 20 milliseconds on the left and 23 milliseconds on the right, and set the feedback to 30 percent.

4.   So far, this resembles a good old-fashioned short delay. The key to turning it into a chorus is found in three controls we ignored in Chapter 3: Mix, Depth, and Rate. The Mix slider should already be at 50 percent. Be sure that is the case.

Note: With a more typical delay on an aux input, you would leave the mix at 100 percent and adjust the balance between wet and dry via the aux input's volume control. With the delay inserted directly on the source track, the Mix control sets this balance.

---

5. Shift-drag the Rate slider to 0.21 Hz. Remember that for finer adjustment, you can hold down the Ctrl (Cmd) key.

6. While continuing to hold the Shift key down, slowly raise the Depth setting until you reach 13 percent. This should start to sound familiar.

7. Adjust the mix to control the intensity of the chorus relative to the original. In a true chorus, no voice is dominant, so the mix ratio should be high. In common practice, however, the chorus is used to enliven but not obscure the original, so the mix ratio is relatively low.

Chorus 2

Let's create another chorus. Before leaving this memory location, however, copy the delay's settings so we can use them as the basis for the new chorus.

1. Click to open this plug-in's Librarian menu and choose Copy Settings. This places the current settings in the Clipboard, ready to be pasted into another mono-to-stereo Delay II plug-in.

2. Go to memory location 2, Chorus 2.

3. Insert a Short Delay II (mono/stereo) on the Lead track.

4. Click to open the Librarian menu and choose Paste Settings, as shown in Figure 4.2. This endows this plug-in with the settings you copied into the Clipboard in step 1.

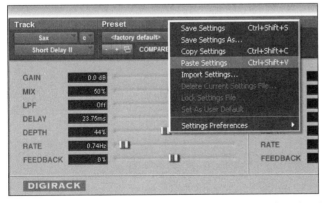

Figure 4.2 Pasting settings from one instance of a plug-in to another.

Note: You could have accomplished this by saving the settings in the preceding section as a preset and then opening the preset here, but if you don't intend to use those settings more than once, this is a simpler and more direct approach.

---

5.   To make this chorus more intense, raise both mix levels until the chorused copies are equal in volume to the original. This makes for a thicker sound, but it's still pretty polite.

6.   Drop the mix back down to 50 percent or so. This time, raise the modulation rate on both sides to 1.0 Hz. That should make the sound quite a bit more active.

7.   Now raise the modulation depth on both sides to 35 percent or more and listen to the change. The pitch changes now become more obvious, and the sound is much more like a hive of bees than a decent chorus of lead synths. Lower the mix level to about 30 percent, though, and the effect is powerful without being distracting. Tweak the right settings slightly apart from the left settings as you've done before to move the effect to the outside.

Note: Offsetting each right parameter slightly from the corresponding left parameter moves the effect from the middle of the stereo field. When our ears hear the same settings on left and right, the correlation between them causes our brains to perceive the effect as being centered. De-correlated effects sound like they come from the outside of the soundstage.

---

8.   Reset the depth and rate to 13 percent and 0.2 Hz, and raise the mix to 50 percent again to return to the softer chorus.

9.   Now increase the feedback as much as you can stand. Eventually it will reach the point where it sustains indefinitely. Before you reach that point, lower the mix to about 18 percent and listen to how even an extreme setting can sound musical when blended properly.

You might describe this setting as I did the previous setting—powerful without being distracting—yet they are distinctive sounds. With a little imagination, you can always find more than one way to create a particular type of effect.

Flanging

Another classic effect bearing a familial resemblance to chorus is *flanging*. In a tape-based system, this effect was created by running two tape decks playing the same material in sync with each other, then varying the playback speed of first one and then the other by dragging one's finger on the flange of the tape reel. As the two tapes moved in and out of sync with each other, subtle pitch and timing differences (sound familiar?) caused sonic friction between them. There are two main differences between flanging and chorus. The first is that flanging duplicates the signal only once rather than several times. The second is that the rate of modulation of flanging is usually slower than that of chorus. As with a chorus, setting up a flange effect in Pro Tools starts with inserting the Mod Delay directly on the track you want to process. Although you can use flanging on individual parts, I'll illustrate the principle in the traditional fashion—on a stereo mix.

1. Go to memory location 3, Flanging.

2. Insert a Short Delay II (stereo) on the audio track.

3. For both channels, set the delay time to 0.00 ms, and confirm that the mix level is set to 50 percent and the feedback to zero, as shown in Figure 4.3.

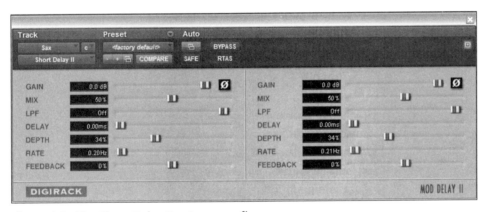

Figure 4.3   The Short Delay II set up as a flanger.

4. Enter a modulation frequency (Rate) of 0.21 Hz for both channels. (Remember that holding down the Shift key lets you adjust both simultaneously.)

5. Click Play. As you listen, Shift+Ctrl-drag (Shift+Cmd-drag) the Depth slider to slowly raise the modulation amount.

6. Hunt down your old lava lamp to go with this 1970s sound.

7. Now that you have a good idea of how a flanger works, replace the Short Delay II with the AIR Flanger, found under the Modulation plug-in list. Take some time to explore its presets. Its controls go far beyond the basic flanging available with the Mod Delay plug-ins.

Note: Also found under the Modulation plug-in list are the AIR Chorus, Ensemble, Multi-Chorus, and Phaser. Each of these takes the basic principles of chorus and flanging and builds on it. See where your imagination takes you by applying these to the preceding exercises. Explore the presets, but don't be limited by them! If you find that a little goes a long way, be patient—in Chapter 7, "Automation," you'll learn how to bring special effects in and out of the mix as needed.

De-Essing

Sibilance refers to the hissing sound made by pronouncing the letter *s*. From a mixing perspective, sibilance becomes an issue because it is often much louder to our ears than the other vocal sounds surrounding it. If you watch the meters as a vocalist sings or says, "These are my sisters, Chelsea and Sasha," you may not see volume spikes at every *s*, *ch*, and *sh*, but to your ears, those sounds will stand out (see Figure 4.4). If you adjusted the volume of that phrase to rein in the sibilants in order to make the phrase fit in the mix better, you would have to turn it down to the point where the overall volume was much softer than the sentence, "I believe you've met my brother Bob," which has no sibilants.

Figure 4.4 Sibilance as your ears hear it. After filtering to emphasize the frequencies to which your ears are drawn, the volume spikes in this waveform represent sibilance.

Certain steps in the recording process tend to exacerbate the problem, such as popular microphones with hyped high-end for that sexy vocal presence, some reverb algorithms, and so forth. The processor that controls sibilance is called a *de-esser*. A de-esser works by ducking the volume when it detects sibilance. This is a special sort of compression, where the level detection and threshold setting only look at the frequencies associated with sibilance.

Note: Traditionally, engineers accomplished de-essing by creating a copy of the signal, equalizing it with a band-pass filter to emphasize sibilance, and feeding it to the detector circuit of a compressor through a special connection called the *side-chain*, which I'll cover in detail in Chapter 11, "Advanced Dynamics." When sibilance occurs, the compressor kicks in, ducking the original signal just long enough to reduce the volume of the *s*, *ch*, or *sh* sound, and then returns to normal.

A Look Under the Hood

Dynamics III includes a de-esser that can be inserted directly on the source track without requiring a side-chain or equalizer, thus saving both time and system resources. Before applying it to actual vocal sibilance, let's look under its hood.

1. Go to memory location 4, Under the Hood, and brace yourself. What you are about to hear is a test tone, not musical material, and you may want to start with your volume turned down a bit. The region consists of pink noise with one-second sine wave tones at 1, 2, 4, and 8 kHz. The pattern of four tones then repeats itself, with the noise droning on throughout.

2. Insert the Dynamics III De-Esser plug-in (see Figure 4.5) on the audio track.

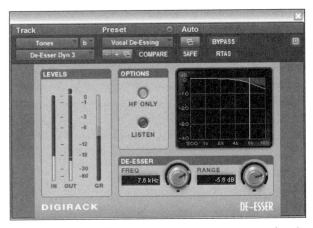

Figure 4.5   The DigiRack Dynamics III De-Esser plug-in.

3. Make sure the HF Only button is disabled (dimmed) and set the frequency to 8.0 kHz.

4. Set the range to −6.0 dB.

5. Hit Play. As the 1 and 2 kHz tones play, nothing changes, but when the 4 kHz tone plays, the compressor applies a bit more than 3 dB of gain reduction. When

the 8 kHz tone plays, the compressor applies more than 6 dB of gain reduction. Notice that the compressor affects all frequencies, ducking the noise along with the tone.

Note: You may find it odd that the 4 kHz tone triggered the compressor until you remember that band-pass filters are defined not only by their center frequency but also by their bandwidth. Clearly the band-pass filter De-Esser III uses is wide enough to allow some of the 4 kHz tone to reach the compressor's detection circuit. You do not have any control over bandwidth in this particular plug-in, only the center frequency.

Notice that the gain reduction (GR) meter includes an orange segment as well as a red segment. You will recall that this is an indication of a soft knee in the compressor portion of the plug-in. So, although you have no direct control over either parameter, you now know that the De-Esser's filter has a moderately broad bandwidth and a soft knee. Your experiences in Chapters 1 and 2 taught you that such settings favor transparency over surgical precision, and that is a reasonable and necessary compromise for a de-esser.

---

6. Listen to the effect of the De-Esser plug-in at frequency settings of 1, 2, and 4 kHz. With these settings, the entire signal will still be compressed each time the processor is triggered. The only distinction is which frequencies will cause the effect and how much compression will be applied.

7. Lower the range enough, and you will see that the pink noise actually triggers the compression. The noise includes frequencies across the audible spectrum, so no matter what the trigger frequency is, some of the noise makes it through the band-pass filter. If the range setting is low enough, the noise itself triggers de-essing. The important lesson here is that when dealing with broad-spectrum musical material, you need to be sure that the de-esser's range setting is low enough to catch real sibilance without being so low that it catches non-sibilant high frequencies.

8. Click the HF Only indicator to enable it. (It will turn blue.)

9. Hit Play, run through the various frequency settings, and see what happens. Now the compression is applied only to frequencies above the trigger frequency. Note that HF Only mode does not affect the compressor's detection—with a 2 kHz frequency setting, an 8 kHz tone still does not trigger compression.

Note: In HF Only mode, there are two separate EQs involved. The first filters the trigger signal so that only sibilance causes compression. The second splits the original signal into two bands, only one of which (the higher) gets compressed. This is called *multi-band compression*, and this is just one of many potential applications of this powerful technology. Unfortunately, this is the only multi-band application incorporated into Dynamics III.

Real-World De-Essing

Now that you've seen the inner workings of a de-esser, you're ready to apply it to a real vocal. Listen carefully to the difference proper de-essing can make on a sibilant track.

1. Go to memory location 5, Vocal De-Essing, and listen to the vocal phrase. It's full of sibilance, and ripe for de-essing.

2. Insert the De-Esser Dyn 3 plug-in on the Lead Voc track. All you need to do is determine the frequency of the sibilance so you can set the De-Esser correctly.

3. Click on the Listen indicator (see Figure 4.6) to hear only the band-passed signal that is fed to the detection circuit.

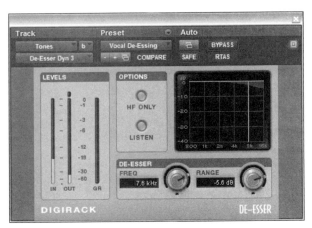

Figure 4.6   In Listen mode, the De-Esser Dyn 3 passes only the band-filtered trigger signal to help in setting the trigger frequency.

4. While looping the selection, scan with the Frequency knob until you hear the sibilance sticking out plainly. Try to center in on it as accurately as possible.

5. Turn Listen mode off and lower the Range control enough so that compression is occurring during the sibilance without getting triggered by any other sounds.

You may find it's necessary only to reduce the sibilance a few decibels, but that may change when you add compression and other effects to the vocal track.

6.   If you find the de-essing is too obvious, try it in HF Only mode. (You may need to lower the range.) Experiment until you get the best sibilance reduction with the least effect on the rest of the track.

Note: Should you compress a signal before or after you de-ess it? It depends on whom you ask—or more importantly, it depends on the source material and what sound you're after. De-essing before compressing prevents sibilant phrases from being compressed differently than non-sibilant phrases. De-essing after compressing can be used to tame sibilance that made it through the compressor due to a slow attack.

Extra Special FX

This topic could go on almost endlessly just using the plug-ins that come bundled with Pro Tools. Before we move on, let's explore just a couple more.

1.   Go to memory location 6, Extra Special FX. Listen to the dry drum loop.

2.   Insert a mono Eleven Free plug-in on the track (see Figure 4.7). It's found in the Harmonic list.

Figure 4.7   Digidesign's Eleven Free amp-modeling plug-in

> **Note:** Eleven Free is a trimmed-down version of Digidesign's Eleven amp-modeling plug-in. Although the full version models the sonic character of 16 different amps, seven different cabinets, and eight different microphones, the free version offers but two amps and two cabinets. Those two sound just as authentic as they do in the full version—you just get less variety.

3. Call up the Memphis Tweed preset and listen closely to the effect.

4. Change the amp's Normal/Bright setting to Bright and listen to the difference.

5. Change the Cab Type to 4x12 Classic 30 and listen to the difference.

> **Note:** It bears repeating: *Always listen critically as you change settings!* Anyone can recall settings from a recipe—a skilled engineer has listened so closely for so long that he has a good idea what it will sound like when he changes a setting. Every session is an opportunity to train your ears.

Loops are used so much in many styles of music that engineers are always looking for ways to spice them up. Amp-modeling plug-ins (or real amplifiers) are good candidates because they offer such a wide variety of timbres. Consider combining a mildly to moderately distorted loop like this with a clean loop or live drums, or even using automation to bring the distortion in and out. As for this loop, you're not done with it yet.

6. On the next insert after Eleven Free, call up the AIR Talkbox plug-in. It's found in the Modulation list.

7. While playing the loop, audition the Talkbox's various presets by clicking on the Next (+) and Previous (−) buttons located under the Librarian menu (see Figure 4.8). I found 07 Lonesome and 13 Mouth Percussion particularly appealing—be your own judge.

Figure 4.8 Auditioning plug-in settings with the Next and Previous buttons.

Another way to audition plug-ins is by opening the Plug-in Settings select window (see Figure 4.9). You can click on any preset's name to load it as you play, or you can enable the Increment Setting Every *N* Seconds function, and Pro Tools will move from one preset to the next at the interval you specify.

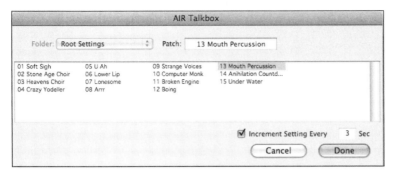

Figure 4.9 Auditioning plug-in settings from the Plug-in Settings select window.

8. When you have settled on a preset as a starting point, fine-tune it with the available parameters. Pay particular attention to the Vowel setting—this is one you're going to want to come back to after you learn automation in Chapter 7.

You've just transformed a natural-sounding drum loop into the sound of a robot beat-boxing. Not bad for a day's work! With a bit more aggressive amp settings, you should be able to conjure a Harley or even a Peterbilt beat-boxing, depending on the needs of the song.

You are now familiar with the essential purpose and operation of the effects that make up the vast majority of processing in a contemporary mix. Most importantly, you've started to refine your ear's sensitivity to the sort of challenges presented in a typical mix and the solutions to those challenges.

In the next four chapters, you'll explore the big-picture aspects of mixing, including organizational skills, advanced routing techniques, and more. What you've learned so far will form the foundation on which we'll build, so be sure you're comfortable with the preceding topics before moving on. When you're ready, turn the page and dive back in!

5 The Rough Mix

In earlier chapters, you learned to use the essential types of effects in a mixer's arsenal. You dealt with the proper routing of time-based effects as well as the use of insert effects, such as EQ and dynamics. You also worked on the most important aspect of mixing: critical listening.

In the next few chapters, you will build on that knowledge and apply it within the bigger picture. This chapter deals with getting your mix started, a step that for many is the most difficult. I'll show you how I get a session organized and how much can be accomplished with the proper use of two simple controls: volume and pan.

Organizing Your Mix

Anyone who thinks that organization is anathema to creativity has never looked very closely at an artist's work. A classical composer sees an orchestra in terms of major sections—strings, brass, woodwinds, and percussion. A pop composer sees a song as comprising verses, choruses, an introduction, possibly a bridge, and an ending. Hip-hop lyrics, no matter how freestyle, are built on repeating patterns of rhythm and rhyme. Art is all about organization, even though it may often get a lot of mileage out of building a structure and then breaking it.

It stands to reason, then, that it pays to be organized about a mix. Your sense of organization will be shaped by the music, of course. What instruments and vocals are present? Is there one primary melodic element, or is that role shared? How is the song structured? If segments repeat, will your mix be the same each time or different?

Your sense of organization will also be shaped by the history of the recording. Did the tracking engineer leave you with alternate takes to sort out? Are they spread across different tracks, or are they on edit playlists? If it was tracked in Pro Tools, did the tracking engineer already have some plug-ins on certain tracks? Was there a rough mix? What did the client think of it?

It may be that when you receive a project it needs more than mixing. Perhaps the vocal needs to be edited and/or tuned. Maybe the arrangement could be improved by some inventive editing. Although these are adjustments that often occur during the mixing process, they are not actually mixing topics, so I won't go into them in this book.

Note: Another non-mixing function that may be beneficial before mixing is mapping the tempo of the song. Because effects such as delays can use tempo-based timings, Pro Tools needs to know the tempo of the song. It's also useful to be able to refer to a position within the song by bar numbers—even if the musicians aren't working from a printed score, they'll use terms such as "four bars before the guitar solo" to describe where they want something to happen in the mix. If the song was not recorded to Pro Tools' click track, it's a good idea to tempo-map the entire song using Identify Beat or Beat Detective prior to mixing.

Creating Memory Locations

One of the first things I do with a new mix is throw all the faders up to a reasonable level and listen to the entire track from beginning to end. This helps me get a good feel for the overall intent of the song as well as assess the work that needs to be done. While I'm listening, I also try to map out the form of the song. How long is the intro? How many verses are there? What is the form of the chorus? Are there solos? Bridges? Interludes? Tempo changes?

At each major section of the song, I place a marker. In Pro Tools, a *marker* is one type of memory location (see Figure 5.1) that identifies a specific position in the session timeline. Memory locations can store any or all of various properties, including markers, selections, zoom levels, track height, and more. In the tutorial sessions you've been using with this book, you've seen memory locations used to store selections to establish playback loops, descriptions of each memory location for reference, track heights, track show/hide status, zoom level, and sometimes even a little bit of pre-roll. You've navigated among them either by clicking the location's name in the Memory Locations window or by pressing Period (.), the memory location number, and Period (.) again, all on the numeric keypad.

Open the session Chapter 05.ptf and press Ctrl+5 (Cmd+5) on the numeric keypad to open the Memory Locations window if it's not already visible. Notice that there are no memory locations—they're your job now! Before you start creating markers, however, you should first tell Pro Tools to create marker memory locations by default and to prompt you for a name each time.

1.   Click the drop-down arrow in the upper right of the Memory Locations window and, in the menu that appears, and if necessary, click Default to Marker to

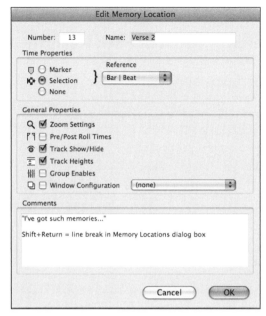

Figure 5.1 The Edit Memory Location dialog box.

enable it. A checkmark should appear next to the option, indicating that it is enabled.

2.   Open the Memory Locations window menu again, and if necessary, click Auto-Name Memory Location to disable it. As shown in Figure 5.2, the checkmark next to the option is removed.

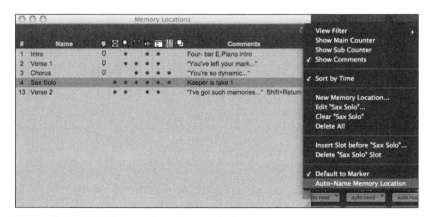

Figure 5.2 The Memory Locations window menu.

3.   Un-mute and solo the first track, called Rough Mix, and hit Play.

4. Listen for the major sections of the song. As soon as each key section begins, press Enter on your numeric keypad to open the New Memory Location dialog box.

Note: Note that for the purposes of memory locations, Pro Tools distinguishes between the two Enter keys on the keyboard. For the duration of this section, you will only be using the numeric keypad Enter key.

---

5. As the song continues, type a brief name for that section of the song such as **Intro, Verse 1,** or **Chorus 2**.

6. Be sure that none of the settings in the General Properties section (Zoom Settings, Pre/Post Roll Times, and so on) is checked. You want your markers to be *just* markers for recalling positions in the timeline.

7. Click OK (or press Enter) to close the dialog box and create the marker. Don't feel rushed—when you click OK to close the dialog box, the marker will be placed where you first pressed Enter, no matter how long you typed. Just be sure you don't take so long that you miss the next section!

If you do miss a section, place a marker you end up regretting, or misspell *Penultimate Sousaphone Obbligato*, don't worry—you can move, edit, add, and delete memory locations. Should you wish to add one, just start playback again at some appropriate prior point and press Enter when you get to the right moment. The only minor inconvenience that will result is that the markers will not be in numeric order. The newest marker will be the highest-numbered. If your markers do end up being out of numeric order, however, you can list them in time order in the Memory Locations window. To do so, confirm that Sort by Time is enabled in the Memory Locations window menu. All your markers will be listed in the order in which they occur within the session. All other (non-marker) memory locations will be listed in numeric order after the markers. To rename a memory location, either right-click its name in the Memory Locations window or double-click the marker in the Markers ruler. The Edit Memory Location dialog box opens; in it, you can edit the name. You may also wish to enter a description of the marked section of the song or jot down what work needs to be done on it in the Comments field (see Figure 5.3). Click OK to confirm the changes and close the dialog box.

To delete a memory location, Alt-click (Opt-click) its name in the Memory Locations window. In the case of markers, you can simply Alt-click (Opt-click) on the unwanted marker in the Markers ruler.

Figure 5.3   The Comments field in the Edit Memory Location dialog box is useful for describing the material found at a memory location or the work that needs to be done there.

Refining Memory Locations

Most of your memory locations will probably be a little late, so take a few minutes to adjust their timing. You can use a shortcut key to audition each marker quickly without listening to the whole song. Before you can do this, however, you need to set appropriate pre-roll and post-roll times. If necessary, open the Transport window by pressing Ctrl+1 (Cmd+1) on the numeric keypad. In the Seconds column of the Pre-Roll field, type 5, as shown in Figure 5.4. Do the same for the Post-Roll field. Now click the Pre-Roll and Post-Roll buttons so they are no longer highlighted. (The shortcut for enabling/disabling Pre- and Post-Roll is Ctrl+K (Cmd+K).)

Figure 5.4   Setting pre-roll and post-roll times in the Transport window.

Go to the first marker, either by recalling it numerically or by clicking its name in the Memory Locations window. Press Ctrl+Alt+left arrow (Cmd+Opt+left arrow) to audition from five seconds before the marker to five seconds after the marker. Watch the waveform as you listen, and find the spot where the new section actually begins.

Note: Ctrl+Alt+left arrow (Cmd+Opt+left arrow) is just one of a set of shortcuts for auditioning a location or selection of audio. In conjunction with modifier keys, the left and right arrows are used to audition the start and end of a selection, respectively, whereas either arrow can be used to audition the current cursor location when there is no selection. The Alt (Opt) key is used to audition audio *prior* to the start or end, whereas the Ctrl (Cmd) key is used to audition audio *following* the start or end of the selection. Alt+left arrow (Opt+left arrow), for example,

> auditions audio leading up to the selection start. Combining them as you just did auditions both before and after. The amount of audition time is equal to the Pre-Roll (Alt/Opt) and Post-Roll (Ctrl/Cmd) values, but pre- and post-roll needn't be enabled.

After you have found the proper spot, simply drag the marker left or right in the Markers ruler. It may be helpful to zoom in a bit. After you've moved the marker, click it again to relocate the playback cursor, then press the spacebar to begin playback from that point. If it sounds right, move on to the next marker. If it still sounds off, repeat the process until you are satisfied with the marker's position.

To see how I would mark the sections of this song, click the Show/Hide icon to the left of the track name Markers in the Tracks list. The hidden track will be shown, and you can see a series of blank regions where I would place markers. Now that you have mapped out the form of the song, un-solo and mute the Rough Mix track.

Track Order

The session's tracks are fairly disorganized, so let's take some time to make sense of them. The tracks appear in the order they were created during the composition and tracking of this song, but at this point they need to be arranged in an order that helps you be efficient in the mixing process. How you choose to organize your tracks is largely a matter of personal preference, but being organized is not only helpful to you—it also prevents wasted effort when you send a session to a collaborator or if you should choose to hire someone to work on your mixes.

> Note: The Producers and Engineers Wing of the Recording Academy (the GRAMMY folks) has created a set of guidelines for DAW sessions, with thorough recommendations on how to organize a session for maximum efficiency. Even if you never intend to share a session or hire someone else to work on it, you can benefit from the wisdom of these master engineers. Download the guidelines from www.grammy.com/Recording_Academy/Producers_And_Engineers/Guidelines.

Rearranging tracks is best done from the Mix window. With a lot of tracks, it helps to narrow the channel strips (see Figure 5.5), so press Ctrl+Alt+M (Cmd+Opt+M). To move a track, simply click its name and drag it left or right. From left to right, start with the drums. The three kick tracks are first, followed by snare and hi-hat. These are the core of the kit, so they need to be together. Next are the Bongos, followed by the Drums Subgroup track. I'll cover subgrouping in detail in Chapter 6, "Advanced Signal Flow";

for now, let's just say that this track allows you to control the entire kit from one fader. It therefore belongs with the other drum tracks.

Figure 5.5 The narrow mix view.

After the drums come the bass and keyboard. The Flute in this case is really an extension of the electric piano, so put it after the EPianoArp track. Strings come next (including the Strings subgroup), followed by the harmony and lead saxophones. Background vocals and lead vocals would ordinarily come last. Any additional subgroup tracks, such as for guitars or keyboards, would go next to their source tracks.

After all the audio tracks have been properly ordered, it's time to consider the aux inputs that are being used as effects returns. Delay and reverb auxes ordinarily go to the right of all audio tracks. This session doesn't have any, but you know you're going to use some time-based processing, so go ahead and create two stereo aux inputs. Name them Delay Aux and Reverb Aux, and place them after the last audio track. The last track should be a master fader. Create a stereo master fader—it should by default be assigned to your first output pair. Name it Stereo Mix.

Track Color

In a session with many tracks, visual organization becomes even more critical. Although the default Pro Tools color scheme is largely shades of gray, you can color-code the tracks for clearer visual reference (see Figure 5.6)

Figure 5.6 Tracks can be color-coded for easy visual reference.

The options in Display Preferences allow you to color tracks by track type, MIDI channel or device, or group membership (which I'll get to in a couple of pages). These defaults are a good starting point, but in a complex session you'll want to customize the track colors using the Color Palette (see Figure 5.7).

Figure 5.7   The Color Palette.

Track color is ordinarily restricted to a single strip below the Comments field. To show track color across the entire channel strip, open the Color Palette from the Windows menu. Click on the Apply to Channel Strip button, which is just to the left of the Saturation slider. Raise the Saturation slider to increase the intensity of the channel strips' color. You can also increase the overall brightness of the Mix window by raising the Brightness slider. These adjustments apply to all tracks.

To specify a particular color for a track or group of tracks, select the track(s) by clicking on its name. In the Color Palette, click on the color you want applied to the chosen track(s).

Note: You can use blank MIDI tracks as dividers to separate groups of tracks. Name them something short and useful and set their outputs to None so there's no chance of them accidentally triggering unintended sounds.

Track Sets

It's often useful to be able to hide all tracks other than the set of tracks you're currently focused on. This is another function that memory locations provide.

1. If the Tracks list is not showing in the Mix window, click the right-arrow symbol in the lower-left corner of the window.

2. In the Tracks list, Alt-click (Opt-click) on the Show/Hide icon of any track. This will hide all tracks.

3. Click and drag across the Show/Hide icons of all the drum tracks (see Figure 5.8), including the subgroup. When you release the mouse, only the selected tracks

will be visible. If you didn't get it exactly right, just click once on the Show/Hide icons of any tracks that should be hidden or shown to toggle them on and off.

Figure 5.8 Showing a selected group of tracks.

4. After the proper drum tracks are showing and all other tracks are hidden, press Enter on the numeric keypad. This opens the New Memory Location dialog box, as you have previously seen.

5. Click None in the Time Properties section of the New Memory Location dialog box. That way, when you recall this memory location, the playback cursor will not change position as it does when you recall a marker.

6. In the General Properties section, deselect everything but Track Show/Hide, as shown in Figure 5.9.

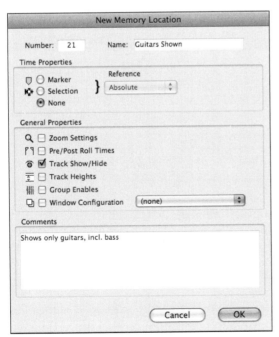

Figure 5.9 A memory location set to recall track show/hide status independent of all other parameters.

7. Name the memory location Drums Shown, enter any comments you want, and then click OK.

Before going on, consider this. The memory location you just created has been assigned the next available number. This number will not be consistent from session to session, potentially creating confusion. It would be better to start these "track sets" on a memory location number that will always be the same. Here's how:

1. Delete the Drums Shown memory location by Alt-clicking (Opt-clicking) it.

2. Press these keys on the numeric keypad in sequence: Period (.), 2, 1, Enter. The New Memory Location dialog box opens to create memory location number 21.

3. Name the new memory location Drums Shown, and set its parameters as shown in Figure 5.9. Click OK.

In the Memory Locations window, you can see that the numbers between your last marker and marker 21 have been skipped. Follow this convention every time you organize a session, and unless you deal with such complex songs that they require more than 20 markers, you will always be able to count on pressing Period 21 Period to show all drum tracks.

Now that you can show just your drum tracks with a few taps on the numeric keypad, how do you return to showing all your tracks? That's what memory location 20 is for!

1. Click the Tracks list pop-up menu and choose Show All Tracks.

2. Create a memory location 20 (press Period 20 Enter).

3. Name the new memory location All Tracks Shown, set its properties as you did with Drums Shown, and click OK.

4. Create similar memory locations for any track sets you think will be useful in this song, such as strings or saxes.

Should you need to update a memory location—for example, after you create a new track your All Tracks Shown memory location will no longer be valid—you can always modify it. Use the Tracks list to be sure that all the tracks you need shown at that memory location are visible, and then simply start to recall the memory location, but press Enter instead of entering the final period. This is the same command you used to create a memory location with a specific number. Check to see that all parameters in the dialog box are as you want them, and then press Enter to close the dialog box. You can even renumber a memory location this way.

Fader Groups

A fader group, or *mix group* as it is called in Pro Tools, is a set of tracks whose controls are linked. Move the fader of one group member and all related faders move as well. Mute one track and the rest of the group's tracks are also muted. Groups make it very easy to mute all the guitar tracks to listen more carefully to the keyboards, or to raise the level of the drum kit a bit without having to drag multiple faders the exact same amount. This is especially helpful for those of us who don't have control surfaces with hardware faders, because a mouse is limited to moving one control at a time.

1. Recall memory location 21, Drums Shown.

2. Alt-click (Opt-click) the name of the Kick track to select all visible tracks.

3. With all of the drum tracks thus selected, press Ctrl+G (Cmd+G) to open the Create Group dialog box (see Figure 5.10).

Figure 5.10   The Create Group dialog box.

4. Notice that a group has both a name and a group ID. The name is for the user's benefit, but the group ID is the way Pro Tools recognizes the group. The group ID is also the key to enabling and disabling groups efficiently, as you'll see. Type **Drums** in the Name field, and set the group ID to D.

> **Note:** Pro Tools supports up to 104 groups in four banks of letters a–z. Your most-often used groups should be in Bank 1 in order to use the shortcut described a bit later to enable and disable them.

5. Accept the default settings and press Enter to close the dialog box.

> **Note:** Pro Tools allows you to group tracks for Mix window functions such as fader movements or Edit window functions such as copying and pasting. Any group can be a Mix group, an Edit group, or both at the same time. Most groups end up making sense in both windows, so the New Group dialog box defaults to Edit and Mix.
>
> You can further customize the behavior of a group by choosing whether to link the mute or solo status of the tracks and/or their sends. Pro Tools HD offers significantly more groupable attributes and greater customization of group attributes. When you open a session in Pro Tools LE that was created in Pro Tools HD, however, those custom group attributes are lost.

On second thought, let's not include the Drums Subgroup track in the Drums group. Here's how to modify an existing group:

1. Press Ctrl+Start+G (Cmd+Ctrl+G) to open the Modify Groups dialog box.

2. From the Group ID drop-down list, choose D (Drums).

3. Select Drums Subgroup in the right column (Currently in Group), and click Remove.

4. Click OK to save the new Drums group.

You could, if you wished, use the same technique to change this to a Mix or Edit group or simply rename it. The Modify Group command is also available from the Groups pop-up menu or by right-clicking on a group name in the Groups list.

Mixing with Groups

Go to the marker you created for the first verse of this song and hit Play. Hear how the drums are a bit on the soft side? Drag any drum fader up a bit, and you will see that all the drum tracks' faders follow along. You may notice that it's difficult to find a level where both the kick and snare sound right—they're out of balance with each other. Start-drag (Ctrl-drag) the Kick fader to adjust its level independently of the group.

Note: Digidesign sometimes refers to the Start (Ctrl) key as the Clutch key because it is used to disengage the group momentarily like this.

You may decide after a few bars that the entire kit needs to be rebalanced. (I won't be offended!) Press the D key to disable the group; you'll notice it is no longer highlighted in the Groups list. (You could have simply clicked its name, but using the mouse like that just slows you down.) When you're satisfied with the balance of the kit, press D to re-enable the group.

It's not uncommon to apply at least a touch of EQ to each drum in the kit, so here's a quick way to fire up an EQ plug-in on every drum track:

1. Click to the left of the Drums group's name in the Groups list; this selects all members of the group in a single click, regardless of whether the group is enabled or not (see Figure 5.11).

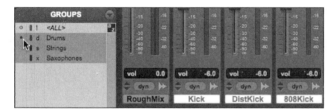

Figure 5.11 Clicking to the left of a group's name selects the members of that group.

2. While holding down the Shift and Alt (Opt) keys, click an insert of the Kick track and create a 4-band EQ III. The EQ will be created on all selected tracks.

Groups can contain other groups. Digidesign's name for this is a *nested* fader group. This is something quite distinct from what is described by the term *subgroup*, as in the Drums Subgroup track, which I discuss in Chapter 6, "Advanced Signal Flow." A great example of a nested fader group is found within the drum tracks you grouped. The Kick, 808Kick, and DistKick tracks make a natural group—after they are properly balanced with each other, you may decide that the kicks collectively need to be turned up or turned down. Here's how:

1. Select the three kick tracks, and press Ctrl+G (Cmd+G).

2. Name the group Kicks, and set its group ID to K.

3. Press the D key to disable the Drums group, and you will be able to tweak the volume of the Kicks group.

4. Press D again to enable the Drums group, and you will see that the larger group overrides the smaller group; that means it is not necessary to disable the Kicks group to use the Drums group normally. Note that the kick tracks now have an uppercase group ID in the Mix view, as shown in Figure 5.12; this indicates that those tracks are members of more than one active group.

Figure 5.12   Uppercase group IDs show membership in more than one active group.

Before I leave this topic, here are some additional tips to keep up your sleeve:

1. Recall memory location 20, All Tracks Shown.

2. Start-click (Ctrl-click) to the left of the Drums group's name in the Groups list. All other tracks are immediately hidden.

3. Shift-Start-click (Shift-Ctrl-click) to the left of another group's name, and the members of that group will be shown along with the drums.

Between this technique and the memory locations you created earlier, you can quickly show only those tracks you need to see at any given time.

Also, note that every Pro Tools session starts with one group—the All group. You cannot modify or delete this group. Its group ID is the exclamation point (!). Its members, obviously, are all tracks in the session. Although many global commands can be executed by holding down the Alt (Opt) key, such as selecting all tracks by Alt-clicking (Opt-clicking) on any one track, some functions, such as fader movements, respond differently to Alt (Opt). Press Shift+1 (exclamation point) to enable the All group, then drag any fader to adjust all track faders simultaneously. If you have created a new track but haven't yet updated your All Tracks Shown memory location, Start-click (Ctrl-click) to the left of the All group's name to show all tracks.

> **Note:** Pro Tools HD allows mix groups to be placed under the control of VCA Master tracks. This is similar to VCA masters on many large-format mixing and live sound consoles, which allow remote control of fader groups. VCAs represent a significant convenience, but they do not change the fundamental operation of a mix group. Opening a session created in Pro Tools HD on a Pro Tools LE system causes all VCA tracks to be removed.

I/O Setup

Just as it is important to organize your tracks, it's also important to organize your inputs and outputs. Pro Tools gives you the power to name every input and output as you wish using its I/O Setup function. From the Setup menu, click I/O. When the I/O Setup dialog box opens, click the Output tab, as shown in Figure 5.13.

The first output *path* you see, Analog 1-2, refers to the first stereo output pair on your interface. You can verify this by looking at the list of outputs at the top of the window. You should see the name of your interface along with a list of its outputs. Depending on your interface, you may see both digital and analog outputs, as with the M-Audio Fire-wire 410 shown in Figure 5.13. Output path Analog 1-2's L and R path indicators should be aligned with your interface's first two outputs.

If you were to drag the L and R indicators to other outputs, every track assigned to Analog 1-2 would end up playing back through those new outputs. Although you would never do this so capriciously, this simple reassignment could be a great asset if your main outputs somehow get damaged or if you want to audition a new pair of speakers without disconnecting your old speakers.

1. Double-click the path name and type in a new name: **Stereo Out**.

2. Press Enter to confirm the new name.

3. Click OK to close the I/O Setup dialog box, and you will see that every output that had been assigned to Analog 1-2 now lists Stereo Out as its assignment.

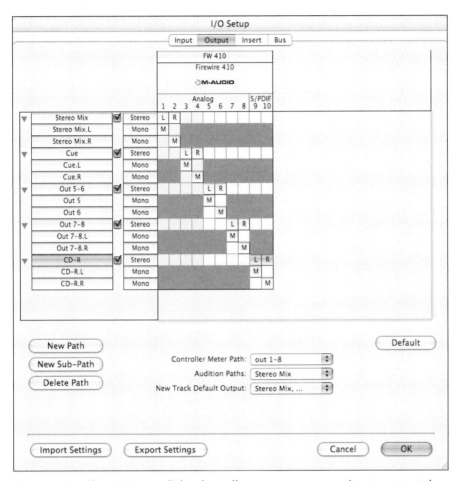

Figure 5.13 The I/O Setup dialog box allows you to rename input, output, bus, and insert paths.

They will all still play back through the same output—only the name has changed. Naming your inputs and outputs in this way saves you from always having to assign track I/O by generic names.

Open I/O Setup again and go to the Bus tab. Up to now, you've routed signal from a track to an aux for time-based processing using generically named buses, such as Bus 1-2 or Bus 7. In a complex session, how would you remember which bus is for a reverb and which for a delay? Name them, and you won't have this problem!

1.   Double-click the first path name and rename Bus 1-2 Reverb Bus.

2. Click the Expand button (it's a + on PC, a triangle on Mac) next to the path name to display the stereo path's mono *sub-paths*, which have been automatically renamed Reverb Bus.L and Reverb Bus.R.

3. Rename Bus 3-4 Delay Bus, and its sub-paths will also be renamed.

What if you want an independent mono bus?

1. Click once to highlight Bus 5-6, then click the Delete Path button. You'll see the path disappear.

2. Click the New Path button and a new unassigned path called Path 1 will appear at the bottom of the list.

3. Drag Path 1 up above Bus 7-8 and drop it.

4. Rename it Hat Delay Bus.

5. In the Path Format column that lists each path as stereo or mono, Hat Delay Bus shows only a question mark. Click the question mark and choose Mono (see Figure 5.14).

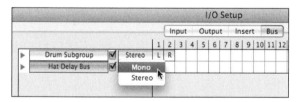

Figure 5.14 Assigning a mono bus path.

6. Move the mouse cursor into the fifth column of the Channel Grid in the Hat Delay Bus row. The cursor will be a pencil; if you click that square, a small box labeled "M" will appear to indicate that you have assigned the Hat Delay Bus path as a mono bus in the fifth of the 32 available slots.

7. Click OK to close I/O Setup and confirm your changes.

8. To see the results of your efforts, click a send of any stereo track. In the Bus submenu, you will see your names listed, as shown in Figure 5.15.

Note: You can also rename any path directly from the Mix or Edit window by right-clicking its name in a track input, output, or send.

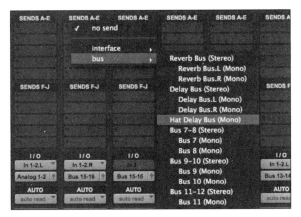

Figure 5.15 Custom-named bus paths shown in the send assignment list.

I/O setups can be saved and recalled like effects presets. To save your current path names and assignments for later recall, do the following:

1. Click the Export Settings button.

2. In the Save I/O Settings As dialog box, enter a descriptive name for the settings.

3. Click Save.

To recall settings, do the following:

1. Click Import Settings.

2. Use the Select I/O Settings to Import dialog box to find and choose the particular settings file you want.

Panning

Although your first instinct might be to reach for the faders to set levels when you start mixing, consider doing at least some basic panning first. One of the beautiful things about mixing in stereo is that panning competing parts to different positions in the stereo soundscape allows them both to be heard more clearly. In mono, you are more likely to make win/lose decisions between competing parts, so starting off by giving parts a bit of separation allows you to make better volume adjustments.

Note: Although Pro Tools LE and M-Powered do not yet support surround mixing, more and more projects are being mixed and released in multichannel formats such as 5.1. Just as stereo panning allows fewer win/lose scenarios between sonically competing parts, surround panning offers even greater opportunities for sonic *détente*. Pro Tools HD systems support surround (up to 7.1), as do most host-based DAWs.

Neyrinck's Mix 51 is a plug-in for Pro Tools LE and M-Powered that does a brilliant job of offering HD-compatible 5.1 surround mixing. Digidesign's Complete Production Toolkit includes extensive support for surround mixing in Pro Tools LE (*not* M-Powered) up to 7.1. It's significantly more expensive than Mix 51, but it includes a host of additional features.

Start with all tracks shown, rewind to the beginning, and start playback. By default, all mono tracks are currently panned dead center, and all stereo tracks are currently panned hard left and right (see Figure 5.16). This results in everything colliding in the middle of the stereo image. It doesn't matter where you start, but your first priority is to weed out this congestion and preserve the center for the most important parts.

Figure 5.16   By default, mono tracks are panned center, and stereo tracks are panned wide left and wide right.

There are few "laws" of mixing (and none of them is absolute), but one holds that four things ordinarily live at the center of the stereo image: kick drum, snare drum, bass, and lead vocal (or instrument). After that, everything is negotiable. A primary reason for this is that these elements need to be heard even when a listener is standing very close to one speaker. Imagine no longer hearing the kick drum and lead vocal when you move off to one side of the dance floor! Center panning means equal levels in each speaker, so nothing panned center will disappear even when heard in such a skewed perspective.

1. Starting with the drum tracks, pan instruments away from center to clear out the clog. Even without changing any track volumes, you'll start to hear the various parts more distinctly. With one kick drum centered, you can move the other two to opposite sides a moderate amount. Move the snare very slightly left and the hi-hat very slightly right of center. (If the client is a drummer, she may want them both on the same side, as that is where they sit in the kit, but from a listener's perspective the two make sense balanced this way.)

Note: There is much debate among engineers as to whether a drum kit should be panned as the audience hears it or as the drummer hears it. The drummer's perspective is opposite that of the audience, as the drummer ordinarily faces the audience in performance. Purists advocate the audience perspective, whereas pragmatists hold that the audience won't notice while the drummer will find it awkward to hear things reversed. A similar debate applies to stereo-miked pianos—should the low notes be on the left, as the pianist hears things, or the right?

---

2. Pan the Bongos most of the way to one side.

3. Leave the Acoustic Bass centered, lest the Mix Police come for you.

4. Pan the EPianoArp and Flute tracks to opposite sides.

5. Array the various strings from left to right, but don't go too wide.

6. The AltoMelody goes dead center, and the two AltoChorus tracks go to the outside.

As you listen to the mix, you will immediately find it easier to pick out individual parts. Even though the balance isn't perfect, the mix already sounds more alive and realistic.

Note: A cool feature of Pro Tools' stereo tracks is the availability of separate left and right pan controls (see Figure 5.17). These give you the uncommon ability to narrow the image of a stereo track, maintaining the stereo picture while fine-tuning its width or location.

Figure 5.17   Pro Tools' separate left and right pan controls allow the stereo image to be narrowed or moved to the side.

Balance

There is no one best approach to setting basic levels for a mix. Your approach will probably change according to the nature of the material, and it may well change with experience. One of the few reasonably valid generalizations one can make about contemporary popular music, however, is that drums and lead vocals are almost always primary focal points. It makes sense, then, to address these first and then build the mix around them.

Which comes first is hotly debated, but here again it depends greatly on the specific song and artist. Starting a Celine Dion mix with the lead vocal makes perfect sense, whereas starting a Dream Theater mix with the drums seems more prudent. The sound of an orchestra is often primarily derived from a single pair of microphones, with various "spot" microphones recorded to additional tracks. The mix starts with the stereo pair, and spots are added only when and to the extent that they are needed to enhance the balance of critical parts.

Keep in mind that, as you have seen in earlier chapters, EQ and compression affect the apparent loudness of sounds. You might decide to change the balance between two parts simply by tweaking their timbres and dynamics, without ever touching their faders. Here again, the approach depends on the specific sounds involved, the genre, and your mixing approach.

The "naturalist" approach is to balance and blend the parts with volume and pan first, and resort to processing when a little extra help is needed. Many contemporary mixers, however, start by shaping individual sounds with EQ, compression, distortion, and other effects and then balance everything. Either way, it's useful to start with a rough mix just to get a solid feel for the character of the song and the interplay of the parts.

Note: Traditional engineering practice dictates that the master fader—the volume control for the main stereo output—should never move from unity. On a typical analog console, there is good reason for this, as it optimizes the signal-to-noise ratio. In a well-designed digital system such as Pro Tools, however, there is no harm in moving the master fader (although there are those who persist in arguing this point). I am nevertheless gently steering you toward keeping the master fader at unity for two reasons. First, it forces you to pull some faders down, fighting the natural tendency always to push faders up. (Eventually, there's no more "up"!) Second, enough people are familiar with the analog tradition that many still look askance at non-zero master faders. Trust me, you'll be happier spending your time mixing than explaining why you're right and they're wrong!

Setting Drum Levels

Now that you've got everything spread out on your virtual stage, you can work on balancing the parts. What follows is not the only way to set levels, but it's based on some pretty common practices. You'll start by getting the drums together and then build the house on that foundation.

1. Press Shift+1 (exclamation point) to enable the All group if it is not already enabled.

2. Drag any fader all the way down, and all faders will follow suit.

3. Press Shift+1 again to disable the All group.

4. Now recall your Drums Shown memory location so that only your drum tracks are visible.

5. In the Tracks list, click the Show/Hide icon of the master fader you created earlier, called Stereo Mix, to make it visible. If for some reason it is not assigned to the first pair of outputs on your interface, or if you monitor through some other pair of outputs, change the master fader's output accordingly as shown in Figure 5.18. (You would also need to assign the outputs of all other tracks in the session to this same output.)

6. Click the third insert of the master fader, and from the multichannel plug-ins' Other list, choose the BF Essential Meter Bridge (stereo). As you can see in Figure 5.19, this plug-in resembles analog VU meters like those found on big expensive analog boards.

7. Under Meter Calibration, click the −20 button, and be sure the RMS/Peak switch is set to RMS.

The recommended levels that follow provide a useful starting point, but your ears, experience, and judgment are your ultimate guides. Basic levels will vary depending on the

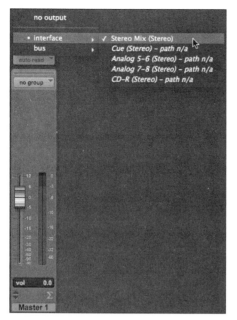

Figure 5.18 Changing the output assignment on a master fader.

Figure 5.19 The Bomb Factory Essential Meter Bridge shows RMS levels similar to the VU meters on an analog console.

number and nature of the tracks. The goal is to have all the tracks add up to about zero on the master fader, so if you've got a lot of tracks you may want to start with slightly lower levels.

1. Disable Pre-Fader Metering in the Options menu.

2. Alt-click (Opt-click) the Drum Subgroup track's fader to snap it to unity. (If it's hidden, click on its Show/Hide icon in the Tracks list.)

3. Show the Acoustic Bass track.

4. Disable the Drums group by pressing D, and enable the Kicks group by pressing K.

5. Hit Play and pull the Kick and Bass faders up gradually, keeping them balanced with each other as you go.

6. When the Meter Bridge is hitting about -7, leave the Kick fader there and bring the Bass fader back down to negative infinity.

7. Now bring up the Snare fader until it complements the kicks. Resist the urge to adjust the kicks' volume, as it is your basis for comparison.

8. Add the hi-hat.

9. Bring up the Bongos track so it balances with the rest.

10. It's important to avoid clipping, so keep an eye on the Drum Subgroup and Master tracks' meters. Being peak meters, the track meters do a better job of showing clipping than the Meter Bridge in RMS mode. If you see the red clipping indicator go off on either track, enable the Drums group and pull the drum faders down until the clipping stops. Always be sure that everything balances against the kick drums as you go.

Note: Pro Tools' meters became somewhat more informative in version 8. Although they are still only peak meters, their color coding is more revealing, and they finally have actual labels, at least in the mix window and the output window. In these windows, you will see numeric labels (in dBFS) along the right side of the meter. The green segment of the meter ranges up to -12 dBFS, the yellow segment ranges up to -3 dBFS, and the orange segment ranges up to 0 dBFS (-0.1 dBFS in Pro Tools HD). The red indicator shows clipping.

Setting the Rest of the Levels

Now that the drums are more or less roughed out, you can start bringing in everything else. Recall your All Tracks Shown memory location and work your way through the rest of the rough mix. In general, bringing up the vocal or lead instrumental track to match the drum kit is a good next step. Alternatively, you might continue to build the foundation of the mix from the bottom up, bringing in bass, guitars, keys, and so forth as you work your way up to the lead.

If you're mixing with headphones, this is a very important step at which to check your work on speakers. In headphones, you can hear individual parts more clearly than on speakers. This often causes you to think a part is loud enough when it is still too soft.

Continue to keep an eye out for clipping. The more parts you add, the more likely clipping is to occur. Don't be too dogmatic about keeping the master fader at unity, however—that's just a guideline, not a law. Keep in mind this is your *rough* mix, so don't spend too much time getting tweaky. When you start shaping individual sounds with EQ and compression and then start adding time-based and special effects, things will inevitably change.

Besides, I've got lots more tricks up my sleeve. In the next chapter, I'll show you some advanced signal-flow techniques that will lay the foundation for the imaginative mix techniques that I'll cover in later chapters. Now that you're well organized, you're ready to dig deeper!

6 Advanced Signal Flow

Through the first several chapters you have seen the fundamental principles by which audio is routed to and through processors. This knowledge alone will get you through most of the day-to-day mixing tasks you will encounter. You might suspect, however, that there are some more involved methods—secret tricks that engineers keep up their sleeves for working more efficiently and for harnessing the power of the Pro Tools mixer. You would be correct.

In this chapter, I'll show you some techniques that have far-ranging ramifications. They focus primarily on the use of an innocuous little thing called a *bus*. You may have heard this term tossed about casually in discussion or encountered it in reference to a mixer or another DAW. You will see that in Pro Tools, the bus's design makes it an enormously powerful tool.

Getting On the Bus

If your community has good public transportation, you may take the city bus downtown, to the library, or to work. If everything goes well, you don't really think about the bus much. You wait a few minutes, hop on, pay a nominal fee, and the bus does what it does, which is to take you from wherever you are to wherever you want to be (or at least within a few blocks of it).

An audio bus does the same thing, only it doesn't smell funny. It takes your audio signal from one part of your mixer to another part of your mixer. Think of a bus in this context as an invisible audio cable that allows you to patch signal out of one place and into another, much as you use patch cables in a patchbay or a modular synthesizer.

In some DAWs, buses are displayed as tracks, but in Pro Tools they are seen only by their connections. Although the difference is partly cosmetic, the effect is that Pro Tools buses are much more flexible than those in other programs. Buses can be either mono or stereo, and in Pro Tools HD multichannel buses are available.

Figure 6.1 A bus is seen only by its connections. Here a stereo bus is used to route signal from the outputs of the first three tracks to the input of the DrumSubgrp track, while a mono bus is routing signal from a send to the input of the Hat Delay track.

In the process of conveying signals hither and yon, buses also *combine* signals and *distribute* them. A bus combines signals when more than one source feeds the same bus. All signals feeding the same bus are summed together. If the bus is stereo, the various signals maintain their relative pan positions, but of course if the bus is mono, all pan information is lost. Any number of sources can all feed the same bus.

A bus distributes signals when it is assigned to more than one destination. The combined signals flowing through the bus all arrive at each destination exactly the same, without any signal loss or compromise. The same bus may be assigned to any number of destinations.

Subgroups

In Chapter 5, "The Rough Mix," you learned how to create mix groups, sometimes called *fader groups*. The faders of a mix group move together when any one is adjusted, allowing for convenient control over a number of related tracks. An audio *subgroup* is similar in that it allows one fader to change the level of multiple tracks. A subgroup is different, however, in that it accomplishes this by routing all the audio outputs of group members through a single control track. In a mix group, the tracks' outputs remain independent of each other.

Open the session Chapter 06.ptf and call up memory location 1, Drums Subgroup. Here you see an entire drum kit with overheads and PZM room mics. Several tracks add up to one instrument. When you're starting your mix, you'll no doubt obsess over the relative levels of those 11 tracks, but the deeper you get into your mix, the more you'll think of them as "the drum kit." Creating a subgroup lets you have the best of both mindsets.

You're going to use a bus to route the outputs of the various drum tracks to the input of a stereo aux. Here's how:

1. First, go into I/O Setup and create a stereo bus called Drum Sub Bus. When you open I/O Setup, you won't see any buses listed in the Bus tab. I have taken the liberty of deleting them all to give you a blank slate. Simply click New Path, name it, choose Stereo from the Path Format selector, and click the pencil in the Channel Grid to create the new bus path. Click OK to close I/O Setup.

    Note: Depending on your personal sense of organization, you may find this blank-slate approach a great way to start, or you may prefer to start with a set of generic buses and simply rename them as you go.

    ---

2. Select all the drum tracks by clicking the name of the Kick track and Shift-clicking the name of the PZM track.

3. While holding down the Shift and Alt (Opt) keys, click to assign the output of any drum track to the Drum Sub Bus. All of them will be reassigned, as shown in Figure 6.1.

4. Hit Play, and you will hear no drums at all. Currently, the drums all go into the bus, but the bus doesn't connect them to any audible output. All the drums share the same fate, which is the purpose of a subgroup. Of course, that purpose is unrealized until you return the bus to an aux so you can hear it!

5. Select the PZM track and create a new stereo aux input. The aux will appear to the right of the selected track.

6. Name the aux Drum Subgroup and assign Drum Sub Bus as its input, as shown in Figure 6.2. Now when you hit Play, you will hear the drum kit.

Figure 6.2 The drum subgroup: All drum tracks are routed through the Drum Sub Bus to the input of the Drum Subgroup aux.

7. Move the aux's fader, and the drum kit will get louder or softer as a unit. Mute or solo the aux, and the entire kit will be muted or soloed.

8. Speaking of mute and solo, Ctrl-click (Cmd-click) on the aux's Solo button to solo-safe it as you did with your reverb returns in Chapter 3.

Compressing the Drum Kit

As you'll recall from Chapter 2, "Dynamics," compressors are used both to control dynamics and to shape the sound of the instruments they process. It is not uncommon for engineers to use compressors to massage the character of individual drum tracks and then to use one more compressor to rein in the dynamics of the entire drum kit as a single instrument. The subgroup you just created makes that easy.

1. On any insert of the Drum Subgroup aux, create a Compressor/Limiter Dyn III.

2. Listening carefully to the sound of the drum kit as a whole, adjust the compressor's settings to give it more punch.

3. Some engineers don't like to include overheads and room mics when they compress the kit, and others like to compress them separately, so let's modify the subgroup to exclude them. You could easily assign them to the Stereo Mix output path, but then their volume, mute, and solo would not follow the subgroup. Here's a better way. Go back into I/O Setup and create a new stereo bus called Drum Comp Bus.

4. Close I/O Setup and create a new stereo aux named Drum Comp.

5. Assign the aux's input to Drum Comp Bus and its output to Drum Sub Bus.

6. Now select all drum tracks other than Overheads and PZM and assign their outputs to Drum Comp Bus, as shown in Figure 6.3. Now the raw drums

Figure 6.3 A subgroup within a subgroup.

have their own subgroup, flowing through the Drum Comp aux. They are then combined with the overheads and room mics into the Drum Subgroup aux.

7. Now drag the compressor from the Drum Subgroup track to the Drum Comp track. You'll want to give it a close listen and adjust its settings to correspond to the new signal flow. With this revised setup, the overheads and room mics are independent of the basic drum tracks.

8. As one final variation, put a compressor on the PZM track and squash it good. This track is now distilled to a strong but natural ambience. Adjust its level so it enhances the overall sound in lieu of reverb.

The Bus as Multiplier

A subgroup demonstrates the ability of a bus to combine many signals into a single stream. The other side of the bus's personality is that it can deliver its contents to many different destinations. This makes the bus a powerful tool for multiplying, or *multing*, a signal.

1. Go to memory location 2, Mult 1.

2. Open I/O Setup and create a mono bus named Lead Mult Bus.

3. Assign this as the output of the Lead track.

4. Create two new mono aux inputs and name them Lead A and Lead B.

5. Assign Lead Mult Bus as the input of each.

6. You now have two copies of the lead to do with as you please. There's no point having two identical copies, however, so let's differentiate them. On Lead A, insert a 4-Band EQ III followed by the Compressor/Limiter Dyn III.

7. Roll off the low end and boost a narrow band around 2.0 kHz.

8. Call up the Fatten preset on the compressor.

9. On Lead B, insert the Bomb Factory BF76 followed by a 4-Band EQ III.

10. On the BF76, call up the All Buttons In preset.

11. On the EQ, set the HF band to a shelf with a Q of 2.00 and a gain of −12 dB.

12. Adjust the frequency until you find an interesting tone.

You have just created two alternative versions of the Lead track (see Figure 6.4). Which one do you like? You may have a strong preference immediately, or you may want to switch the two versions in and out as the mix progresses. Perhaps you'll discover that using one in the verse and one in the chorus is appealing.

Figure 6.4 Using a bus to mult a signal. The Lead track is heard only through Lead A and Lead B, each of which is processed differently.

It's not uncommon for engineers to devote several channels of a big console to mults of a lead vocal. One might be a bit more compressed, one a bit brighter, one might even be distorted for contrast. Blending the different versions helps create a sound that's "bigger than life," while alternating versions maintains interest through the different sections of the song.

> **Note:** In Chapter 3, "Time-Based Effects," you used a send to split off a copy of a track and send it through a bus to an aux. You might be wondering how this is different from the technique discussed here. The difference depends on how you look at it. If you're thinking of using a send to create one copy, that copy will be

affected by whatever effects are on the original track because the send occurs after the inserts. If you're thinking of using that send to create two copies by returning the bus to two separate tracks, you will certainly have independent control of those two copies, but the original track will still be heard. You would have to mute the original track and make the send pre-fader. That would then be equivalent to bussing from the track's output.

Instant Stereo Again

Go to memory location 3, Instant Stereo Again, and listen to the loop. It's a mono loop panned dead center. Nice, but it plays right into the age-old problem of a congested center image. Here's how to fix it:

1. In I/O Setup, create a new mono bus called Loop Mult Bus, as shown in Figure 6.5.

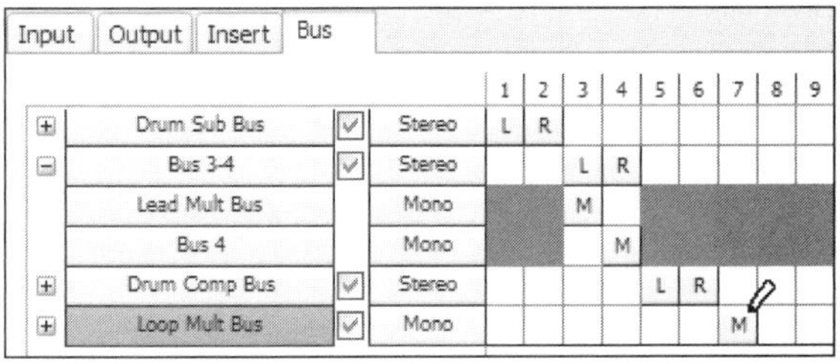

Figure 6.5 Creating a new mono bus in I/O Setup.

2. Assign this bus as the output of the Loop track.

3. Create two new mono aux inputs and name them Loop L and Loop R.

4. Assign Loop Mult Bus as the input of each, and pan them hard left and hard right, respectively.

5. On either aux, insert a 4-Band EQ III.

6. Using a moderately narrow bandwidth, boost two bands by 3–4 dB and cut two by the same amount. At this point, it doesn't make a lot of difference what those bands are—trust me.

7. Now Alt-drag (Opt-drag) the EQ to an insert of the other aux.

8. Shift-click the control dots of all four bands on either aux's EQ, inverting them.

9. Listen to how this expands the image of the loop. (Now you can fine-tune the EQ settings to get the effect just the way you want it.)

In Chapter 1, "Equalization," you created a similar effect, inserting a mono-to-stereo delay and making it inactive just to be able to use a dual-mono EQ. Using a bus to split the signal to two separate tracks accomplishes the same thing while giving you more direct control over each, including the ability to mute them independently.

Pump Up the Snare

Go to memory location 4, Pumped Snare, and listen to the drum track. You're going to kick the snare into overdrive by multing and processing it.

1. You know the basic drill by now: Create a mono bus, create two mono auxes, and route the Pumped Snare track to the two auxes. Don't neglect naming everything properly!

2. Insert a Compressor/Limiter Dyn III followed by an Expander/Gate Dyn III on one snare aux.

3. Set the compressor to emphasize the snare's attack: short attack, moderate release, high ratio, medium threshold, and hard knee.

4. Set the gate with the shortest possible attack and a quick release so that only the pop of the snare's attack gets through.

5. When you blend this signal with the unprocessed snare, you will hear that something has changed drastically, but not for the better! There is a heinous comb filtering between the two copies of the snare as a result of one copy being delayed.

Note: When a signal is blended with a delayed copy of itself, some frequencies reinforce each other while others cancel each other out. It's as though you took a multi-band EQ and turned alternate bands up and down—the pattern resembles a comb. Although it can be a useful technique for synthesizing new and interesting sounds, it sounds quite unnatural, so engineers do everything they can to avoid it.

Why is one copy now delayed? Do you remember enabling the Look Ahead function in the Expander/Gate in Chapter 2 (see Figure 6.6)? It allowed very clean attacks by opening the gate two milliseconds ahead of the signal crossing the threshold. Because of this, everything coming through the gate is delayed by two milliseconds. That's the delay causing the comb filtering.

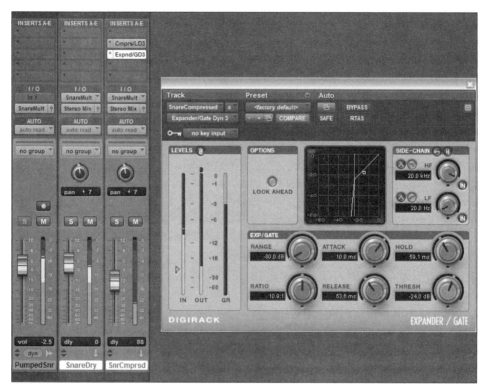

Figure 6.6 The Look Ahead function in Expander/Gate Dyn III causes the signal to be delayed by two milliseconds. The delay is shown where the track volume is ordinarily displayed.

Unfortunately, turning off Look Ahead doesn't eliminate the delay as you might expect it to. Pro Tools LE is not currently capable of detecting and compensating for a processing delay such as this. However, you can fix it manually with a plug-in call Time Adjuster. Here's how:

1. Insert Time Adjuster (see Figure 6.7) on the *unprocessed* snare aux.

    Note: Although you might like to be able to undo the delay on the processed track, the only way to re-align the two is to match that delay on the unprocessed track. Time Adjuster therefore always goes on the "dry" track.

    ---

2. Time Adjuster simply delays the ungated track by the same amount the Look Ahead function delays the gated track. To find out how much that delay really

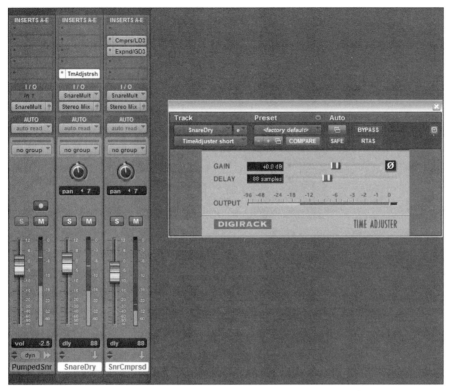

Figure 6.7 The Time Adjuster plug-in.

is, you must Ctrl-click (Cmd-click) the track volume (vol) indicator just above the track name. The first click shows the track's peak level indicator, and the second click shows the delay indicator, as shown in Figure 6.6. The processed track should show 88 samples of delay, corresponding to two milliseconds at 44.1 kHz.

3.   In the Time Adjuster window, click once in the Delay field, type **88**, and press Enter (Return). The comb filtering is now eliminated, and the blended snare tracks produce a powerful attack with a full-bodied ring.

Note: Pro Tools LE and M-Powered compensate for some—but not all—delays associated with signal processing. In general, if plug-ins don't do look-ahead processing, there will be no problem. Unfortunately, many of the most popular and powerful plug-ins do use look-ahead techniques, so listening carefully and understanding the proper application of Time Adjuster is critical.

Subgroup Mult

Now let's use a bus as both a merge and a mult at the same time. Go to memory location 5, Stereo Saxes, and listen. There are three sax parts, and they're currently panned in a group around the center. The trouble is that they're supposed to be a background part, and their panning is too "front and center." You're going to combine them to a bus, manipulate their stereo width, mult them, and then move them to the outside of the sound field.

1. Create a new *stereo* bus called Saxes.

2. Assign the outputs of the three sax parts to your new bus.

3. Create two new stereo aux inputs named Sax Subgroup L and Sax Subgroup R, and assign the Saxes bus as their inputs. You're getting quicker at this, aren't you?

4. Set the right pan slider of Sax Subgroup L to 0, and set the left pan slider of Sax Subgroup R to 0, as shown in Figure 6.8. Notice that not much has changed

Figure 6.8   Three saxophone parts subgrouped, multed, and de-correlated to move them out of the center of the mix.

sonically. This is that old correlation thing rearing its ugly head again, as discussed in Chapter 4.

5. Set up EQs on each subgroup with the same sort of "equal and opposite" settings you used earlier in the section "Instant Stereo Again." Try to come up with settings that spread the subgroups as far apart as possible. Try also using a short delay on one subgroup (with or without the EQs) to move them to the outside as you did in Chapter 3.

Multiple Outputs

It's always helpful to check your mix on different sets of speakers. A big commercial studio ordinarily has at least three sets: mega-monitors built into the walls, smaller close-fields sitting on the console, and one tiny little speaker in the middle to simulate the sound of a television set. Switching between them is as simple as pressing a button on the console.

If you have an alternate set of monitors but don't have a fancy console or monitor mixer to switch speakers, you can accomplish the same thing within Pro Tools. All you need to do is assign your tracks to multiple output paths.

1. Go to memory location 6, Multiple Output Paths.

2. Open I/O Setup and name one of your stereo outputs Alt Monitor. (If you have an Mbox or an M-Audio interface with only two outputs, you will not be able to do this. For practice, create a stereo bus named Alt Monitor and use that instead.)

3. Assigning multiple outputs is accomplished by holding down the Start (Ctrl) key as you make an assignment, so hold down the Start (Ctrl) key and click the Output selector of any track currently assigned to Stereo Mix.

4. Without releasing the modifier key (Start/Ctrl), finish assigning the output to Alt Monitor as you would normally. When you are finished, you will see a plus sign (+) next to the name displayed in the Output selector, as shown in Figure 6.9. The plus sign tells you that more than one output has been assigned to that track.

Figure 6.9 A plus sign (+) indicates that more than one output path is assigned to a track.

5. You can do this more efficiently, though, can't you? First by clicking, and then Shift- or Ctrl-clicking (Cmd-clicking) track names, select all tracks that are currently assigned to Stereo Mix.

6. Hold down the Shift and Alt (Opt) keys (Apply to All Selected) along with the Start (Ctrl) key (Multiple Outputs), and assign any track's output to Alt Monitor. All selected tracks will follow suit.

Note: That's right—you can often combine Alt (Opt) and Shift+Alt (Shift+Opt) with other commands and keyboard shortcuts to apply those commands to all tracks or all selected tracks. My personal favorite is making all selected tracks inactive. To make a single track inactive, you Ctrl+Start-click (Cmd+Ctrl-click) the track's track type icon in the Mix window. To make all currently selected tracks inactive, you combine the two key combinations to get a four-modifier-key shortcut: Ctrl+Start+Shift+Alt-click (Cmd+Ctrl+ Shift+Opt-click)!

You have now accomplished what you set out to do, but there's a problem. The sound is coming out of *both* sets of monitors all the time! If you've got mute or volume controls on the monitors themselves, you can switch between them that way. To switch between them from Pro Tools, you can use master faders. The next section continues with memory location 6 as you have now modified it.

Master Faders

Digidesign's definition of a *master fader* (see Figure 6.10) is that it controls the volume of an output or bus. A master fader has inserts, so it can also apply processing to the signal traveling through that output or bus. If this definition seems oversimplified, consider all that you have done so far without ever needing a master fader. Audio tracks and aux inputs have allowed you to get signal from wherever to wherever you needed it, and you are only now calling on master faders to control volume at a pair of outputs.

I like to think of a master fader as a valve, much like the handle on your kitchen faucet. Turn the handle one way, and water turns on—first a little and then more as you keep turning. Turn the handle the other way, and the flow diminishes. The handle did nothing to get the water from the street to the sink—that was handled by pipes. The handle only controls the flow of water that has already been routed to the sink.

Figure 6.10 A master fader controls the volume of an output or bus. It can also apply processing via its inserts.

You have already routed your mix to two separate sets of monitors—the pipes are in place. A master fader on each output will allow you to control the flow of audio going to each set of monitors, so you can compare the sound as you set out to do.

1. Create two new stereo master faders (Track > New).

2. Assign one master fader's output to Stereo Mix and the other's to Alt Monitor, and name them for their outputs, as shown in Figure 6.11.

3. Listen and you will see that merely creating and assigning master faders has changed nothing. Now lower the volume of Alt Monitor all the way, and you are listening to your main monitors.

4. Alt-click (Opt-click) Alt Monitor's fader to snap it to unity, and pull Stereo Mix's fader down all the way so you can hear your mix at your alternate monitors.

Figure 6.11   Mixing to two sets of monitors simultaneously.

It would be easier to mute and un-mute the two monitor feeds, but you can't do that because master faders have no mute buttons. Let's try a different scenario that makes things easier. The next section continues where you left off at the current memory location.

Note: Master faders are actually missing a number of things in addition to mute: solo, record-arm, pan, and sends. Perhaps most surprisingly of all, a master fader has no input selector. Consider, however, that a master fader is in charge of controlling an output or bus. It has nothing to do with an input. For this reason, I like to think that you don't assign an output to a master fader—you assign a master fader to an output.

Another unusual aspect of a master fader is that its inserts are post-fader. This means that if you place a dynamics processor on the master fader's insert and then move the track's fader, you have effectively changed the processor's threshold. If you apply dynamics processing to a master fader, you will ordinarily not change or automate its level.

Alternate Monitors

So if the problem with using a master fader for this task is that it has no mute or solo buttons, what track should you use? An audio track has mute and solo, but on LE and M-Powered systems, to listen to the input of an audio track requires record-arming it. An aux input has mute and solo and doesn't require record-arming to monitor it, so that seems the appropriate choice. However, an aux input doesn't directly control an output or bus as a master fader does—you must route the signal to the aux using a bus.

Wait a minute—won't it require two buses, one for each output? No, because you can multi-assign the aux track's output to go to both Stereo Mix and Alt Monitor outputs. Ah, but then you're right back where you started, with one mute button that applies to both outputs! You need two separate auxes, don't you? That's better, but aren't you back to two buses now? No, because one of the defining characteristics of a bus is that it can both combine signals and distribute signals. One bus from all of the tracks can be applied as the input of each of two auxes, one of which is assigned to Stereo Mix and the other of which is assigned to Alt Monitor, as shown in Figure 6.12. Here's the procedure:

Figure 6.12   Mixing to two sets of monitors, using aux inputs for control.

1. Create a new stereo bus named Mult Monitor.

2. Select all tracks that are assigned to Stereo Mix and Alt Monitor outputs.

3. Holding down the Shift and Alt (Opt) keys, reassign the output of one of those tracks to the Mult Monitor bus (*only* the bus). All selected tracks will be reassigned. Right now, you should not be able to hear any tracks.

4. Create two new stereo aux inputs and name them Stereo Mix and Alt Monitor.

5. Assign their outputs to the output paths after which they are named, and assign both of their inputs to Mult Monitor.

You can now mute and solo your two sets of monitors from within Pro Tools. You can even change their output gain with the auxes' faders and process them using plug-ins on the auxes' inserts if you want. There is, however, one important limitation to this scenario: If the combined signals of all the tracks feeding Mult Monitor end up being loud enough to clip the input of the auxes, the aux faders will not stop the clipping. They will turn down the result, but the clipping occurs *before* the aux tracks' inputs. The solution is our old friend the master fader, which does what? It controls the volume of signal passing through an output or bus, which is what you need to do. You should assign a master fader to the Mult Monitor bus so you can turn it down if necessary.

1. Create a master fader and name it Mult Monitor.

2. Click its Output Path selector and assign it to the Mult Monitor bus, as shown in Figure 6.13. If the bus is clipping, the master fader's meters will show it, and lowering the master fader's fader will fix it.

Note: The name "master fader" conjures up expectations of controlling everything from one centralized fader. In fact, that is one application of the master fader—to control the main stereo output through which you're monitoring. In Pro Tools, however, a master fader is much more than that, as you've seen. It's useful to think of a master fader as *already existing* on every output or bus in your session, waiting for you to display its controls if necessary.

Now sit back, take a deep breath, and give yourself a mental pat on the back for having come so far so fast. It may seem as though you've created some complex signal flows in this chapter, but if you look back you'll see that each is actually relatively simple. The

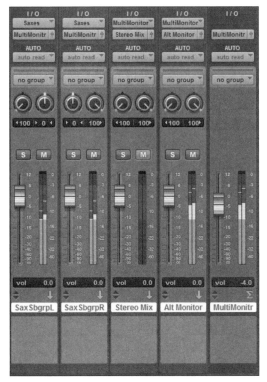

Figure 6.13 Improved version of mixing to two sets of monitors. The aux inputs are used for switching and control; the master fader can turn down the bus if it clips.

only complexity is in combining knowledge of what the basic mixer elements do with a bit of imagination. A bus seems so simple, yet it is the key to opening many doors in the Pro Tools mixer. Many of the techniques in the final chapters of this book will depend on the creative application of buses. Before you get there, however, you'll want to know how to use Pro Tools' automation features to keep your mixes engaging.

7 Automation

In the days before automated recording consoles—not that long ago, really—mixing a song was as much a performance as the recording of the original tracks. The engineer, aided by one or more assistants (sometimes even band members, on a complex mix), would have to reach, bend, stretch, twist, and generally dance about the control room to tweak levels on an inconsistent vocal, mute a guitar solo at the right moment, enable a delay for a special effect in the chorus, adjust an EQ to glue two different takes together, and pan various "ear candy" sounds around to catch the listener's attention. Sometimes it was necessary to mix a song to two-track tape, section by section, and then splice the sections together. Heaven help the assistant engineer who didn't remember to mute the lead guitar's delay send on the "and" of three in the third bar of the second verse!

The advent of console automation systems allowed the engineer to record mix changes and then play them back along with the audio tracks. This not only gave one person as many virtual hands as needed to perform the most complicated mix, it also made the mix changes consistent and, better still, editable. Outboard effects, however, were for the most part not controllable by the console's automation.

In Pro Tools, as in most DAWs, every relevant mix parameter can be automated, giving you more dynamic control over your mixes than was available during the mixing of many classic recordings. In this chapter I'll show you how to use Pro Tools' real-time automation features and how to edit that automation graphically.

> **Note:** If you have a Digi 003, Commandl8, ProjectMix I/O, Axiom Pro, or any compatible third-party control surface, you will find real-time automation especially appealing. A mouse limits you to adjusting a single parameter at any given time, whereas a control surface allows real-time adjustment of multiple controls. Digidesign's high-end ICON systems combine a powerful Pro Tools HD rig with a D-Control work surface for the ultimate in real-time tactile control. Everything you'll learn in this chapter forms the basis for the ICON's powerful workflow.

Writing Automation

The initial pass of automation allows you to establish the basic overall levels and pan positions of your mix. Once these are established, you work through the song section by section refining those level and pan values. Pro Tools automation functions in several modes, allowing you to change its behavior according to your needs.

1. Open the session Chapter 07.ptf and go to the first memory location, Initial Pass. Although the tracks are well organized, there are no markers to map out the form of the song, so you may want to start by taking care of that important detail, as discussed in Chapter 5, "The Rough Mix."

2. The first thing you should do, ironically, is turn all automation off. To do so, Alt-click (Opt-click) the Automation Mode Selector of any track (by default it says Read), as shown in Figure 7.1, and choose Off. Because you are holding the Alt (Opt) key as you do this, all tracks are set to Off mode. This ensures that you will have complete control over the initial mix values without any interference from automation data you may have inadvertently already written.

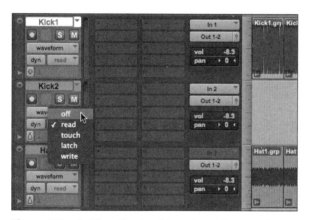

Figure 7.1 Setting the track's automation mode.

3. Play the session all the way through and set levels and pan for all tracks. Go for a solid ensemble sound and note those sections where you'll want to amend these overall settings. If it takes more than one time through the song to make it sound right, that's okay—having automation turned off allows you the freedom to make incremental adjustments to any parameter without being hurried.

4. After you have a solid rough mix, press Enter (Return) to place the cursor at the beginning of the song. Alt-click (Opt-click) the Automation Mode selector of any track and change the automation mode to Write. You're going to use Write

mode to establish the current mix values as the starting point for your mix. First, however, you need to ensure that Pro Tools is ready to write automation.

5. Press Ctrl+4 (Cmd+4) on the numeric keypad to open the Automation window (see Figure 7.2). Ensure that the Auto Suspend button is not engaged and that all the Write Enable buttons are highlighted in red. Click to toggle the status of any button that is in the incorrect state.

Figure 7.2   The Automation window.

6. Press the spacebar to begin playback, and then press it again to stop. Really—that's all it takes! Put all tracks in Read mode so you don't make any unintended changes to this initial automation.

This demonstrates two important truths about Pro Tools automation. First, automation is written during *playback*. Although you could think of setting the automation mode as "record-arming" a track for automation, you must keep in mind that pressing Record is not only unnecessary but unwise. In Record mode, you could potentially overwrite important audio or MIDI data when you simply wanted to create automation data. It's useful to think of "writing" automation rather than "recording" it—after all, they are called the *Write* Enable buttons.

The second truth is that *any* automation data changes a track from its initial state to its automated state. In the initial state, wherein no automation has yet been written to a track, you can adjust a fader or other control at any time and expect it to hold that value. In the automated state, the fader and all other mix controls will reset themselves to their automated values. In the preceding chapters, you changed volume, pan, and plug-in settings as you wished, and Pro Tools always respected those changes because the tracks were devoid of automation. Try changing a fader now, and when you hit Play you will see it immediately snap back to the value you just wrote. The moral of the story is that you don't need to write your initial values throughout the duration of the song in order to establish them; a fraction of a second is sufficient.

Updating Automation

When you create automation using Write mode, any previous automation is ignored. This is a powerful and useful way to create automation, but there are times when you simply want to make adjustments to existing automation. Pro Tools provides two "update" modes to let you do exactly that. They are called Latch and Touch.

Note: Automation is one area in which there are some significant differences between Pro Tools LE and Pro Tools HD. All the features you're learning in this chapter work exactly the same way in HD, but there are several additional functions that can make working on a complex project more efficient. For example, there is an additional update mode called Trim that enables you to raise or lower an existing automation curve without completely rewriting it.

Latch Mode

When you begin writing automation in Latch mode, all controls play back existing automation without changing anything. This is what makes it an update mode—it respects previous automation until you tell it otherwise. Once you start adjusting a control, new automation is written for that control. When you are finished writing automation for that control, Latch mode holds the last value you wrote until you stop playback (thus its name). Here's how it works:

1. Go to memory location 2, Latch.

2. Be sure you have set the automation mode for all tracks to Read.

3. Set the automation mode of the Arpeggio track to Off.

4. Listen to the arpeggio in context for a moment. You're going to fade it in gradually over eight bars, so you want to choose a starting volume that allows it to enter audibly while leaving you plenty of room to increase it.

5. Click the Track View selector of the Arpeggio track and display the volume playlist (see Figure 7.3). This isn't a necessary part of the procedure, but it will enable you to see the results of your automation.

6. When you have arrived at a satisfactory starting volume, put the Arpeggio track in Write mode.

7. Disable all the Write Enable buttons in the Automation window except Volume, so you won't overwrite any other parameters. (Yes, you can save yourself

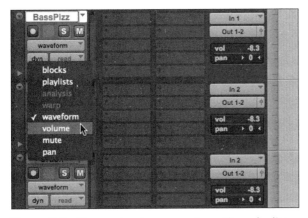

Figure 7.3 Choose to view an automation playlist.

several clicks by Alt-clicking [Opt-clicking] to disable them all and then clicking once on Vol to enable it.)

8.   Press Play and start slowly raising the track's fader. When you reach bar 33, release the fader. Note that the fader holds that last value because Write mode cares nothing for whatever data might have existed there previously.

9.   When the playback cursor reaches the end of the selection, playback and writing of automation will cease. The results of your automation are displayed as a series of line segments joining small white dots, as in Figure 7.4. These dots are *breakpoints*, and they define the shape of the volume automation playlist. Although the line may seem a bit squarish and low-res, Pro Tools interpolates smoothly between breakpoints with 24-bit accuracy, meaning there are almost 17,000,000 values between the highest and lowest possible volume settings.

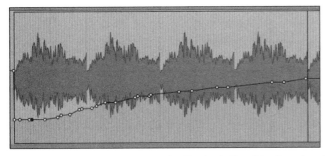

Figure 7.4 An automation playlist is defined by breakpoints.

10. If you're like me, you'll almost certainly find something to dislike about that first attempt. If you're having second thoughts about the starting volume, your best bet is to go back to Off mode and repeat the entire process. If you only need slight adjustments, however, you can simply update your automation by doing another pass in Latch mode. Let's try that for practice.

11. To make things easier on yourself, open the track output window by clicking on the tiny fader icon at the right of the track output selector, as shown in Figure 7.5. Like the send output window, the track output window is simply a floating window showing the track's mix controls. It's as though you had torn off the channel strip from the Mix window. The large fader will make writing automation with your mouse much easier. If you need even finer control, hold down the Ctrl (Cmd) key while dragging the fader to make the fader move more slowly.

Figure 7.5 The track output window's large fader makes writing automation with a mouse easier and more precise.

Note: Although I've been showing you automation in the Edit window so you can see the effect of your work in the automation playlists, much of the time you will prefer to do your real-time automation from the Mix window. Everything functions the same way, but you have the advantage of bigger faders and pan knobs without having to open individual output windows. Of course, if you have a control surface, you may never open the Mix window at all.

12. If necessary, set the track back to Latch mode, and then press Play. Notice that Pro Tools simply plays back the volume curve you just wrote. This is the nature of Latch mode—it doesn't change anything until and unless you tell it to by moving a control.

13. Restart playback, and this time grab the fader at the point you feel it needs improvement. Write the new, improved crescendo all the way to bar 33, and then release the fader. The fader will stay where it was when you released it and hold that value until you stop playback.

14. If you stop playback before bar 41, you will end up with a line that jumps from the latched value to the previously written value, as shown in Figure 7.6. You can fix this easily. Be sure you are still in Latch mode (you should be), and start playback before the jump. Once playback starts, click the fader and release. The fader picks up at the latched value, and you can now let playback continue to bar 41 to write that value for the rest of the phrase. Put the Arpeggio track in Read mode before moving on to the next section.

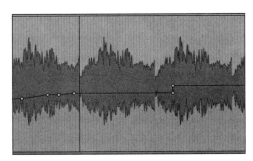

Figure 7.6 Watch for discontinuities when using Latch mode.

Touch Mode

Touch mode looks exactly like Latch mode at first: It simply plays back existing automation. Even after you start twisting knobs and moving faders to write new automation, it behaves like Latch. It's only after you release the controls that the difference reveals itself, as you'll see.

1. Go to memory location 3, Touch, and insert a 4-band EQ III on the BassSynth track. Disable its low and low-mid bands, and enable its high-pass filter.

2. Click the plug-in's Automation Enable button (see Figure 7.7) to open the Plug-In Automation dialog box (shown in Figure 7.8). This window is used to enable specific plug-in parameters for automation. By default, all parameters are listed in the left column, and are not yet enabled for automation. By clicking to select any parameter in the left column and clicking the Add button, that parameter can be moved to the right column, making it automatable.

Figure 7.7 The Plug-in Automation Enable button.

3. Enable the following parameters: Master Bypass, High-Pass Enable, High Band Freq, and High Band Q. Click OK to close the dialog box.

4. In the Automation Enable window, be sure that all Write Enable buttons except plug-in are grayed out. This disables writing of automation for all parameters other than plug-in controls.

5. Bypass the EQ III, put the BassSynth track in Write mode, and press Play to write these starting values. Remember that only a moment of playback is required.

6. This track's default state is now to be unaffected by the EQ III. To carve out a creative exception, first un-bypass the plug-in.

7. Set the High-Pass filter to 18 dB/oct and around 200 Hz to take the bottom out of the sound.

8. Set all three controls on the high band to their lowest values, and put the track in Write mode.

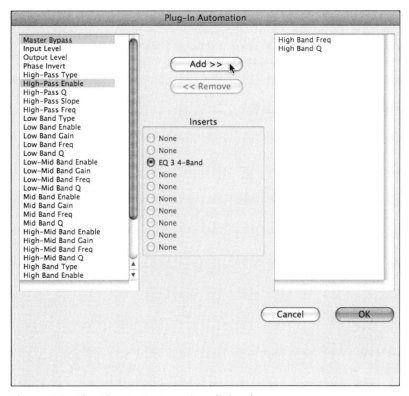

Figure 7.8 The Plug-In Automation dialog box.

9. When you begin playback, raise HF Q to its maximum value over four bars to bring out the edge in the sound.

10. Over the next four bars, raise HF FREQ to its maximum value to create a classic "filter sweep."

11. When you reach the downbeat of bar 49, click to disable the High-Pass filter and restore the low end. You have just helped this bass part make its initial entrance with a big splash.

12. Listen closely to playback. You will notice that the HF FREQ knob doesn't really make much difference beyond its 12:00 position. To fine-tune that filter sweep, you'll use Touch mode. Touch mode is similar to Latch mode insofar as it respects existing automation until you give it new values. Instead of holding the last value, however, Touch gradually returns to reading existing automation. The amount of time this transition takes is the AutoMatch time.

13.   Open the Setup menu, choose Preferences, and choose Mixing to see the Automation Preferences (shown in Figure 7.9).

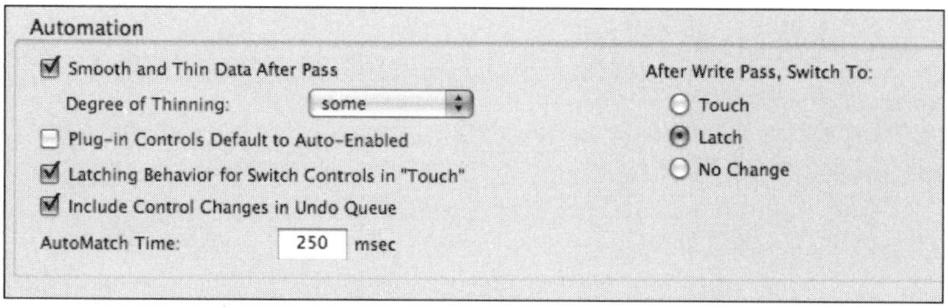

Figure 7.9 The Automation Preferences.

14.   Enter a value of 1000 in the AutoMatch Time field. This means that when you release a control, Pro Tools will blend from that last value to the existing automation over one second.

15.   Before closing the Preferences dialog box, be sure the Smooth and Thin Data After Pass box is checked and that the Degree of Thinning option is set to Some. This tells Pro Tools to smooth out little bumps in the automation curves you write—after all, the mouse is not a precision instrument—and to optimize the number of breakpoints used to draw the curve. Values of More or Most would be more aggressive in minimizing the number of breakpoints. This helps ensure that playback will not get bogged down by the processing required to update the display of vast quantities of automation breakpoints. Automation playback will still be smooth because of the interpolation between breakpoints.

16.   Click OK to close the window.

17.   Put the track in Touch mode and press Play.

18.   When you reach bar 45, grab the HF FREQ knob and write a slower sweep. You should reach about 9 kHz by bar 49. Release the knob, and it will continue to move on its own, reaching 20 kHz one second after you released it.

19.   If you were a bit late disabling the High-Pass filter, you can use Touch mode to fix it, too. If the IN button should pop back after you click it, go back into Automation Preferences and be sure Latching Behavior for Switch Controls in Touch Mode is checked.

Note: You may have noticed that each time you use Write mode, Pro Tools switches the track's automation mode to either Touch or Latch when you stop playback. You change this behavior by changing the After Write Pass, Switch To setting in the Automation Preferences (refer to Figure 7.9). When set to Touch or Latch, it prevents you from accidentally overwriting existing automation. Setting it to No Change causes a track to stay in Write mode until you change it.

The Five Automation Modes

You have learned all five automation modes available in Pro Tools LE. Modes are set on a track-by-track basis, so different tracks could be in different modes at any given time. Here's a quick summary of the characteristics of the modes:

- **Off.** No automation will be played or written. All controls retain their current positions, and if you move a control it stays where you put it.

- **Read.** If any automation—even a fraction of a second—has been written in a track, it will be played. If you move a control, it will snap back to the automated value (if any exists). No new automation can be written in this mode.

- **Write.** Current control values for any enabled parameter will be written from Play to Stop, including any changes made during playback. Any previously existing automation will be replaced and will not be played.

- **Latch.** Acts like Read until you change a control. Any control changes you make will replace previous automation. After you release a control, it stays at that value and continues writing automation until playback is stopped.

- **Touch.** Acts like Latch until you release a control, at which point that control gradually returns to its Read state. The AutoMatch time determines how long it will take for that control to return to Read.

Drawing Automation

Real-time automation allows you to make adjustments by ear, but there are times when it's easier and more exact to create or edit automation graphically. Most of what you know about editing audio and MIDI data applies to automation parameters as well: The edit modes, the edit tools, and the Edit menu all function as expected.

Here's one quick trick to show how even a simple change in a plug-in can have a dramatic effect.

1. Go to memory location 4, Kick Trick, and insert an AIR Kill EQ on the Kick1 track. Enable its Low band and set the Low frequency to 55 Hz.

> **Note:** The AIR Kill EQ, as the name implies, is a three-band cut-only EQ with simplified controls that enables the sort of low-cut, band-reject, and high-cut EQ techniques popular in certain dance styles.

2. Drag-copy the plug-in to Kick2 (holding Alt/Opt as you did in Chapter 6, "Advanced Signal Flow").

3. Change the copy's frequency to 85 Hz. Listen to how these settings allow the energy of the kicks to come through without all of their low-end bulk. You're going to hold back the low-end for impact.

4. Ctrl+Start+Alt-click (Cmd+Ctrl+Opt-click) the Low button of one EQ to bring up the context menu shown in Figure 7.10 and choose Enable Automation for "Low." This shortcut allows you to enable plug-ins for automation without opening the Plug-In Automation dialog box. Do the same for the other kick's Kill EQ.

Figure 7.10 The quick way to enable a plug-in parameter for automation.

> **Note:** You must still enable plug-in parameters in order to draw automation for them, as any parameters that are not enabled for automation will not be available for viewing in the Edit window. Automation can be drawn regardless of a track's automation mode or the status of the Suspend or Write Enable buttons in the Automation window. However, automation will not be played back when automation has been suspended.

5. Click the Kick1 track's Track View selector and choose (fx c) AIR Kill EQ, Low, as shown in Figure 7.11. (Note that the letter after "fx" will vary, depending on which insert you used for the EQ.)

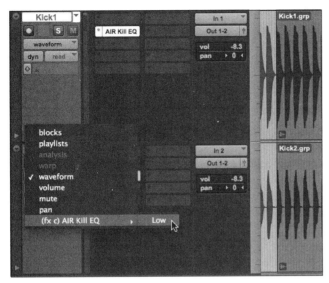

Figure 7.11 Set the track view to display the plug-in's Low playlist.

6. Click the Low button a couple of times and you will see the line in the track jump from the top (Kill) to the bottom (Thru). Leave the button on, so the band is killed.

7. Put Pro Tools in Grid mode and be sure the Bars:Beats ruler is active.

8. With the Grabber tool, grab the black line at the top of the Kick1 track and drag it to the bottom of the track. A breakpoint will appear where you grabbed the line, and the line will jump from the top to the bottom at the breakpoint.

9. Before you release the breakpoint, drag it earlier or later until the cursor indicator reads 33|1|000. Release the mouse, and the breakpoint will come to rest at the downbeat of bar 33. (If necessary, you can drag the breakpoint to reposition it.) The Low band will no longer be killed when playback reaches this bar.

10. Apply the same technique to the Kick2 track, "un-killing" its Low band at bar 33, and then killing the band again on Kick2 from bar 57 to bar 67.

11. Listen to playback from the beginning. You will hear one decent kick for 16 bars, two kicks layered for the next 16 bars, and then thunderous kick drums just as the second hi-hat enters at bar 33. Bars 57 through 67 are musically similar, so they get a variation on the technique. This is one example of how mixing decisions help enhance the overall musical flow.

Note: If you find yourself enabling many plug-in parameters on a regular basis, try enabling Plug-in Controls Default to Auto-Enabled in automation preferences.

Selective Delay

The four-bar break at bar 99 needs something to make it a bit more active. Adding a delay to the single BassPizz note there would be good, but you don't want to add delay to the BassPizz track for the whole song. You need to have a delay all set to go, then un-mute the delay send just for that note. You can draw this easily.

1. Go to memory location 5, Selective Delay, and listen.

2. Create a mono aux named BassDelay and create a pre-fader send from the BassPizz track to the delay aux.

3. Insert a Long Delay II (mono/stereo) on the aux, and set it to a quarter-note delay on one channel and a dotted eighth on the other. Be sure the plug-in is set to follow session tempo.

4. Set the feedback to around 82% and the mix to 100%.

5. Bring the aux input's volume up to about −6.0 dB.

6. Set the BassPizz track to display the send's Mute playlist, as shown in Figure 7.12. Note that, unlike a plug-in, a send's playlists appear automatically.

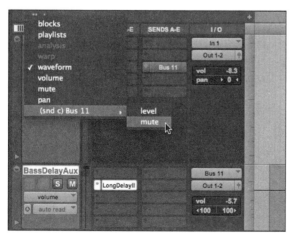

Figure 7.12 Displaying the send's Mute playlist.

7. In the send's output window, click the Mute button so its default state is muted.

8. Set its volume to 0.0 dB.

9. In Slip mode, use the Grabber to drag the automation curve up just before the note and down just after the note. (Because there is no audio immediately surrounding this region, you needn't worry about being too precise.)

10. You have just un-muted the delay send for this one note, so it is the only sound that will be processed by the delay. Listen, and you will hear that note bounce around throughout the four-bar break. When the regular BassPizz part resumes, it is no longer delayed. Use the aux input's volume to adjust the amount of delay, and use the delay's feedback to adjust how persistent the delays are.

The Line Pencil Tool

Not surprisingly, the Pencil tool comes in handy for drawing automation. The Pencil tool can be used freehand, or it can be constrained to one of four shapes: a straight line, a triangle pattern, a square pattern, or a random pattern (see Figure 7.13). To choose a particular shape, simply click and hold on the Pencil tool icon to see the drop-down list of shapes. You can also press your favorite Pencil tool shortcut [F10 or Ctrl+6 (Cmd +6)] repeatedly to cycle through the various shapes. Note that the last two shapes (Parabolic and S-Curve) are reserved for drawing in the Tempo editor and cannot be used for drawing automation.

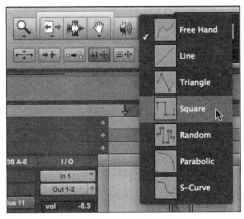

Figure 7.13 The Pencil tool's various shapes.

1. Go to memory location 6, Line Pencil, and you'll hear the obligatory machine-gun snare roll. Such a roll ordinarily crescendos to the downbeat—a natural application of the Line Pencil tool.

2. Choose Line from the Pencil drop-down list and set the Snare Roll track's view to Volume.

3. Click just before the first snare note, about a quarter of the way from the bottom of the track.

4. Draw an ascending line to the last snare note, ending at the level of the original line. When you release the mouse, you will have created exactly two breakpoints with a perfectly straight line between them.

5. Should you decide upon playback that the crescendo starts or ends at the wrong volume, you can either redraw the line or simply drag the breakpoints with the Grabber. You will recall that in Chapter 2 you used dynamics processing to change the pacing of a similar crescendo—to accomplish the same thing with volume automation, you can either draw a series of line segments or "bend" the line by drawing new breakpoints with the Grabber (see Figure 7.14). Pro Tools does not currently support actual curved lines, but because of the smooth interpolation between breakpoints, this is not a major problem.

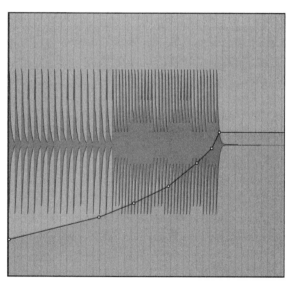

Figure 7.14 Multiple line segments can be used to approximate curved shapes.

6. The snare roll occurs again at bar 97 and at bar 131. Use the Line Pencil tool to draw crescendos on those rolls. Bar 131 is a much longer crescendo, so you will probably want to use multiple line segments to control its pacing.

Other Pencil Shapes

The Square and Triangle Pencil tools are especially good for creative panning.

1. Go to memory location 7, Other Pencil Shapes, and create a mono aux to use as a delay for the reverse cymbal.

2. By now, I'm sure you know what to name it and how to route audio to it from the Crash track. (Make me proud!)

3. Insert the Extra Long Delay (mono), and set it to a whole-note delay with a feedback value of 32.

4. Using the same technique you used previously on the BassPizz send, un-mute the Crash's delay send just for the duration of the reverse cymbal region.

5. Listen to the effect without any creative panning—not bad, but it could use some spice.

6. Display the delay aux's pan playlist and choose the Square Pencil.

Note: A speedy way to switch to a particular automation playlist is to Ctrl+Start-click (Cmd+Ctrl-click) on a track's volume, pan, or mute controls. The same technique also works with any enabled plug-in parameters. To return to the waveform view, hold down the same modifier keys and click on the track's name.

---

7. Enable Grid mode (be sure it's Absolute Grid), and set the grid value to one bar.

8. Starting at bar 102, drag in the pan playlist for about eight bars to create a square pattern, as shown in Figure 7.15. Before you release the mouse, drag all

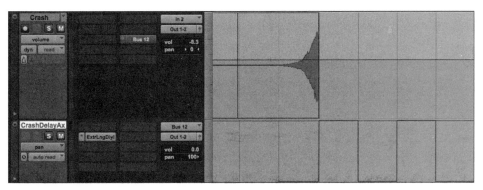

Figure 7.15   Use the Square Pencil to draw pan automation.

the way to the top or bottom of the track so the pattern fills the whole track. This square line causes the aux input to pan abruptly from hard left to hard right at one-bar intervals.

9. Press Play and listen to each iteration of the delay come from alternate speakers.

10. Try a variation on this effect. Switch to the Triangle Pencil and redraw the pan curve. The delay still moves from side to side, but more gradually. This has the effect of making the cymbal fly out from the center as it swooshes, a much more active effect than the square panning. I liked this enough that I increased the delay's feedback to make the subsequent delays stronger. Then I muted the aux at bar 107 so it didn't go on too long. (You now know several ways to accomplish that!)

Note: Pro Tools 8 introduced the ability to display multiple automation playlists simultaneously. The automation lane show/hide button is an arrow located at the bottom of the track's color code strip (see Figure 7.16). Use the plus and minus buttons on an automation lane to add or subtract as many lanes as you need.

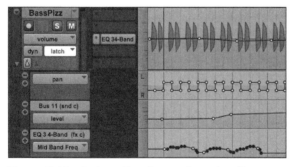

Figure 7.16 Automation lanes allow simultaneous editing of multiple automation playlists.

The Trim Tool

As I mentioned earlier, Pro Tools HD systems feature a real-time automation mode called Trim that is not available in Pro Tools LE or M-Powered. That said, you can get exactly the same result by using the Trim tool to edit automation playlists. When editing audio or MIDI regions, the Trim tool works horizontally, dragging the start or end of a region earlier or later to make it longer or shorter. With automation, the Trim tool works vertically, dragging selected breakpoints higher or lower.

1. Go to memory location 8, Trim Tool. This is the point at which Kick1 drops out for eight bars, and although the change in timbre adds variety, the energy drops too much. The solution is to raise the volume of Kick2 for these eight bars.

2. Display the Kick2 track's volume playlist. (Try out that new shortcut!)

3. Place the Trim tool over the Kick2 track; notice that the trim cursor is tipped over on its side, ready to drag breakpoints up and down (see Figure 7.17).

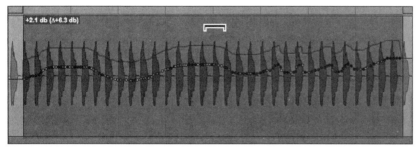

Figure 7.17   The Trim tool can be used to make relative adjustments to automation playlists.

4. Click and hold anywhere within the region that starts at bar 41.

5. At the beginning of the region, something like the following will appear: −6.4db (Δ0.0db). The first number is the current volume and the second number shows how far you have trimmed the volume from its original value. The Greek letter Δ (*delta*) is the mathematical symbol for amount of change, so this is called the *delta value*.

6. Drag the Trim tool upward, releasing it when the delta value is about +6 dB. Listen to the results and adjust the volume as necessary. Note that breakpoints appeared at the beginning and end of the region. Whenever you trim automation within a region, the trimming is restricted to that region. If you wanted to trim the volume across multiple regions or partial regions, you would simply make a selection with the Selector tool first. The selection would then define the range to be trimmed.

7. If you trim automation in an area of the track where there are no regions, the entire playlist is affected. Try this in the Kick1 track. Click with the Selector tool anywhere in the Kick1 track, and then press Ctrl+Start+right arrow

(Cmd+Ctrl+right arrow) to display its volume playlist. This shortcut allows you to cycle through all of a track's different views, from waveform to volume to pan—even enabled plug-in parameters. The shortcut applies to any track or tracks in which the edit cursor currently appears or an edit selection has been made. Ctrl+Start+left arrow (Cmd+Ctrl+left arrow) moves backward through the playlists.

8. Press Alt+A (Opt+A) to show the entire duration of the session.

9. Click with the Trim tool at bar 41 or in any other space where no region appears, and trim the volume up or down. Once again, the current volume and delta value are displayed, but this time they are displayed at the very beginning of the track. As you trim, the entire length of the track's volume playlist will move up or down.

Note: Trimming automation, whether graphically or using an HD system's real-time Trim mode, makes adjustments relative to existing values. This means that the most complex automation curve will retain its shape after trimming; only the overall level of the curve will have changed. A crescendo is still a crescendo, but its starting and ending values have increased or decreased together.

Editing Automation

One of the nice things about working in a DAW is that simple things you take for granted in your word processor—like cutting and pasting—can be used to make your musical life simpler. Automation can be cut, copied, pasted, duplicated, repeated, or edited in virtually any of the ways that Pro Tools lets you edit audio and MIDI.

1. Go to memory location 9, Editing Automation, and listen for a moment. This is a repeat of the phrase from bar 25, and it would make sense to create a crescendo in the Arpeggio track again. You could re-create it, but it will be quicker to copy what you've already done.

2. Go to memory location 2, and be sure the Arpeggio track is showing its volume playlist.

3. Double-click with the Selector tool anywhere within the first region to select it. (Note that even though the region is dimmed [because this is not the Waveform view], Pro Tools allows you to use the region to make a selection.) Shift-click in

the track anywhere after the final breakpoint of the crescendo to extend the selection, and press Ctrl+C (Cmd+C) to copy the volume automation.

4. Press the asterisk on the numeric keypad to highlight the main counter (see Figure 7.18).

Figure 7.18 The main counter shows the location of the playback cursor and can be used to relocate the cursor quickly.

5. Type **111** and press Enter to move the cursor to bar 111. (You could have simply returned to memory location 9, of course, but using the asterisk shortcut to change the cursor location is a great way to move around a session quickly.)

6. Because the cursor is already in the Arpeggio track, it is still there at the new cursor position. Press Ctrl+V (Cmd+V) to paste the volume automation to the repeated arpeggio phrase.

Paste Special and Copy Special

Pro Tools has certain rules regarding the copying and pasting of automation. The first rule is that any automation you copy or cut will always be pasted into its own playlist, no matter what playlist is currently displayed. In the previous example, you could have displayed the waveform, pan, or mute at bar 111, and the volume automation would still have been pasted into the volume playlist. To prove this to yourself, press Ctrl+Z (Cmd+Z) to undo the pasting, change the track view to anything other than volume, and press Ctrl+V (Cmd+V) to paste again. Look at the volume playlist, and you will see the same result as before.

The Paste Special to Current Automation Type command overrules this behavior, allowing you to paste an automation curve from one parameter to the playlist of another parameter. To experiment with this function, display the Arpeggio track's pan playlist, and press Ctrl+Start+V (Cmd+Ctrl+V). Now what was a crescendo appears as a line panning from right to left. Depending on how you originally panned the Arpeggio track, this could actually turn out to be an interesting effect. Keep it or undo it at your discretion.

The other rule is that when you copy or cut audio (from the Waveform or Blocks view) or MIDI (from the Notes, Regions, or Blocks view), all automation within that selection is also copied and will replace existing automation of the same type wherever the audio or MIDI is pasted. To experiment with this function, copy the Arpeggio region at bar 111 and paste it to any open space in the track. When you look at the volume playlist, you will see that the crescendo has been copied with it.

If you're thinking there must be a Copy Special command to overrule this behavior, you're correct! Copy Special (see Figure 7.19) can be used to copy all automation, only pan automation, or only plug-in automation without the corresponding audio or MIDI data. When this automation is pasted elsewhere, each parameter is pasted to its own respective playlist and does not affect any existing audio or MIDI data at that location. This is a great way to take a snapshot of the mix at one location and paste it to another location. You can tweak the first chorus of your song, select the chorus across all tracks, Copy Special All Automation, and Paste (*not* Paste Special) the entire mix to the other choruses. To copy and paste audio or MIDI data without its underlying automation, deselect Automation Follows Edit in the Options menu and use regular Copy and Paste.

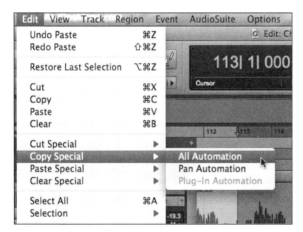

Figure 7.19 Copy Special allows automation to be copied without its associated audio or MIDI data.

1. Go to memory location 10, Copy Special Part 1. You'll recognize this as the place you creatively EQed the two kick tracks and then boosted Kick2 for eight bars when Kick1 dropped out.

2. Now go to memory location 11, Copy Special Part Deux. This is a repeat of the same sequence of events, and it cries out for a similar mix. You could certainly

re-create it using the various real-time and graphic techniques you've learned, but Copy Special will allow you to copy both the EQ automation and volume automation from bars 25–49 and paste them to bars 103–127.

3. Go back to memory location 10, select bars 25–49 across both tracks (using Grid mode to be exact).

4. Make sure the track is not in Waveform or Blocks view, and then press Ctrl+Start+C (Cmd+Ctrl+C) to Copy Special All Automation.

5. Press the asterisk on the numeric keypad, press 103, and press Enter to move the cursor to bar 103.

6. Press Ctrl+V (Cmd+V) to paste the automation to bar 103.

7. Use Ctrl+Start+right/left arrow (Cmd+Ctrl+right/left arrow) to cycle through the playlists so you can see the results.

Not Fade Away

Fading out the end of a song is one of the most common tricks in the book, but here's a variation on that technique that takes advantage of one last automation tip. You know that the Write Enable buttons allow you to choose exactly which parameters can be automated at any given time. These buttons act globally, affecting all tracks. It is also possible, however, to suspend automation for a single parameter on a single track.

1. Go to memory location 12, Not Fade Away. You're going to fade out the entire mix except for the Sweep track, which will linger a few bars longer.

2. Check the Automation window to be sure that volume automation can be written.

3. Show the Sweep track's volume playlist.

4. To suspend volume automation on this track, Ctrl-click (Cmd-click) the word "volume." The Track View selector will turn a darker gray, and the text will be italicized, as shown in Figure 7.20. Volume automation will not play back, nor can it be written, while the playlist is suspended.

Figure 7.20   Volume automation has been suspended on the Sweep track; it will not play back, nor can new data be written.

5.   Enable the All group as you did in Chapter 5.

6.   Set all tracks to Latch mode.

7.   Open the output window of any track. Begin playback, and drag that fader slowly down to silence from bar 135 to bar 143. All tracks will fade out together because the All group is active.

8.   Release the fader and let it latch at the bottom for a couple of bars.

9.   After you stop playback, deactivate the All group. Un-suspend the volume playlist on the Sweep track by Ctrl-clicking (Cmd-clicking) it again.

10.   Play these bars back. You still hear the sweep throughout the fade-out because it was unaffected by the automation. The sweep will eventually die out on its own, leaving an odd little afterthought to an otherwise straightforward dance track. (Note that this will not work properly if you neglected to do the initial Write pass discussed at the beginning of this chapter. If the Sweep track's volume has not been anchored, it will still follow the All group. You can tell this has happened if the track's entire volume curve is a flat line at the bottom of the track. To correct it, simply do a short Write pass to anchor the volume before the fade.)

Note: If you tend to use a lot of synthesizers in your music, you may be accustomed to using real-time MIDI control change messages to create filter sweeps, modify attack settings, and so forth. In many cases you will get smoother control changes by using Pro Tools automation rather than MIDI controllers. As a general rule, if you can automate a virtual instrument's parameters from its instrument track, you should do so. In all cases, you should control volume and pan from the instrument (or aux) track rather than using MIDI volume and pan. With hardware synthesizers, this will also help optimize your signal-to-noise ratio.

You have used automation to add interest to this track, changing settings from section to section and within phrases. Automation has allowed you to change settings on all sorts of mix parameters, from level and pan to plug-in settings. Although a dance track such as this example is especially dependent on automation to give it shape, most mixes will benefit from judicious use of these techniques.

This track cries out for experimentation, so take some time to refine the mix. I can imagine short delays being used to give space to some of the high-frequency parts (perhaps the hats and synths) and a subtle rhythmic delay on one or more of the percussive parts. Try a long reverb (or delay) on the sweep, and see if some pan automation can be used to give it motion. This is a good opportunity for you to start combining the various techniques you've learned to see just how far you can take this track.

If you find that playback starts to glitch after you draw large amounts of automation, you can reduce the number of breakpoints in a playlist manually—Smooth and Thin Data After Pass only applies to automation written in real time. Select the playlist or portion of a playlist you want to thin, raise the Degree of Thinning setting in the Automation Preferences dialog box, and choose Thin Automation from the Edit menu. When you finish, it's time to print that final mix so you can burn a CD. That's called *bouncing*, and it is the topic of the next chapter.

8 Bouncing Your Mix

You've explored every major part of crafting a good mix in Pro Tools. You've dealt with time, timbre, balance, position, ambience, dynamics, and more, and you're on your way to making better mixes than ever before. The thing is, none of it matters if you can't take your mix out of the studio!

Bringing your mix to the people requires a CD for their stereo or a file for their iPod. They can't play your Pro Tools session! That means you need to create a single output file containing your final mix. This process is called *bouncing*, a name that harkens back to the days of combining tracks on tape. Prior to the days of 24-track recorders, several tracks on a four- or eight-track recorder would be mixed down to one or two free tracks, and then new parts would be recorded to replace those source tracks, allowing engineers to combine more parts than the actual number of tracks on the tape. Taken to the extreme, this was called *ping-ponging* tracks because they would be bounced back and forth between tracks several times.

Bouncing in Pro Tools is actually quite a simple affair, yet it is surrounded by an extraordinary amount of hype, mystery, misinformation, and less-than-scientific marketing claims from third-party vendors. I will spend just a bit more time on explanations in this chapter than I have in other chapters in order to help you see through the fog.

Bounce to Disk

There are five general circumstances in which you use Pro Tools' Bounce to Disk function:

- The first, and most obvious, circumstance is when you want to commit your final mix to a file that can be burned to a CD or distributed online.

- A second circumstance is when you want to create *submixes*, which are partial mixes representing major portions of the mix. In a musical context, you might have a submix of the rhythm section and one of the background vocals. These partial mixes can be recombined easily for creating backing tracks for a concert or for creating an alternate final mix without going back to the original session. In a film or video context, these submixes—called *stems*—might represent dialog, sound effects, or the musical score. Having these pre-mixed makes the final mix more manageable. I'll cover stems and submixes in Chapter 10, "Stems and Submixes."

- In a Pro Tools LE or M-Powered system, you are limited to 48 mono or stereo tracks. If your arrangement grows beyond these constraints you could submix tracks internally. So, for example, a third application might be to bounce a dozen drum tracks to a stereo drum submix, thus freeing up several tracks for additional parts. This is directly analogous to bouncing tracks to manage limited tracks of tape.

- A fourth possibility is what is called *printing* effects. This is another term borrowed from tape, and it describes the practice of recording a track through an effects processor to another track. After the effect has been committed to tape, the processor can be reassigned to another part. Although you can use multiple copies of a plug-in in Pro Tools, you may choose to print effects in order to conserve CPU resources in a complex mix. Chapter 14, "Managing Mix Resources," walks you through internal submixing and printing effects.

- The fifth application of Bounce to Disk is similar to printing effects, except it involves printing synthesizer parts. When you mix a song that includes synthesizer parts controlled by MIDI tracks, it is entirely possible to leave these parts "virtual" right up to the final bounce. There are times, however, when it's desirable to print them to individual audio tracks for maximum control in the mix. I'll get to that later in this chapter.

The Bounce Procedure

Bouncing, regardless of the application, requires only that you select the time range you want to bounce and choose Bounce to Disk from the File menu. Let's use your finished mix of the Chapter 7 session for this exercise. If you didn't save a mixed version, go ahead and work with the original.

It's a good idea to "pad" the beginning and end of a file with a little bit of silence. There are several reasons for this. If you are going to make your song available for streaming playback online, a little silence at the beginning gives the media player a little safety margin in case it has to pause to re-buffer the file. A bit of extra at the end ensures that you haven't inadvertently cut off the last bit of the reverb tail. Most mastering engineers prefer to receive files with a couple of extra seconds on either end to give them flexibility in spacing songs on a CD, so always select a bit more than you think is necessary. First, pad the beginning of this song using the Move Song Start function (see Figure 8.1).

Figure 8.1 Move Song Start allows you to pad the beginning of a mix before you bounce.

1. Press Alt+1 (Opt+1) on the numeric keypad to open the Time Operations dialog box.

2. Press Ctrl+up arrow (Cmd+up arrow) once to switch to the Move Song Start dialog box.

3. Using a timebase of Minutes:Seconds, set a new Song Start position of 00:02:000. Don't renumber the bars, and tell Pro Tools to move everything, including all sample-based markers and tracks. When you click Apply, two seconds of silence will appear before your song's downbeat, allowing you to create a two-second "handle" at the beginning of the file.

If you bounce now, without making any selection, the entire session timeline will bounce. At first glance, this may seem to be a good idea, but there are some dangers. For one thing, if some stray bit of automation wound up 20 minutes down one track (I've seen it happen!), it would take several times longer to bounce your session and you would end up with a 20-minute file that needed to be trimmed substantially. For another thing (assuming you have no such straggling data), your bounce will stop at the very last region boundary or automation breakpoint, very likely cutting off the last second or so of reverb at the end of your mix. It is therefore advisable always to select exactly what you want to bounce.

1. Press Enter (Return) to return the cursor to the beginning of the session and immediately press Shift+Ctrl+Enter (Shift+Opt+Return) to select to the end of the session.

Note: Hopefully, you're getting fluent in the language of Pro Tools shortcuts and modifier keys. In this case, Shift creates a selection while Ctrl (Opt) reverses the direction of Enter (Return), which would ordinarily move the cursor to the start of the session. Thus, Shift+Ctrl+Enter (Shift+Opt+Return) selects to the end of the session. For those of you paying *really* close attention, yes, this is a rare exception to the usual translation of Windows Ctrl to Mac Cmd.

2. Next, add two seconds in order to allow plenty of time for the last sounds to die away completely, plus another two to ensure sufficient padding for the mastering engineer. First, click to change the main time scale to Min:Secs as shown in Figure 8.2.

Figure 8.2 Changing the main time scale.

3. Press the slash (/) key on the numeric keypad three times to highlight the Length field in the Event Edit Area (see Figure 8.3). The slash key cycles through the Selection Indicators (Start, End, Length), allowing you to change the current selection from the keyboard. It always highlights the leftmost field first, which in this case is Minutes, so to change the Length of this selection by a matter of seconds you need to press the right arrow key once.

Figure 8.3 Changing the current selection using the Event Edit Area.

4. Now that the Seconds field is highlighted, press the plus (+) key, the number 4, and Enter or Return. This *adds* four seconds to the current Length value, making your selection four seconds longer.

Note: Digidesign calls this technique the "calculator" function. Instead of having to add four seconds to the current Length value in your head and then type that new value in, you can simply let Pro Tools add the four seconds. You can use this

technique to change any of the three Selection Indicators or to change the main
counter. For some reason, subtraction was broken in Pro Tools 7.x, but happily it
has been fixed in Pro Tools 8, so you can once again add or subtract values.

5. Having selected the appropriate amount of time, press Ctrl+Alt+B
    (Cmd+Opt+B) or choose Bounce to Disk from the File menu.

6. Use the Bounce dialog box (see Figure 8.4) to specify the desired bounce
    parameters. By default, the bounce source is set to your main stereo output.
    Most of the time, this is exactly what you want to bounce—what you've been
    hearing from your speakers—but bouncing a submix or stem might require
    bouncing an alternate output pair or even a bus. Always confirm that the
    bounce source is set correctly.

Figure 8.4 The Bounce dialog box.

Bounce Parameters

Unless your CD-burning software or MP3 converter requires otherwise, you should
ordinarily bounce to a WAV file. Broadcast WAV files are considered the industry standard and the most future-proof file type. If you intend to re-import the file into Pro
Tools, set the file format to Multiple mono, but if the file is headed for a CD make it
Stereo Interleaved. Most CD-burning applications prefer to work with interleaved files.

If you purchased the MP3 Export Option, you will be able to choose MP3 as your file type. If you have not, you can still bounce MP3s for 30 days from the first use of this option. Otherwise, you can import the file into iTunes or your favorite encoder to create an MP3 or AAC file.

You should choose your bit depth (Resolution) and sample rate according to the intended use of the bounced file. Since these parameters determine the quality of the output file, you should not reduce them unless it is necessary. If you intend to burn them directly to CD, create 16-bit/44.1 kHz files. If you intend to tweak the files in your CD-burning application before burning—for example, match track volumes, apply EQ or compression, or create crossfades—maintain the bit depth and sample rate of your session. If your session is not at 44.1 kHz, however, check to see if your burning program needs you to bounce to 44.1.

Should you intend to send your files to a mastering engineer for final polishing, bounce to the resolution of your session. Lowering the resolution will result in a lower-quality bounce, and raising the resolution will have no positive effect. If you intend to re-import the bounce back into your Pro Tools session, maintain the session's bit depth and sample rate.

Note: You may notice a theme here: Don't reduce your bit depth and sample rate unless and until you absolutely must! Lowering the resolution of your file lowers its audio quality, and that quality can't be recovered down the line. Of course, most files end up at 16-bit/44.1 kHz resolution on a CD, so you should use the best tool possible to perform that conversion. Although each situation is unique, your first choice is usually to let the mastering engineer handle it. If you're not hiring a professional mastering engineer, do it when bouncing in Pro Tools. Unless you have a very sophisticated CD-burning application, you should have all gain tweaking, processing, and bit-depth/sample-rate reduction done prior to importing into that application. Letting the burning application handle that is usually your last choice.

If you bounce to a different sample rate, you will be prompted to specify a conversion quality (see Figure 8.5). This setting determines how hard Pro Tools works to interpolate between existing samples to generate new samples. The harder it works, the longer it takes, but the better it sounds. The available options, from fastest to slowest, include Low, Good, Better, Best, and Tweak Head. Unless your processor is so slow that the conversion takes an unreasonably long time, you should use Best or Tweak Head. If you are bouncing to an 8-bit file, consider checking the box to "Use Squeezer" to optimize the file's dynamic range prior to word-length reduction.

Figure 8.5   Sample rate conversion quality options in the Bounce dialog box.

Finally, Pro Tools asks you whether you want to convert the file type, bit depth, and sample rate during or after the bounce process. If you convert during the bounce, the file will be ready to use as soon as the bounce is completed, saving you time. However, your CPU may be distracted from its mix duties by the conversion process, and the accuracy of your automation may suffer. (It's important to note, however, that nothing other than automation accuracy will be degraded.) You should therefore convert during the bounce only if your mix uses little automation and your top priority is speed. This would be the case in many broadcast scenarios, but rarely in music production. Unless you have no other choice, opt to convert after the bounce.

Now that you have set your bounce parameters according to your needs, click Bounce. In the ensuing dialog box, give the bounce file a name and specify its location. Then click Save, sit back, and listen carefully as the session bounces.

Bouncing to an MP3

Let's try bouncing the same track to an MP3 file. The selection you made in steps 1–4 above should remain. If it has been lost, repeat those steps before continuing.

1. Press Ctrl+Alt+B (Cmd+Opt+B) to open the Bounce to Disk dialog box.

2. Confirm that you are bouncing your main output, and set the File Type to MP3. If you have not purchased this option, creating your first MP3 will initiate a 30-day trial of the MP3 Export Option, which uses the industry-standard Fraunhofer codec.

3. Be sure the Format is set to Stereo Interleaved. You can bounce a summed mono MP3 if you choose, but you would obviously lose any panning information. In

some cases, this may be a useful trade-off, as a mono MP3 will have better frequency response than a stereo MP3 at the same bit rate. It's your call.

4. Click Bounce, and the MP3 Export Options dialog box will appear (see Figure 8.6).

Figure 8.6 MP3 Export Options.

5. Set Constant Bit Rate (CBR) to the desired bit rate. The higher the bit rate, the higher the audio quality. Although 128 kbit/s is often cited as a standard, iTunes songs are now sold at 256 kbit/s, and many DJs use 320 kbit/s files. Pro Tools does not support Variable Bit Rate (VBR) encoding.

6. Set the Encoding Speed to Highest Quality, Slower Encoding Time. This may take up to five times as long as the Fastest setting, but it's ordinarily worth the wait to produce a better-sounding file.

7. Enter ID3 info, such as artist name and song title, then click OK. The *metadata* contained in ID3 tags not only helps your listeners identify you and your songs in their media players, but it can also help you keep track of different mixes, different edits, and other production information.

8. Give the file a name and a location, and click Save. As with the WAV file, Pro Tools will bounce the track in real time. When it is done bouncing, it will convert it to an MP3 file at the settings you specified.

It would be worth your while to import your WAV and MP3 bounces into separate tracks in a blank Pro Tools session to compare their sound. It's useful to be able to hear exactly what MP3 encoding does to the sound of a file. If you are running Pro Tools on a PC, try bouncing to a Windows Media file. The procedure is essentially the same, but the sound will be slightly different, even at a comparable bit rate. You may find you like it more on some songs and less on others, but ordinarily it's the target audience that determines choice of codec.

The Real-Time Bounce

Pro Tools always bounces in real time—for example, a four-minute song takes four minutes to bounce (see Figure 8.7). For historical, technical, and philosophical reasons, Pro Tools' entire mix engine is built around real-time performance. To be honest, there are times when this is a major nuisance. Imagine recording a two-hour concert, mixing and editing it, and then having to wait two hours for it to bounce!

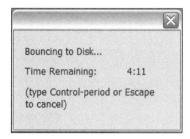

Bouncing to Disk...

Time Remaining: 4:11

(type Control-period or Escape to cancel)

Figure 8.7   Pro Tools always bounces in real time.

Of course, if you were working with tape, you would never expect anything other than real-time bouncing. In fact, in some studios it's common practice to synchronize Pro Tools to analog tape, recording certain parts digitally and others analog. Even if Pro Tools could bounce faster than real time, one would still have to record all of the tape parts to Pro Tools first, and that would happen in real time.

In an LE system, the real-time bounce ends up being an advantage in two cases: recording hardware synthesizers and inserting hardware effects. Because Pro Tools plays all MIDI data during a bounce and includes all aux inputs, even hardware inputs, during a bounce, there is no need to record hardware synths and effects prior to bouncing.

In some DAWs, all external sound sources must be committed to audio tracks before they can be included in a bounce. Every hardware synthesizer part ends up needing its own audio track, as does every hardware EQ or compressor. This takes time, and it eats up audio tracks. In Pro Tools, whatever you hear during normal playback will be included in the bounced file, exactly as you hear it.

You may still choose to record external sources, however. For example, if you are playing eight different parts on a hardware synthesizer, but the synthesizer has only four outputs, you would want to record at least four of those parts prior to bouncing so that each part can be mixed independently. External effects are affected by system latency, so if that causes a noticeable problem you can record the processed part and slide it earlier to compensate. I'll expand on these practices later in this chapter.

Dither

Very few concepts in digital audio are as shrouded in mystery as dither. A complete explanation is beyond the scope of this book, but the simple explanation is that dither preserves the integrity of the signal at its lowest levels. Without dither, sounds that are supposed to disappear into silence end up falling off a sonic cliff, screaming in agony as they do so. With dither, they fade away more gracefully, retaining their dignity as they blend into the ether.

As a general principle, dither should be used whenever you reduce word length (bit depth). In practice, this means that every time you create a 16-bit output file you should use dither. This is obvious when you are bouncing a 24-bit session to a 16-bit file, but you may wonder why dither is necessary when bouncing a 16-bit session to a 16-bit file. The answer is that Pro Tools is always mixing at higher resolution—a 16-bit session is mixed at 32-bit resolution in order to calculate all mix parameters as accurately as possible, so you are still reducing word length when you bounce to 16 bits. (The details are slightly different in Pro Tools HD, but the principle is the same.)

1. In the Chapter 7 session, create a new stereo master fader and name it Mix Output. Be sure it is assigned to your main output path.

2. Click its lowest insert and, from the multichannel plug-in, Dither menu choose POW-r Dither (stereo) (see Figure 8.8).

Note: POW-r Dither is not included with Pro Tools M-Powered, so instead you should use Maxim, which is found in the Dynamics plug-in menu. Maxim is a limiter that includes dither, but if you make sure that its Threshold and Ceiling controls are set to 0.0 dB, only its dither will be active. The DigiRack Dither plug-in, which is also included in both versions of Pro Tools, would ordinarily be your third choice.

---

3. The essential controls for the three plug-ins are nearly identical. First, you must choose what bit depth your output file will be. With rare exceptions, this will be 16 bits.

4. Next, you must choose your noise-shaping options. Noise-shaping changes the frequency content of the noise introduced by dither to make it less

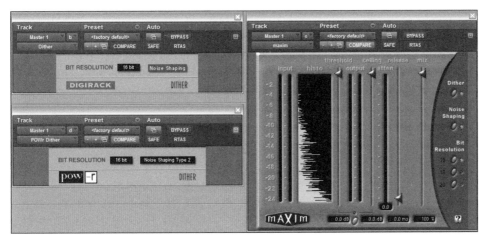

Figure 8.8   DigiRack Dither, POW-r Dither, and Maxim.

objectionable. In Maxim and the DigiRack Dither plug-in, you should always enable noise-shaping. In the POW-r Dither plug-in, you must choose among three different types of noise-shaping. Although the documentation attempts to explain the differences between them, your best course of action is simply to audition each of them by playing back a very quiet phrase, preferably a sound that diminishes to silence.

5.   Take a few minutes to re-bounce the Chapter 7 session with dither. Listen carefully to the end of each of the two bounces, as the sweep and its reverb (if you added any) die away. The one with dither will die away more gracefully, but there will be a small amount of additional noise. This is the trade-off of dither: We trade distortion for noise because noise offends our ears less.

Note: Use dither whenever you bounce to a 16-bit file or MP3. Place the best dither plug-in you have available on the last insert of your main output's master fader. Although you will not notice the difference during loud passages, the sound will be smoother at low levels. Do *not* use dither when you are bouncing to 24-bit files. It will not help, and it will make the mastering engineer's job more difficult.

A Brief Bounce Experiment

You may have heard in online forums or trade publications how awful it sounds when you bounce in Pro Tools—*it's not true!* Despite all objective evidence, there are people who are willing to jump through all sorts of elaborate hoops to keep Pro Tools from collapsing the stereo field, making the mix quieter, wrecking the low end, destroying the high end, making the mix sound thin, and committing every sort of heinous audio crime known to mankind. Oh, the humanity! The simple fact is that *Pro Tools bounces exactly what you hear*, no more and no less. Here's a simple experiment that will demonstrate that the ones and zeros that travel to your A/D converters are the same as the ones and zeros that end up in the bounced file.

1.   Close your session and open the original Chapter 07.ptf session.

2.   Set the main time scale to Min:Sec.

3.   As before, use the Event Edit Area to make a precise selection. Remembering to use the numeric keypad, press slash (/) once to highlight the Start field, and type 0 (zero). Don't press Enter yet!

4.   Press slash (/) again to highlight the End field, press the right arrow to move the cursor to the Seconds column, and type **30**.

5.   Press Enter to confirm these values. You have now selected precisely the first 30 seconds of the session.

6.   Bounce the selection with the parameters shown in Figure 8.9. This will create a 16-bit/44.1 kHz dual-mono broadcast WAV file that will be imported immediately into the Regions list. Save it to the session's Audio Files folder.

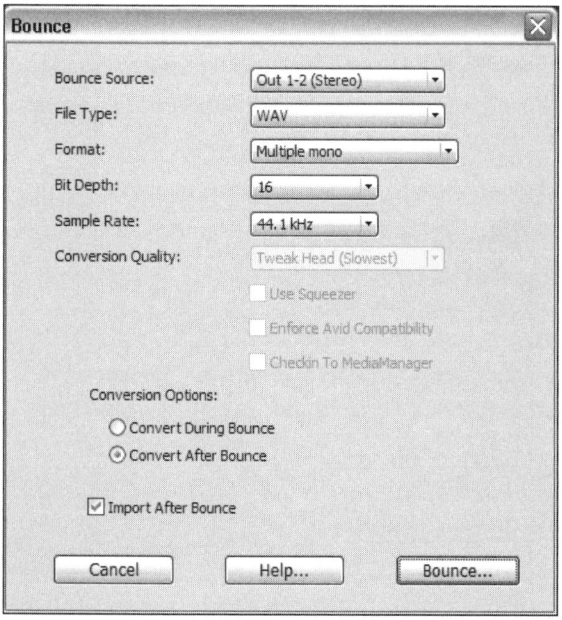

Figure 8.9 Bounce parameters for re-importing a file.

7. After the file has been bounced, the Audio Import Options dialog will ask whether you want it to go in a new track or simply in the Region list (see Figure 8.10). Choose Region list, make sure Location is set to Session Start, and click OK. This places the bounced file in a new stereo audio track right at the beginning of the session. It will now play back in addition to the actual mix. If you play the session now, it will sound perfectly normal but six decibels louder—this is what happens when identical signals are added.

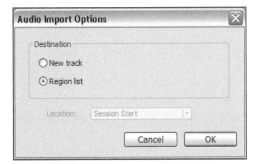

Figure 8.10   The Audio Import Options dialog.

8. Select the entire bounce region and, from the AudioSuite > Other menu, choose Invert. This plug-in inverts the polarity (often incorrectly called the *phase*) of the bounce region. In other words, it flips the waveform upside down, creating a mirror image of the original (see Figure 8.11).

Figure 8.11   Inverting a region creates a perfect mirror image of the original.

What happens when a signal is added to an inverted copy of itself? Silence. If the copy is truly "equal and opposite," the two should cancel each other, just as adding 37 to −37 equals 0. Thus, when you play this inverted signal, it will work in exact opposition to the signal created by the other tracks, pushing when they pull and pulling when they push. The net effect is that the inverted bounce will cancel the rest of the tracks because it was *identical to the mix* prior to being inverted. The bounced file is exactly the same as the product of the mix being played back—you have successfully debunked an entrenched myth!

You will get the same results if you record the mix internally to an audio track. To test this, simply route the outputs of all tracks (be sure to mute the track that holds the bounce region you just created) to a stereo bus, then assign that bus as the input of a new stereo audio track. Record to the new track, invert the resulting region, and listen— blessed silence, and a popular variation on the bounce myth debunked!

Note: There are a handful of variables that can afflict experiments of this type. One is dither, which is by definition random. If you dither the bounce, the dither on playback will be different, making it seem as though the bounce is imprecise. Another is that if you have a master fader on the mix output set to something other than 0.0 dB, when you import the bounce it will be boosted or cut *again* by the master fader, making it seem louder or softer than the mix. It should go without saying that comparing a 16-bit bounce to the original 24-bit mix will reveal some differences—after all, you sacrificed 48 dB of dynamic range to make it fit on a CD!

Pro Tools mix automation is not always sample-accurate, so a mix with any significant amount of automation may be slightly different on playback from its bounce. Similarly, certain effects (often reverbs) are deliberately randomized, so each time they play back they are slightly different. In either of these cases, if you were to record the output digitally to another device during a bounce and then compare that to the bounce, *those* would be identical, proving the case that what Pro Tools bounces is exactly what you hear.

You have proven that Pro Tools does not wreck your mix when you bounce it. Of course, this means that you have no one but yourself to blame if you don't like the sound of your bounced mix!

Bouncing Synthesizer Parts

When your mix includes MIDI tracks, you have two options when you bounce. The first option is to let Pro Tools play your MIDI tracks during the bounce and capture the resulting audio from your synthesizers in the bounce. This is one advantage of the real-time bounce, but you must be sure your session and your synthesizer(s) are set up properly. The second option is to commit each part to an audio track before you bounce. Although this takes more time, it allows you to mix each of your MIDI parts independently regardless of how many outputs your synthesizer has. It also allows you to perform any type of audio-only processing you wish, such as Elastic Audio, time compression/expansion, and reverse. Bouncing MIDI parts to disk and then importing the bounced files back into the session is a common technique for this. You simply have to remember the rules of Bounce to Disk. Another technique is to record the part directly to an audio track via a bus. As you just learned, this will yield the same result as Bounce to Disk. Because it results in the part already being placed in an audio track, this actually saves a step compared to Bounce to Disk.

Note: We often use the term "bounce" indiscriminately to refer to recording internally as well as to using Bounce to Disk. There's no absolute right or wrong, and since the results are identical you can't even argue about it. Some engineers will call this "printing" sources to tracks or even "flattening" tracks.

Bouncing MIDI "Live"

It's not uncommon to have several MIDI tracks triggering a single multi-timbral synthesizer and one aux input returning the audio output of that synthesizer to Pro Tools, as shown in Figure 8.12. A variation on this uses an instrument track, which is essentially a MIDI track and an aux input rolled into one. The instrument track holds one MIDI part and returns the audio from the synth, while other MIDI tracks trigger the same synth. Open the session Chapter 08.ptf and look at memory location 1 for examples of each.

For sequencing, this is a convenient setup, but for mixing it is too restrictive. How would you EQ the piano part without affecting the bass? You need to separate the audio streams from each other so you can mix them independently. If your synthesizer has multiple audio outputs, you can do this easily by connecting each output to an input of your interface and setting up separate aux inputs to return each of those signals. Even some software synthesizers offer multiple audio outputs for this purpose.

There's no way I can describe this process for every synthesizer, so you'll have to explore your device's manual for the specifics. The process, however, is the same for any synth. Each MIDI part is on a different channel, and you need to set up the synth so that each channel plays out a different output. If the part is a mono instrument, such as a bass or a horn, this will be a mono output.

Figure 8.12 Three MIDI tracks trigger sounds from a Proteus 2000, and the sound of the Proteus is heard through the aux input.

In some cases, a synthesizer will force you to use outputs in pairs. If you encounter such a limitation, all you need to do is pan one channel hard left and another channel hard right, then assign them to the same output pair. You can then route the left and right channels of that output pair into Pro Tools as separate mono inputs.

Memory location 2 shows a typical scenario using a Triton Rack synthesizer to play six parts. At the top is the stereo aux input I used during sequencing, now muted. Below are six pair of MIDI and aux tracks, one for each MIDI part. The Bass part is played by the Bass MIDI track and triggers the Triton on channel 1. The resulting audio signal comes out of the Triton's first individual audio output and into Pro Tools through the audio input labeled Triton 1. The Shaker track uses MIDI channel 2, Triton individual output 2, and Pro Tools input Triton 2, with the EPiano and Claps tracks following suit.

The last two parts, Trumpet and Sax, use the Triton's main outputs, the same pair I used for sequencing. In order to use these as two mono outputs instead of a stereo pair, pan the Trumpet MIDI track hard left and the Sax MIDI track hard right, as shown in Figure 8.13. Now assign their audio inputs to Triton L and Triton R, respectively.

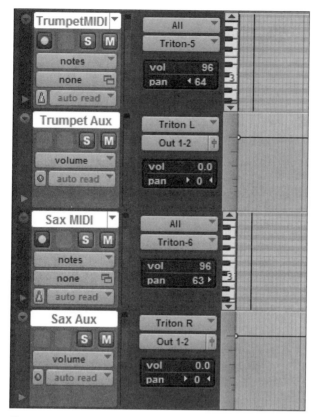

Figure 8.13 By panning the MIDI tracks left and right, even a synthesizer's main output pair can be used in mono.

Note: Instead of using separate MIDI and aux tracks for each synth part, you could use mono *instrument tracks*. Introduced in version 7.0, instrument tracks combine all of the features of a MIDI track with all of the features of an aux input. Instrument tracks can be mono or stereo, and they support both hardware and software synthesizers.

When using a synthesizer in this way, it's important to disable or at least selectively assign the instrument's built-in effects. If you find a particular internal effect useful on a part, you may be able to assign that effect to that part's individual output.

It's also advisable to set the volume on each MIDI track to 127. This ensures that each part is leaving the synthesizer with the best signal-to-noise ratio and hitting your interface at a decent level. If you've used any MIDI volume automation, set the track's automation mode to Off so it stays at 127. You'll be using the aux inputs to control the volume of each part, so any automation belongs there.

Using a multi-timbral software synthesizer with multiple outputs, you would follow the same procedure. The only difference is in how you assign individual parts to separate channels and outputs.

MIDI Offset

One other thing you must consider when using hardware synthesizers in this way is the latency inherent in a host-based system. All audio traveling into and out of Pro Tools must travel through a buffer at the CPU. A *buffer* is merely a holding area—a bit of RAM, really—that allows multiple audio events to be re-aligned in time after getting processed. This delays the signal a bit, and although that delay is often so small as to be negligible, it can sometimes be audible. The magnitude of this delay is determined by a setting called the Hardware Buffer.

To compensate for this latency, Pro Tools allows you to offset your MIDI tracks. Sending the MIDI data to your synthesizers a bit early counteracts the buffer's delay, so the audio ends up being on time. To set the MIDI offset, first go to Setup > Playback Engine, and look at the value of the H/W Buffer Size field (see Figure 8.14). This is the value to which you will set the MIDI offset.

Close the Playback Engine dialog box without changing anything. From the Event menu, open the MIDI Track Offsets dialog box (see Figure 8.15). If you have no software synthesizers in your session, enter the value of the H/W Buffer Size in the Global MIDI Playback Offset field *as a negative number*. It's essential that you use a minus sign, because a negative value causes the MIDI tracks to play back *early*. If you also have software synthesizers in your session, you should leave the Global value at 0 and enter the negative number in the Sample Offset field for each MIDI track assigned to your hardware synthesizers, as shown in Figure 8.15.

You can now hide your MIDI tracks and mix the aux inputs as though they were additional audio tracks. This is one way in which you can get a lot more performance out of a Pro Tools LE system than its 48 audio track limitation would suggest. You are still limited, however, by the number of outputs on your hardware synthesizers and the number of inputs on your audio interface. With the right synthesizers and a Digi 003, you could theoretically get up to 18 simultaneous hardware synth parts into Pro Tools LE this way, but 10 of those inputs must be digital. A more practical expectation is 8 to 10 parts. With software synthesizers, you are primarily limited by the architecture of the synth and your CPU power.

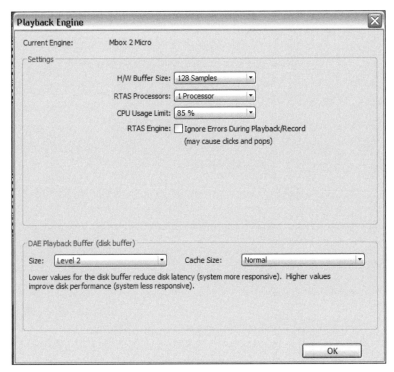

Figure 8.14   The Hardware Buffer (H/W Buffer) setting determines the amount of latency in an incoming signal.

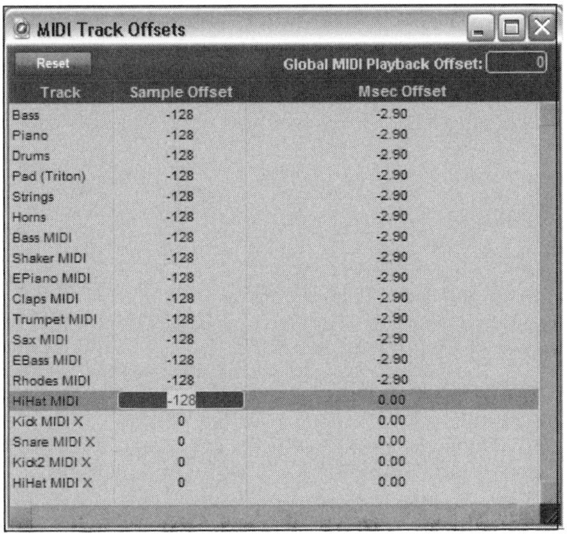

Figure 8.15   The MIDI Track Offsets dialog box.

Note: Your synthesizer itself may actually introduce a slight delay due to its own latency as it responds to incoming MIDI events, so you might want to measure the exact latency and set the MIDI offset more precisely. Run any sound with a crisp attack through your synthesizer, record it to an audio track, zoom way in, and measure the distance in samples from the start of the MIDI note to the start of the resultant audio waveform. Enter this value as a negative number in the Sample Offset field for that track. This value may be larger for higher channel numbers, and it may vary slightly according to the density of MIDI data currently being played. This is one reason some people prefer to print MIDI tracks and time-correct them with Beat Detective. Listen carefully to your synth parts to see what you think with your setup.

Printing MIDI Parts

If you don't have enough synth outputs or Pro Tools inputs to return the audio from your synthesizers to independent auxes, you can print each part to its own audio track. This might also be necessary if your CPU is unable to support as many virtual instrument tracks as you would like. Whether you need to or not, you might choose to print your MIDI parts in order to manipulate them in the audio domain.

1. Go to memory location 3. You will see three MIDI tracks and a stereo aux.

2a. If you have a hardware synthesizer with a General MIDI bank, assign the input of the aux to the Pro Tools input to which that synth is connected, and then assign the outputs of the MIDI tracks to the synth's MIDI port on channels 1, 2, and 3, respectively.

OR

2b. If you do not have an appropriate hardware synthesizer, insert an Xpand2 instrument on an insert of the synth aux. Recall the preset Ch08 MemLoc3 from the Librarian menu, and assign the outputs of the MIDI tracks to Xpand2-2 channels 1, 2, and 3, respectively.

3. Solo-safe the aux track by Ctrl-clicking (Cmd-clicking) on its Solo button.

4. Press Play. You should hear a simple musical phrase. You're going to print the three parts to their own individual audio tracks so you can mix them independently within Pro Tools.

> **Note:** As in the preceding example, you should set the volume of the MIDI tracks to 127 and turn their automation modes to Off. Unless you intend to time-correct the parts (using Beat Detective, for example), you should set an appropriate MIDI offset before bouncing.

5. In the Options menu, be sure Pre-Fader Metering is disabled. As the name suggests, this setting would cause track meters to ignore any volume changes made with the track fader.

6. Pan the EBass MIDI track hard left and the Rhodes MIDI track hard right. With Xpand2, do this with the pan controls on the Xpand2 interface, not the track pan controls. Solo them both and begin playback.

7. Be sure your synthesizer's master volume is as high as it can go without clipping the input. This will ordinarily be all the way up with a hardware synth, but with Xpand2 you may not need to adjust it at all. As the session plays, set the aux input's fader high enough that the meters peak at around −6 dBFS (slightly more than half-way up the yellow segment). This ensures that you will be bouncing a strong audio signal.

8. Select bars 13–16 and press Ctrl+Alt+B (Cmd+Opt+B).

9. Set the bounce parameters to the same resolution and file type as the session (16/44.1 WAV).

10. Select Out 1-2 as the bounce source and multiple mono as the file format.

11. Enable the options Convert After Bounce and Import After Bounce.

12. Save the file to the current session's audio files folder.

13. After the file has bounced, you will be prompted to place it in a new track or in the Regions list. Choose Regions list.

14. Click the arrow to the left of the region name to display its left and right regions, as shown in Figure 8.16.

Figure 8.16   Every stereo region in Pro Tools is actually made up of a L/R pair of mono regions with .L and .R extensions.

15. Rename the left and right regions EBass and Rhodes, respectively.

16. While holding down the Start (Ctrl) key, drag the two regions to the Tracks list. They will be placed in new mono audio tracks named EBass and Rhodes at the cursor's current location.

17. Next, for the HiHat MIDI track, pan it hard left, and then bounce only Out 1, using the same parameters.

18. Name the bounce file HiHat.

19. When it has been imported, simply Start-drag (Ctrl-drag) it to the Tracks list. You now have three synth parts printed as audio, ready to mix.

The Other Bounce

For this last exercise in printing MIDI parts, I'm going to use Digidesign's Xpand2 plug-in. Memory location 4 shows another basic drum arrangement. This time, though, the Kick MIDI X part is on an instrument track running a stereo Xpand2 drum kit. The MIDI tracks Snare MIDI X, Kick2 MIDI X, and HiHat MIDI X are also routed to play the Xpand2 kit.

1. Create four new mono audio tracks and name them Kick X, Snare X, Kick 2 X, and HiHat X.

2. Set all four inputs to a mono bus, and assign this same bus as the output of the instrument track.

Note: Yes, that's correct—you're assigning a stereo track to a mono output. Both channels will be merged into a single channel. You could substitute a mono Xpand2, but that would be cumbersome. I could have done my sequencing using a mono Xpand2, but that would feel unnatural. As long as you are careful the signal doesn't clip, summing the output to mono is the optimum solution.

---

3. Mute the Snare MIDI X, Kick2 MIDI X, and HiHat MIDI X tracks, and record-arm the Kick X track.

4. Disable the Xpand2's FX1 and FX2, unless you are so enamored of their sound that you are willing to print the tracks with effects permanently embedded.

5. Use the Xpand2 Level control (see Figure 8.17) to ensure that the signal going to the Kick X track is strong but doesn't clip.

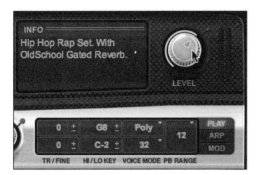

Figure 8.17   Use Xpand2's Level control to set proper record levels.

6.   Select bars 25–28 and then press Record.

7.   Repeat the process for the Snare MIDI X, Kick2 MIDI X, and HiHat MIDI X tracks.

Note: When working with virtual instruments, MIDI offset is not necessary because the signal doesn't pass through the hardware buffer on its way to the audio track. There is also no need to worry about signal-to-noise ratio because the signal flow is entirely internal.

Believe it or not, you have now covered most of what there is to know about mixing in Pro Tools. You can route audio wherever you need it, you can organize the most complex session, you understand how to route all the essential effects, you can bring it to life with automation, and you can bounce it all down to a file ready to burn to a CD. You would have to dig pretty deeply into the *Pro Tools Reference Guide* to find anything new to learn. Congratulations!

The remainder of this book is devoted to applying a bit of imagination to these tools. It consists of a series of short chapters, each of which deals with a particular advanced application. The ideas discussed will not only fill out your "bag of tricks," but also serve as a springboard for your own imaginative applications.

9 Doubling Parts

You have now spent two-thirds of this book exploring the basic tools in the Pro Tools mixer's arsenal. You have a good sense of the program's signal flow and the customary (as well as some not-so-customary) methods of applying effects. On that foundation you have built a working knowledge of organization, automation, and other advanced techniques.

In the remaining chapters, I'll share with you some techniques that will take your skills to the next level. You will learn some creative applications of the fundamentals you have mastered. This chapter and those that follow will be shorter, each dealing with a particular technique. I'll also help you manage your sessions and system resources.

Strength in Numbers

The sound of popular music is defined in large part by the practice of *double-tracking*. As the name implies, this is the practice of recording two (or more) tracks of critical parts and then combining them in the mix. You don't have to dig through your CD collection too far to find examples of this sound.

Double-tracking can be used as a creative technique to conjure sounds that don't exist in nature—the larger-than-life vocal or the guitar that seems to be in two places at once. Alternatively, it can be used to mask the deficiencies of pop stars whose talents are more apparent on CD covers than on the CDs themselves. (Don't make me name names!)

Either way, the best approach is ordinarily to have the performer repeat the part, carefully matching the phrasing, timing, and intonation of the original (see Figure 9.1). Ironically, double-tracking achieves its ends precisely because this is an impossible task. Unlike machines, humans can't do the same thing exactly the same way twice. The resulting differences in pitch and timing between the original and the copy cause a sonic clash that gives double-tracking its characteristic sound.

If you don't have multiple takes to work with, you can simulate double-tracking by creating a copy that clashes in time and/or pitch with the original. You did something

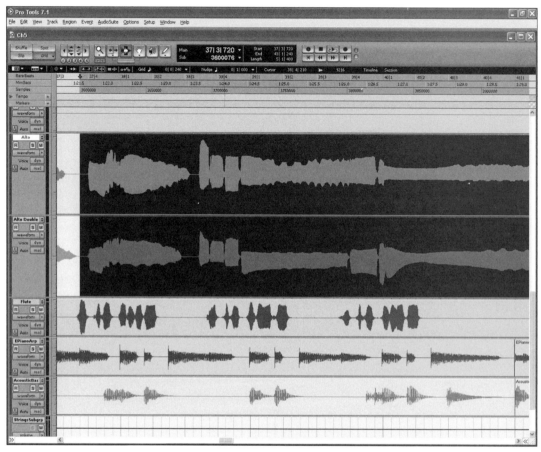

Figure 9.1 Double-tracking can produce a larger-than-life sound.

similar using chorus and flange effects in Chapter 4, "Special Effects." In this chapter, I'll show you some additional techniques, each of which has a sound of its own.

Better Late...

The first technique takes advantage of the way our ears interpret very small timing differences. Here's the way it works:

1. Open the Chapter 09.ptf session, and go to memory location 1, Better Late. Listen to the clip to see what it sounds like raw. You're going to create some sonic variations by doubling the melody.

2. Create two new mono aux inputs and route a send from the SynthLead track to the mono bus you have selected as the input for both auxes. Make the send pre-fader, and set its volume to unity (0.0 dB).

Note: After you've completed the next few steps and you have the sound the way you want it, you might want to make this a post-fader send so the effect's level will change relative to the level of the dry sound; however, a pre-fader send makes it easy to solo the source track for comparison.

---

3. Mute one aux input and place a Short Delay II (mono) on an insert of the other.

4. Set the Mix to 100%, and set Delay, Depth, and Rate all to 0 (see Figure 9.2).

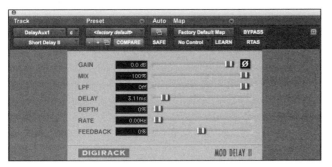

Figure 9.2 At very low delay times, a delay's effect is more timbral than temporal.

5. Confirm that the aux's fader is at unity and panned center—it should be set that way by default.

6. Begin playback, and listen to the sound change as you bypass and un-bypass the delay. Note that despite what the plug-in tells you, the delay time is never actually 0. If it were, bypassing the plug-in would have no effect.

7. While holding down the Ctrl (Cmd) key, drag the Delay slider slowly to the right. Listen to the changes in the sound as the delay time gradually increases. The timbre shifts in ways that range from interesting to downright ugly. This is the same effect you created with a chorus, but without the chorus's modulation.

Note: Even though you're using the Ctrl/Cmd key to enable fine control resolution, the delay time increases in steps rather than changing smoothly. Although some plug-ins do a better job than others at smoothing out the changes, all digital controls by definition move in steps like this. You wouldn't want to automate this control, but that's why the Mod Delays have modulation parameters.

The reason for the timbre change is the same *comb filtering* you worked to avoid in Chapter 6, "Advanced Signal Flow," but in this situation you are using it to your advantage! Using short delays to color the sound like this is a great way to call attention to a part without raising its volume. As you increase the delay time, you'll hear the effect less as a timbre change, and more as an actual delayed copy—as though the sound is reflecting off a nearby surface. Somewhere between the lowest and the highest delay settings, our ears start to be able to distinguish the delayed copy from the original.

On Location

Our ears react not only to timing differences between sounds, but also to positional differences. Here are a couple of ways to take advantage of that.

1. Find a delay time between five and 15 milliseconds that you find particularly annoying. Let the sound sink in for a moment, and then drop the volume of the aux input by about 6 dB. Changing the volume of the delay changes its character dramatically.

2. Now pan the aux gradually to one side, listening to how your perception of the sound changes. Mute the aux to remember the pure original—it will probably sound pretty flat and one-dimensional without the delay. What started as a deliberately harsh timbral effect has been transformed into a useful spatial effect by careful volume and pan adjustments.

3. Un-mute the aux and gradually raise the delay time, listening as the space you just created around the original grows bigger with the delay time. The greater the delay time, the more independent the copy becomes. At the maximum setting of 38 milliseconds, it's almost as though the performer were standing in two places at once.

4. Un-mute the second aux and insert a mono Short Delay on it.

5. Pan this aux opposite the first and lower its volume to about −6 dB.

6. Set the new delay identically to the first, and you will hear the "double" collapse to the center of the stereo field.

7. You need to *de-correlate* the two delays, as discussed in Chapter 4. Lower either one of the delay times several milliseconds, and you will hear the effect move out of the middle. You now have the desired result: a lead part that sounds more substantial than it did by itself.

8. Insert a 1-Band EQ 3 after the delay on each of the two aux inputs (see Figure 9.3).

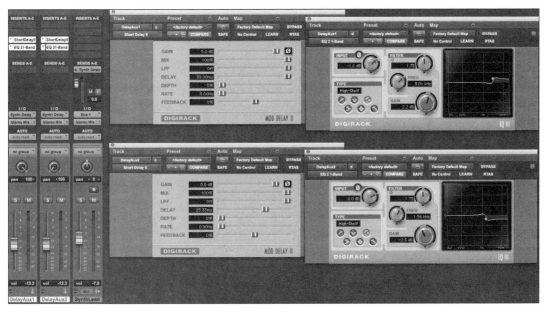

Figure 9.3   The original track is copied to a pair of aux inputs, each of which is delayed and EQed. The auxes are then panned to opposite sides for a straightforward doubling effect.

9. Dial up a high shelf with a boost on one side and a cut on the other, with a cutoff at around 3 kHz. This should make the doubling (tripling?) effect sound a bit less mechanical. The EQ can be used to increase the differentiation between the original and the two copies as well as to soften or sharpen the effect.

Fever Pitch

Delays are useful for simulating the timing variations between doubled parts. But what about pitch? Pro Tools ships with an AudioSuite processor, Time Shift, that allows you to change the overall pitch of any selected audio. Let's use it to detune a copy and see what happens.

1. Go to memory location 2, Fever Pitch.

2. Select the three sax tracks and, from the Track menu, choose Duplicate.

3. In the Duplicate Tracks dialog box (see Figure 9.4), check only the Active Playlist and Insert After Last Selected Track checkboxes.

4. Type **2** in the Number of Duplicates field, and click OK. Two exact copies of the three tracks will appear just below Tenor 2.

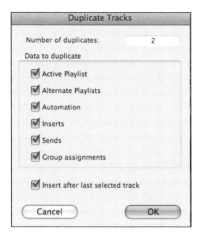

Figure 9.4 The Duplicate Tracks dialog box.

5.   Rename the tracks Alto B, Alto C, Tenor1 B, Tenor1 C, and so forth, and then mute the Cs.

6.   Use the Grabber to select the regions on the Bs. Then from the AudioSuite > Pitch Shift menu, choose Time Shift to launch the plug-in (see Figure 9.5). *This is not a typo!* Use Time Shift, not Pitch Shift. Time Shift is a more advanced plug-in and can do what we need with a more natural sound.

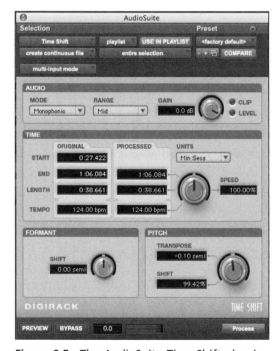

Figure 9.5 The AudioSuite Time Shift plug-in.

7. Set the Transpose parameter to −0.10 semitones (10 cents).

8. Set the Mode to Monophonic and the Range to Mid.

9. Be sure that the top-center button (the Selection Reference) reads "Playlist" (*not* "Region List") and that the button to its right, which reads "Use in Playlist," is highlighted in blue with white letters, as shown in Figure 9.5.

10. Click the Process button; Pro Tools creates a new whole-file region in each B track that plays back ten one-hundredths of a semitone lower than the original.

11. As you listen to this new effect, experiment with pan and volume settings as you did before. When the detuned parts are panned with the originals, they create a very strong impression. As you pan them away from the originals, the sound becomes more expansive, filling the soundstage more fully. Wide panning and lower volume gives a subtler effect that nevertheless covers the entire stereo image.

Note: If you have an automatic pitch-correction plug-in, such as Antares Auto-Tune or Celemony Melodyne, you can insert it on one or more auxes and create pitch-manipulated doubles without sacrificing audio tracks. Combine a tuned version with the original, or deliberately mis-tune a copy.

---

12. Un-mute the C tracks and detune them up 0.08 semitones (eight cents).

13. Pan them opposite the Bs. Depending on your volume and pan settings, the three sets of saxes combine to form a gentle or insistent swarm of sound. Make the effect more pronounced by adding a short delay to each of the copies, and make it more subtle by using an EQ to roll off the high end of each copy.

Note: When you experiment with larger or smaller degrees of pitch manipulation, always base each processed version on the original region. If you process and re-process the copies with an AudioSuite plug-in, each generation of processing degrades the sound slightly.

Elastic Fantastic

Introduced in Pro Tools 7.4, Elastic Audio is intended to make it as easy to correct or manipulate the timing of audio as it is with MIDI. Pro Tools 8 then added the ability to modify the pitch of Elastic Audio regions. A complete tutorial on this powerful new tool is beyond the scope of this book, but it can offer an extraordinarily simple technique for creating the sort of timing and pitch variations that make double-tracked parts so useful.

1. Undo the last several steps until you have the unprocessed duplicated tracks back.

2. Select all of the duplicates (B and C tracks). While holding Shift and Alt (Opt) so that this parameter change will affect all currently selected tracks, click on the Elastic Audio Plug-in Selector (see Figure 9.6) and choose Polyphonic from the menu.

Figure 9.6 Applying Elastic Audio to a track.

3. Select the regions in the B tracks and press Alt+0 (Opt+0) to open the Quantize window (see Figure 9.7).

4. Be sure Quantize is set to operate on Elastic Audio Events (not Audio Regions), and set the Quantize Grid to 16th notes. Click Apply.

5. Repeat this operation for the C tracks, but apply a Randomize value of 5% to create additional timing variations.

6. Experiment with panning and volume, as you did in the previous section. The effect should be fairly similar to that of real double-tracking.

7. Select the B regions and press Alt+5 (Opt+5) on the numeric keypad to open the Elastic Properties window (see Figure 9.8), or right-click on any selected region and choose Elastic Properties from the menu.

8. Enter a Pitch Shift value of +8 cents, and press Enter (Return) to confirm the value.

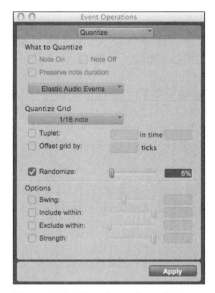

Figure 9.7 The Quantize window.

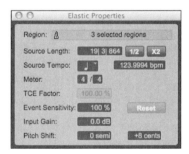

Figure 9.8 The Elastic Properties window.

9.   Select the C regions and pitch shift them by −10 cents.

10.   Try combining all three techniques—pitch, time, and delay—in subtle or dramatic ways to see the entire range of possibilities.

Although it's often desirable to work with actual double-tracked parts, these techniques carry their own sonic signatures. Taken together, they expand the possibilities for creating those bigger-than-life or two-places-at-once effects.

10 Stems and Submixes

You've probably heard the terms *stems* and *submixes* before, but you may not know exactly what they mean. Don't worry—nobody else does, either. Both refer to a subset of the total tracks in a mix, such as just the background vocals in a song or just the sound effects in a movie. The only thing resembling a rule regarding the use of the two terms is that *stem* is more often used in reference to sound for film and video, whereas *submix* is more often used in reference to music production. As rules go, it's slightly less strictly observed than the one about using your turn signals when you change lanes—and way less important. In an uncharacteristic display of nonchalance, I will throw caution to the wind and use them more or less interchangeably.

Imagine sitting on a dubbing stage trying to mix the hundreds of tracks that make up a typical movie soundtrack: dialog, footsteps, doors, cars, wind, rain, explosions, street sounds, crowd noise, animal sounds, and a 90-piece orchestra. Yes, it would be cool, but it would also be insanely complex! To manage this complexity, each category of source material is organized into a stem, which is controlled by a single fader. Stems themselves can be organized into an even smaller number of stems so that large-scale control of those hundreds of tracks is possible with just a few faders.

Stems and submixes are really just special applications of subgroups, which were discussed in Chapter 6, "Advanced Signal Flow." As you'll recall, a subgroup is created by routing the outputs of two or more tracks to a bus and then returning that bus to the input of an aux. All the audio from the source tracks now passes through the aux, where it can be controlled by a single fader and, if necessary, processed as a unit.

Mixing with Stems

The more tracks a session has, the more you'll want to simplify your approach. Here's how to use stems to control many tracks from a few faders.

1. Open the session called Chapter 10.ptf.

Note: As the session opens, you may see the Missing Files dialog box shown in Figure 10.1. This tells you that a number of audio files are not where the session file expects them to be. That's because this session is a mix of the song from Chapter 5, "The Rough Mix." Rather than create additional copies of all those audio files, I've built this session on the same files.

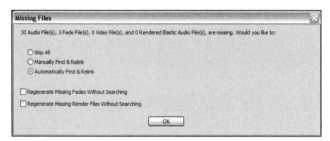

Figure 10.1   The Missing Files dialog box.

2. If the Missing Files dialog box appears, accept the default action: Automatically Find & Relink. Within a couple of minutes, Pro Tools will realize what's going on and point the current session to the correct files.

    Note: Should you encounter any difficulties with the re-linking process, simply close the Chapter 10 session, copy the session file to the Chapter 5 session folder, and open it from there.

3. Take a few minutes to listen to and look through this mix. You will recognize many of the techniques covered so far in this book. The 31 tracks are labeled and organized, but you are going to make them more manageable.

4. Go into I/O Setup and create five new stereo bus paths. Name them Drums Stem, Keys Stem, Lead Stem, Strings Stem, and Altos Stem, as shown in Figure 10.2. You will use these bus paths to create subgroups of each section.

5. Select all the drum tracks, including the three delay auxes.

6. Shift+Alt-click (Shift+Opt-click) the output selector of any drum track and choose the Drums Stem bus from the drop-down list that appears. The outputs of all the drum tracks will be set to Drums Stem.

7. Create a new stereo aux input and name it Drums Stem.

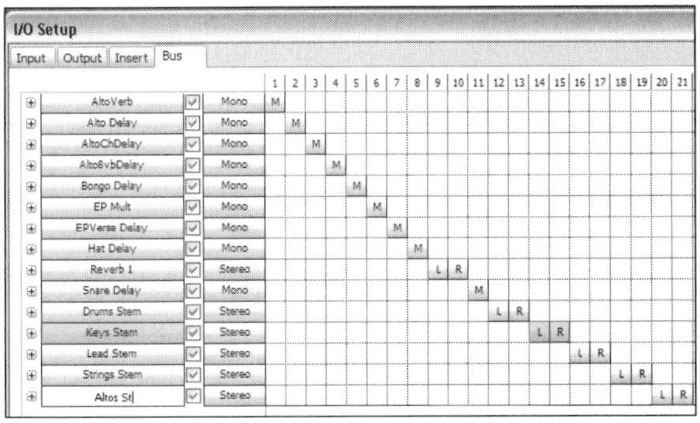

I/O Setup			1	2	3	4	5	6	7	8	9	10	11	12	13	14	15	16	17	18	19	20	21
AltoVerb	☑	Mono	M																				
Alto Delay	☑	Mono		M																			
AltoChDelay	☑	Mono			M																		
Alto8vbDelay	☑	Mono				M																	
Bongo Delay	☑	Mono					M																
EP Mult	☑	Mono						M															
EPVerse Delay	☑	Mono							M														
Hat Delay	☑	Mono								M													
Reverb 1	☑	Stereo									L	R											
Snare Delay	☑	Mono											M										
Drums Stem	☑	Stereo												L	R								
Keys Stem	☑	Stereo														L	R						
Lead Stem	☑	Stereo																L	R				
Strings Stem	☑	Stereo																		L	R		
Altos St	☑	Stereo																				L	R

Figure 10.2   Create bus paths for the stems.

8. Assign the Drums Stem bus as its input, and Alt-click (Opt-click) its fader to set its volume to unity.

9. Listen to any part of the session, and you will hear that subgrouping through an aux set to unity gain does not change the sound at all.

10. Following the same procedure, create a Keys stem for the EPVerse, EPVerseDelay, EPChorus, and Flute tracks.

Note: Why not the EPianoArp track? Because it is multed to the EPVerse and EPChorus tracks (you learned how to do this in Chapter 6). Because the audio from those tracks is included in the stem, so is the EPianoArp track. But why the Flute track? Because it is really functioning as part of the keyboards section of the arrangement.

Note: The Lead Stem is made up of the AltoMelody and AltoDelay tracks. The Altos Stem is made up of the AltoChorus and Alto8vbChrs tracks, along with their respective Delay tracks. The Strings Stem consists of the five string tracks plus the String Verb track.

Note: You may have noticed that I included the String Verb track in the Strings Stem, but I did not include the Alto Reverb in any stem. The String Verb is processing only string tracks, so it can be included in their stem unambiguously. However, the Alto Reverb is functioning as a traditional group effects return, processing audio being sent from members of three different stems. It can't be included in any of those stems without causing problems for the others, so it stays independent.

Note, however, that now the String Verb level follows the Strings Stem, while the Alto Reverb level is unaffected by any adjustments you make to the Altos, Lead, or Keys stems. (The reverb sends are post-fader, but not post-stem!) If you make any large level changes with the stems, you must listen closely to determine whether the effect return needs adjustment as well.

If you have created the stems in order, you should have a stem aux at the right of each set of tracks, as shown in Figure 10.3. It's a good idea to keep stems near their source tracks, in keeping with the organizational principles discussed in Chapter 5.

Figure 10.3   Source tracks are subgrouped to create stems. Stem auxes are placed to the immediate right of their source tracks.

One important part doesn't yet belong to any stem. Lumping the bass part with the keys or drums doesn't make much sense. However, it is part of the overall rhythm section, and that's a stem you haven't yet created.

Stems Within Stems

That's right—a stem can include other stems. The more complex your mix, the more important it becomes to create this sort of hierarchical structure. Here's how:

1. Create a new stereo bus path called Rhythm Stem and a new stereo aux input with the same name.

2. Subgroup the Drums Stem, Keys Stem, Strings Stem, and Bass tracks to the Rhythm Stem track.

3. Select all the stem auxes.

4. From the Tracks list menu, choose Show Only Selected Tracks (see Figure 10.4).

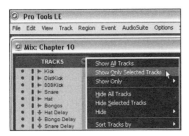

Figure 10.4 Show only selected tracks.

5. On the numeric keypad, type **.31** and press Enter to create a new memory location.

6. Name the new memory location All Stems and set it to recall only Track Show/ Hide status.

7. Set Time Properties to None.

8. Now you can instantly hide all tracks other than the stem auxes. Using memory location 31 is an extension of the organizational logic you used in Chapter 5, where you used memory locations in the 20s to show subsets of tracks. Create a memory location 30 that shows only the Rhythm, Lead, and Altos stems, and then one more that shows all tracks. (This was number 20, remember?)

9. Recall memory location 31 and begin playback from the beginning. Use the stems to balance the large sections of the arrangement. If you need to adjust the level of an individual track, recall memory location 20 and make the adjustment.

Printing Submixes

Often, it's useful to have independent bounces of each submix. For example, if you decide at the mastering house that you mixed the lead vocal a bit too low, you could let the mastering engineer recombine the rhythm section submix with the vocal submix and fix the problem without having to return to the original session. Live backing tracks, remixes, and other scenarios also make frequent use of submixes.

The simplest way to create these submixes is to bounce each stem bus one by one. However, because Pro Tools always bounces in real time, it would take a very long time to bounce the full mix plus two or more submixes of every song on an album, so I will show you how to create them all at once.

1. Create four new stereo audio tracks and name them Ch10 Mix, Ch10 Rhythm Submix, Ch10 Altos Submix, and Ch10 Lead Submix (see Figure 10.5). It's essential that you name these tracks before recording because the resulting audio files will take their names from the track names.

Figure 10.5 Each submix gets recorded to its own audio track.

2. You can probably guess what inputs get assigned to the Rhythm, Altos, and Lead tracks—the Rhythm Stem, Altos Stem, and Lead Stem buses.

3. The Mix track needs its own bus, so create a new stereo bus called Mix and assign it to the Mix track's input.

4. Recall memory location 30, and select the Rhythm Stem, Altos Stem, and Lead Stem tracks.

5. While holding the Shift, Alt, and Start keys (Shift, Opt, and Ctrl keys), assign the outputs of any of the three tracks to the Mix bus. All three stems are still

going to your main output, but the same mix that you're hearing is now going to the Ch10 Mix track, too—almost.

Note: Remember that Shift and Alt (Opt) mean "apply to all selected," while Start (Ctrl) allows you to assign multiple outputs to a track.

---

6. You need to apply the same master bus effects to the Mix bus that you are using on the main output. This requires a master fader. Create a stereo master fader, and name it Mix Bus.

7. Alt-drag (Opt-drag) to copy any plug-ins from your master fader to the Mix Bus master fader, making sure you keep them in the same order. Do not copy the Dither plug-in, however, as you will not be bouncing to 16 bits.

8. Set this track's volume to exactly the same level as the Main Out master fader.

9. You must also consider any "group" effects returns. The String Verb is no problem, as it will be included with the Rhythm submix. However, the Alto Reverb is currently processing audio received from part of all three submixes. The best way to handle this is to give each submix its own reverb return. Select the Alto Reverb track, and from the Track menu choose Duplicate.

10. In the Duplicate Tracks dialog (see Figure 10.6), be sure all options are checked. Enter a value of 2 for the Number of duplicates field, and click OK. You will now have three effects returns with identical settings, right down to the plug-in parameters.

Figure 10.6 Duplicating the effects return.

11. Name the two new tracks Rhythm Verb and AltoCh Verb.

12. Create two new mono buses with similar names, and reroute the reverb sends on the Snare, Hat, Bongos, Flute, AltoChorus, and Alto8vbChorus tracks accordingly.

13. Route the inputs of the three effects returns from their namesake buses and their outputs to their respective stem buses. Because the plug-in settings are identical, the sound will be the same as it was before. (This would not be true with a dynamics processor, but they are not usually grouped in this way.) However, you are now using more CPU resources to run two additional reverb plug-ins.

14. Using the procedure from Chapter 8, "Bouncing Your Mix," select the entire song plus a little extra on the beginning and end.

15. Record-arm the four new audio tracks, mute them, and press 3 on the numeric keypad to begin recording.

Note: Obviously, this technique requires that you still have eight voices available in your mix. In an HD system, this would rarely present a problem, but in an LE system, it takes up one sixth of your system's voices. If you can't afford the voices, you are stuck bouncing each stem bus individually. If you're using any global effects, such as an overall reverb, there's no need to duplicate it. Just route the effects return(s) temporarily to the bus you're bouncing.

You will end up with four stereo audio tracks (see Figure 10.7) and four corresponding split-stereo audio files representing your key submixes. You will still want to bounce an interleaved stereo file of the entire mix for burning to a reference (audio) CD. (This is where you would use that Dither plug-in.) Take all four files for each song to the mastering engineer. Most of the time, he or she will simply use the 24-bit Mix files, but the submixes might come in handy. If the label asks someone to do a remix of your song, you would send them the submixes.

Despite the inconsistency with which these terms are used, there are three different yet equally important concepts at work here. All require routing multiple tracks through a common aux input. A subgroup is ordinarily used to apply common processing, as you did in Chapter 6. In the next chapter, I'll show you an advanced application of subgrouping called *parallel compression*. A stem (or submix) is a way of organizing a

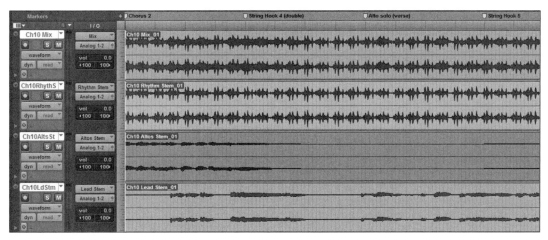

Figure 10.7 The completed submixes.

complex mix that allows simplified balancing of large sections of the arrangement. Printing submixes (or stems) yields partial mixes that can be recombined easily for corrective or creative purposes. Regardless of how you apply the names, be clear on what you are trying to accomplish, and you will wield the power successfully.

11 Advanced Dynamics

In Chapter 2, "Dynamics," you saw the power of compressors, expanders, limiters, and gates to control the dynamics of your mix. In this chapter, you'll combine that with the flexibility of buses to come up with some new dynamics tricks. First, I'll show you how to use the dynamics of one part to control another part using a *side-chain* input. Then, I'll show you how to break the fundamental rules of signal flow to apply compression in a novel way.

Side-Chain Processing

Some dynamics processors, especially compressors and gates, have an additional input called a side-chain, or *key input*. When signal is received at the key input, the processor's detection circuit responds to that signal instead of the audio signal passing through the processor. This means, for example, that a compressor on a stereo music track would not reduce the track's volume when the music crossed the threshold but would instead reduce the track's volume when the announcer's voice, patched to the compressor's key input, crossed the threshold.

The utility of keying a processor to an alternative control signal is obvious for broadcasters, but the technique also enables some interesting creative possibilities. All it takes is a bit of imagination.

Ducking a Music Bed

You've heard the sound a million times, in ads, documentaries, and podcasts: As the announcer starts speaking, the music ducks out of the way. When the announcer stops, the music returns to full strength. You could make this happen with volume automation, but why not let Pro Tools do the work for you?

1. Open the session called Chapter 11.ptf, and go to the first memory location, Ducking. You will hear a music track with a voiceover.

Note: I pre-mixed the music to a stereo track for simplicity, but it's not always necessary to do so. If you were working with a large multi-track mix, you could simply bus all the music tracks to a stereo aux and apply this technique to that submix.

---

2.   On the Voiceover track, assign a pre-fader send to a mono bus.

3.   Bring the send's fader to unity.

4.   Insert a Compressor/Limiter Dyn III on the Music track, and set it as follows: short attack, moderate release, 3:1 ratio, no make-up gain, and medium knee. Start with the threshold at 0 dB.

Note: Instead of a pre-fader send, you could use a post-fader send from the voiceover track or simply multi-assign its output to a bus. The advantage of the pre-fader bus, however, is that it allows you to mute, raise, or lower the signal coming out of the voiceover track without changing the level of the signal going to the key input.

---

5.   As you can see in Figure 11.1, Pro Tools uses a small skeleton-key emblem to denote key input settings. Dynamics III uses the same emblem but calls it *side-chain*. Clicking No Key Input opens a menu from which you can assign an input or a bus as the key input; choose the bus to which you assigned the Voiceover track's send.

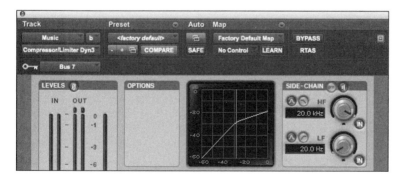

Figure 11.1   Key-input controls are designated by a skeleton-key emblem. At left, below the plug-in selector, is the key input assign menu. At right, labeled "Side-Chain," is the key input enable button.

6. Click the Side-Chain skeleton key button to enable the key input. It will turn blue.

7. Begin playback.

8. Gradually lower the compressor's threshold. As the threshold reaches the level of the voiceover, the music bed will start to be compressed. The music bed automatically *ducks* out of the way whenever the voiceover comes in. The threshold controls the level of voiceover that triggers the ducking, and the ratio controls the amount of compression applied to the music track.

9. Mute the voiceover track and listen to what the compressor is doing to the music track. By itself, it sounds unnatural; but when the voiceover is audible, it grabs the listener's attention away from the music anyway. The ducking works with our ears' tendency to focus on the voice, exaggerating the effect to enhance the clarity of the voiceover.

10. Un-mute the voiceover.

11. Listening carefully, adjust the compressor until the music bed ducks quickly and smoothly whenever the voiceover enters and then blooms again when the voice stops for a moment.

Getting ducking to sound natural takes some experimentation. Once the sound is in your head, you'll hear good and bad examples every time you listen to a television or radio commercial.

Fun with Gates

Let's turn this technique on its head and use the key input to bring a sound forward instead of ducking it. To do that, you need an upside-down compressor—you remember the gate, don't you?

1. Go to memory location 2, Fun With Gates, and listen. You'll hear a rhythmic loop and two pads. Neat sounds, but they need work, so mute everything.

2. Assign a pre-fader send on the Drum Loop track to any mono bus.

3. Insert an Expander/Gate Dyn III after the Xpand2 on the Main Pad track, and assign the same bus as its key input.

4. Click to enable the side-chain, then Alt-drag (Opt-drag) the Expander/Gate to the Bass track to copy it there.

5. Un-mute the Main Pad track, and set its Expander/Gate to extreme gate set-tings: infinite ratio, lowest range, highest threshold, and shortest attack, hold, and release times (see Figure 11.2).

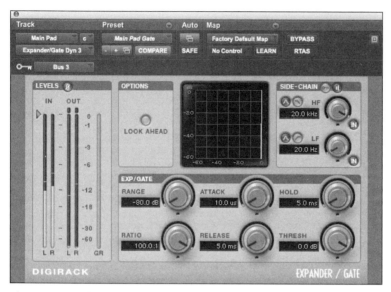

Figure 11.2   The Expander/Gate Dyn III is set to listen to Bus 3 as its key input. As the threshold is lowered, part of the bus's signal will cause the gate to open.

6. Begin playback and gradually lower the threshold until you hear the pad trig-gering in time with the loop.

7. Adjust the Expander/Gate's parameters to your liking. You can soften the beginning of each note by increasing the attack time, round off its end by raising the release time, and lengthen it by using a higher hold time. You might even try raising the range value to allow some of the pad to sustain between notes.

8. After you have the Main Pad sounding the way you want, mute that track and un-mute the Bass track.

9. Starting with the same extreme settings, drop the threshold until you can hear the drum loop triggering the bass part.

10. Before tweaking the other parameters, try something different. Within the Side-Chain section of the Expander/Gate are two filters (see Figure 11.3) that can be used to process the key input before it reaches the detector circuit. This gives you additional control over what part of the signal is going to trigger the

Figure 11.3   The Expander/Gate Dyn III has two filters that can be used to process the key input signal.

gate. Click the IN button to enable the top filter, and be sure it is set to low-pass mode, as shown in Figure 11.3.

Note: The Expander/Gate Dyn III's side-chain filters are labeled opposite of what you've come to expect from the filters in EQ III. The top filter is labeled *HF*, and it stands for *high filter*, not high-pass filter. The bottom filter, labeled *LF*, stands for *low filter*.

---

11.   Click the small speaker icon next to the side-chain enable button—this is the *key listen* button. This allows you to monitor the key input signal (the drum loop) instead of the signal passing through the gate (the bass pad).

12.   Lower the cutoff until you can hear almost nothing but the kick drum.

13.   Disable the key listen button and you will hear the pad triggering only on the kick drum notes.

14.   Now tweak the parameters, setting the hold and release times long enough to emulate the sound of that loud car that always stops next to you at a traffic light—you know, the car with such overpowered subwoofers that its hood vibrates to the sound of the kick drum.

15.   Un-mute the Main Pad track and balance the two pads.

16.   Shift-click on the gate inserts on the two pad tracks so you can tweak their settings side by side.

17.   You might decide to leave the Drum Loop track muted and use it just as a trigger for the pads, or you might choose to copy the phrase and un-mute the different elements sequentially.

18.   I've included two extra pad parts and a Snare FX track for your experimentation. Insert the gate *after* the Xpand2 insert on each of the instrument tracks. Try tweaking the pads so they enhance just the attack of the main pad without

sustaining. Feel free also to change the rhythm and harmonic structure of the Main Pad and Drum Loop tracks.

19. Use the top filter in band-pass mode on the side-chain of the Snare FX track and adjust its frequency so it triggers only on the drum loop's snare. You may need to add the bottom filter in high-pass mode to completely prevent the kick drum from triggering the track.

20. For a little something extra, insert a 1-Band EQ III on the Main Pad track. It really doesn't matter whether it's before or after the gate, since the gate is being triggered by the loop track.

21. Set the EQ 3 to a high shelf, set its Q to max and its gain to minimum, and sweep the frequency up and down. (If you have an analog filter emulation, such as the Bomb Factory Moogerfooger Lowpass Filter, try that instead.) This is a classic candidate for automating a plug-in parameter. Alternatively, try the AIR Frequency Shifter—I especially like the Infinite Downward Spiral preset.

Note: Remember that the Expander/Gate Dyn III has a two-millisecond look-ahead buffer, so audio leaves the processor that much after it enters. Whether this delay matters musically depends on how you are using the gated signal. If you are using the pads as primary rhythmic elements, you might want to compensate for the delay. Unfortunately, Time Adjuster can't help you with this problem, because you can't delay the loop track without delaying the key input signal as well. You could copy the loop track, assign its output to the key input bus, and select all of its regions and shift them earlier by two milliseconds (Edit > Shift). Alternatively, you could bounce the gated pads and shift them earlier or time-correct them with Beat Detective.

Drums with Gates

Turn the tables and give your drums some help instead of depending on them to spice up a pad. For this exercise, use the same signal flow to generate some tones that will reinforce the kick and snare. I'll use Signal Generator, part of the DigiRack package, but you could substitute any other tone generator you wish—analog-modeling soft synths, such as Digidesign's Hybrid, make prime candidates.

1. Go to memory location 3, Drums with Gates, and you'll find a four-track drum part. It sounds fine, but the producer would like to pump up the kick and snare a bit.

2. Assign a send on the kick track to a mono bus, and a send on the snare track to a separate mono bus.

3. Create a mono aux input for the kick and another for the snare, and insert an Expander/Gate Dyn III on each. Solo-safe each of these two auxes.

4. Assign the appropriate bus as the key input for each gate, and enable the key input.

5. On any insert above (prior to) the gate on the kick track, go to the Other category and choose Signal Generator (see Figure 11.4). Signal Generator creates any of four basic waveforms and two types of noise, and it is most often used for testing and calibration.

Figure 11.4 Signal Generator can create one of four different waveforms or two types of noise.

6. Confirm that the waveform (Signal) is set to Sine, and then type in a frequency of **40 Hz**.

7. Solo the kick track and begin playback.

8. Adjust the gate's settings so that the sine wave triggers with every kick note. With the proper attack and release settings and the proper aux level, it can sound as though it's part of the kick drum's fundamental timbre.

9. Of course, a natural blend may not be the producer's objective. Try increasing the release time to around two seconds for that automotive subwoofer sound. Alternatively, increase the hold time to almost two seconds and make the release time very short. The note is the same length, but the character is much different. Hold maintains the sine wave's volume, whereas Release fades it out gradually (just as these parameters do in a synthesizer's envelope generator). Balance the two settings to shape the note as you see fit.

10. On the Snare track, insert a Signal Generator before the gate, set to White Noise.

11.   Set up the gate to approximate the amplitude envelope of the snare. (Don't get too tweaky, as you're not quite done with the timbre.) Notice how electronic this sounds? White noise was in fact a popular basic tone for a synthesized snare drum in some early drum machines, so it's immediately recognizable. If you're not going for a drum-machine effect, you may not like this scenario yet.

12.   Insert a 7-Band EQ III on the snare aux. It doesn't matter whether it's before or after the gate, but obviously it needs to come after Signal Generator.

13.   Use a high-pass filter to roll off everything below about 250 Hz, then use the other bands to shape the timbre as needed. For example, if all you want is to add some sizzle, raise the low-pass even further, and maybe add a high shelf.

14.   Once you've got the timbre tweaked, revisit the gate settings. Now that you've got a sound you like better, you might want to hear more of it. You might be surprised at how close to a half-second release you can come before deciding it's too much.

Note: Try replacing the Signal Generator on the Kick track with Vacuum, one of the AIR instruments included with Pro Tools 8. It's a virtual analog synth capable of some great lead and bass sounds. Dial up a good bass patch—I like the Juno 106 Bass—and play a long sustained note as the kick track plays. The note will trigger with the kick drum as did the Signal Generator, but now you have the option of playing actual pitches. Create a MIDI track assigned to Vacuum and play or draw an interesting bass line of sustained notes that trigger in time with the kick drum. Try the same thing with the Snare track—Prop Cut and Factory Floor are good Vacuum presets with which to start.

Parallel Compression

The great thing about a compressor is that it reins in a track's dynamics, allowing you to keep the intensity high during the soft parts without the loud parts getting unbearable. The unfortunate side effect of a compressor is that it can mash a part's transients, robbing it of some of its vitality. To get around this limitation, you can use an imaginative technique that has come to be known as *parallel compression.*

Given its name, you might expect this technique to involve two parallel signal paths—and you'd be correct. Two copies of a part—or a subgroup or an entire mix—are created using a bus. One is compressed, while the other is not, and then the two are blended. The compressed copy is more apparent during soft passages and less apparent during loud passages, yielding a narrower dynamic range while having little impact on transients. Properly done, parallel compression sounds more natural than traditional compression, making it very popular with mastering engineers.

1. Go to memory location 4, Parallel Compression, and you'll find a stereo mix.

2. Create two stereo aux inputs and name them Mix Dry and Mix Compressed (see Figure 11.5).

3. Route the output of the Parallel Mix track to an unused stereo bus, and then assign that same bus as the input of both auxes. Solo-safe Parallel Mix.

Figure 11.5 The mix is multed to two aux inputs.

4. Bring the fader of Mix Dry to unity, and leave the fader down on Mix Compressed.

5. Insert a Compressor/Limiter Dyn III on the Mix Compressed track.

6. Set it to a fast attack, a long release, a ratio of 4:1, and a medium-to-soft knee.

7. Set the threshold to achieve about 10–12 dB of gain reduction. If you raise the fader of the Mix Compressed track and solo it, the effect of the compressor will be pretty obvious. When you blend it with the uncompressed track, however, the overall effect will be much more subtle.

8. Listening carefully to the uncompressed mix, gradually raise the fader of the compressed aux until you hear the softer parts of the mix being reinforced. Raise the fader too far, and it will start to sound like regular compression. Find a level that brings the subtle parts of the mix—the percussive arpeggio, delay effects, and ambience—forward enough that they don't get lost.

The peaks of the compressed mix are squashed, so they don't reinforce the dry mix's peaks very much, but the parts of the compressed mix below the compressor's threshold are still at full strength, so they reinforce the quieter parts of the dry mix a lot. The net effect is that you have brought the average level of the mix up significantly while bringing the peak level of the mix up only minimally, and you have done this without changing the sound of the transients very much at all.

Note: You have just seen that there is an important difference between *peak* and *average* levels, and managing that difference is critical to mixing and mastering. To get a mix to sound strong on a CD, a mastering engineer needs to raise the average level without letting the peak level exceed 0 dBFS. Compression and limiting are primary weapons in this fight, and parallel compression is a stealth bomber, delivering the impact without drawing attention to itself.

New York Compression

Parallel compression, with a slight twist, is also a popular technique for treating a drum kit. The term "New York Compression" (a term that, as far as I can determine, was coined by author Bobby Owsinski in his excellent *The Mixing Engineer's Handbook*) is often used to describe this method. Although it seems fair to associate the technique with the New York "school," it was in widespread use even before it had a catchy name.

1. Go to memory location 5, New York Compression, and you'll find a pretty standard set of drum tracks.

2. Set them up for parallel compression by creating two aux inputs and subgrouping all tracks to both auxes. (Remember, this takes only one stereo bus because a bus can have multiple destinations.)

3. Insert a Compressor/Limiter Dyn III on one aux input and insert a 1-band EQ 3 on the following insert of the same track.

4. Set the EQ to Peak mode, and pull its gain down all the way to −18 dB.

5. Give it a center frequency of around 650 Hz and a Q of 1.4 or so. It should end up looking like a smile, with the middle frequencies scooped out completely (see Figure 11.6). This has the effect of leaving the middle of the drum kit unaffected while reinforcing the low end, where the pulse of the beat lives, and the high end, where the sizzle and ambience live.

Figure 11.6 In New York Compression, the EQ is set to scoop out the middle, so only the highs and lows are reinforced by the compressor.

6. Set the compressor very aggressively—aim for at least 12 dB of gain reduction.

7. As you did previously, start with just the uncompressed aux and add the compressed version to taste. Even though the compressor is set quite rudely, the net effect can be subtle. By reinforcing the highs and lows, the drums can become more evident in a mix without hogging all the precious middle ground.

Note: When using parallel compression, you are combining a processed copy of a sound with an unprocessed copy. This is exactly the sort of situation that can create problematic DSP delays, as discussed in Chapter 6, "Advanced Signal Flow." In most cases, Pro Tools LE and M-Powered will compensate for the delay automatically, but if you hear that telltale comb-filtering, you will need to use Time Adjuster on the unprocessed aux input. In Pro Tools HD, you can either enable Automatic Delay Compensation or use Time Adjuster.

Some engineers prefer to compress only the main parts of the drum kit, omitting the room mics and sometimes even the overheads from the compressed subgroup. Others take the opposite approach and compress the electric bass along with the drum kit. Experiment with both—each has its unique charm.

Note that parallel compression applies the "wet/dry" principles normally associated with time-based processing to dynamics processing. Let this bit of creative rule-breaking serve to remind you that there really are no rules. There are certainly standard practices, and knowing them will serve you well. Now that you know those standard practices, however, you are left with two supremely important tools—your knowledge and your imagination. Parallel compression is a great example of an engineer applying knowledge with imagination to create an innovative technique for shaping sounds. Now you've got one more technique to enhance your knowledge and spark your imagination.

12 Stereo Enhancement

Y ou've seen (and heard) how critical panning is to a good mix. You've also used short delays to give sounds a feeling of physical space within the stereo field. In this chapter, you'll see new ways to manipulate the stereo image, including a technique for moving an image beyond the apparent limitations of the left and right speakers.

I'll also show you how to check your mix for mono compatibility. No matter how technologically advanced you may think the listening public is, there will always be times when they are effectively listening to our stereo mixes in mono. It behooves us all to be sure everything will translate well when that happens.

Wider Stereo

Although stereo clearly allows for much greater dimensionality than mono—a fact for which virtually all mix engineers are grateful—it sometimes seems as though the left and right speakers are like concrete walls that contain the stereo image between them. Wouldn't it be nice to be able to soften those edges, or better yet break down the walls completely? That's one reason that mixing in surround is so liberating—but Pro Tools LE doesn't yet allow that without the add-ons discussed in Chapter 5, "The Rough Mix." There is, however, a technique that creative mixers use to expand the stereo field beyond its normal boundaries. One must use caution with this method, though, because it can have a severe adverse effect on mono compatibility.

Breaking Down the Walls

This technique takes advantage of the way our ears deal with two identical signals of opposite polarity. It creates a dramatic sense of width.

1. Open the Chapter 12.ptf session, and go to memory location 1, Wider Stereo.

2. Listen to the track. You'll hear a simple mono arpeggio assigned to a stereo output and panned dead center.

211

3. As you listen, pan the part left and right, listening to how it stops as though bumping into a wall when it reaches one speaker or the other.

4. Return the pan to center, and insert a mono/stereo Short Delay plug-in.

5. Shift-drag either Mix slider down to 0%, because you're not going to use this plug-in for its delay functions. (Be sure to Shift-drag so you adjust both channels at once.) Its sole purpose is to give you independent control over the left and right halves of the signal.

6. Just for sport, try moving either Gain slider. You'll find that if you reduce the gain of one side, the image moves toward the other side. This is all that Pan controls really do—change the balance between left and right in order to make the sound seem to come from a different location. (Note, however, that Pan controls are intelligently designed to move the image left and right without changing its apparent volume.)

7. Reset the Gain controls to unity, and click on the Phase Invert button (see Figure 12.1) for the left channel of the plug-in.

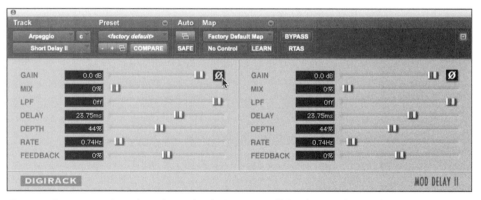

Figure 12.1 Inverting the phase (polarity, actually) of one channel can create dramatic stereo width.

Surprise! What started out as a plain, dead-center mono sound is suddenly floating around somewhere to the left of your left speaker *and* to the right of your right speaker. This is similar to what happened when you de-correlated the two channels of the delay plug-in back in Chapter 4, "Special Effects," only more dramatic. The speakers are no longer a pair of solid walls between which the stereo image must live. You have liberated the image from its bondage!

Note: Technically, the Phase Invert button on a plug-in doesn't affect phase at all—it inverts the signal's *polarity*. De-correlating the two channels of a mono-to-stereo delay as you did in Chapter 4 creates a timing difference, so the two channels are not in phase with each other. That is what causes the timbral and spatial characteristics you observed in those exercises. By contrast, changing the polarity of a signal literally flips it upside down, so each crest becomes a trough, and vice-versa. With a simple symmetrical waveform such as a sine or triangle wave, inverting polarity is indistinguishable from a phase shift of 180 degrees (half of a wavelength), but the same is not true for complex signals. Although everybody knows it's wrong, everybody still calls the button Phase Invert, including Digidesign. Go figure.

Remember how, in your childhood story books, every time the genie granted a wish there was some unintended consequence related to the story's moral? All of those stories were preparing you for this moment. Ask yourself this: If a simple mono arpeggio part can sound this cool just by flipping the polarity of one channel, why doesn't everybody do this all the time? Yes, there's a down side to the technique, and it can be pretty severe. To hear it for yourself, set both Pan controls for the track to center (0). What do you hear? That's right, you hear *nothing*. You have just added a signal to its equal-and-opposite alter ego, and the two canceled each other out (see Figure 12.2). (Think matter and anti-matter, only less explosive.) So much for mono compatibility, eh? If this mix got played back in mono, it would produce only silence. The dirty little secret of this cool stereo technique is that it's disastrous in mono.

Figure 12.2   When a signal is combined with a polarity-inverted copy of itself, the two cancel each other.

Preserving Mono Compatibility

To keep the sound from collapsing entirely in mono, a bit of compromise is in order. In the following steps, you'll use EQ to apply the phase-inversion technique to only part of the signal. That part will still go away in mono, but the rest of the signal will remain.

1.   Remove the delay plug-in and assign the output of the arpeggio track to Bus 7.

2.   Create two new mono aux inputs named Arpeggio Middle and Arpeggio Wide, and set Bus 7 as their inputs to create two copies of the arpeggio signal.

3. Assign a 4-band EQ III to the Arpeggio Middle aux, and set its input gain to −6 dB. Without this volume reduction, the doubled part would be noticeably louder, and might even clip.

4. Set the HF band to a shelf, raise its gain by 6 dB, and set its frequency to 2.5 kHz. This should accentuate the sizzly part of the arpeggio.

5. Insert a mono/stereo Short Delay on the first insert of the Arpeggio Wide track, and Ctrl+Start-click (Cmd+Ctrl-click) on its insert to make it inactive. This gives you the L/R independence you need without using any precious CPU resources.

6. Alt-drag (Opt-drag) the EQ plug-in to copy it from the Arpeggio Middle to any insert of the Arpeggio Wide track following the now-inactive delay plug-in. (Note that Pro Tools happily changes the mono plug-in to a multi-mono plug-in, which is quite convenient. It is not so obliging when you attempt to drag a plug-in to a track with fewer channels, however.) The copied EQ retains the settings of the original, so the high end of the arpeggio should be quite crisp right about now.

7. On the Arpeggio Middle track, change the gain for the HF band to −6 dB. Theoretically, the cut on Middle and boost on Wide should add up to no change in the HF band at all—the arpeggio part should sound exactly the same as it did before you re-routed it to the two auxes.

8. On the Wide track, click the Master Link button in the EQ plug-in window (see Figure 12.3) to unlink the EQ's left and right channels.

Figure 12.3 The Master Link button allows the channels of a multi-mono plug-in to be set independently.

9. Click on the Phase Invert button to flip the polarity of the left channel. Your super-stereo effect is now being applied only to the copy with the high-frequency boost. The arpeggio should dance around the periphery of your stereo image while still being anchored in the middle.

10. Set both channels of the Arpeggio Wide track to Center, and listen to the result. The sound is quieter and darker, but the arpeggio is still present.

11. With the Wide track still centered, mute the Middle track, and the sound goes away completely. This is because the Wide track is still subject to the

cancellation demonstrated in the previous section, but the Middle track is not. Splitting a part this way and widening only one piece of the puzzle lets you have the super-stereo effect without sacrificing mono compatibility.

Note: In a perfect world, you would simply split the signal completely, sending everything above 2.5 kHz to the wide track and filtering that band from the mono track. The EQs that come with Pro Tools LE don't make this very practical, but you can still get good results.

Experiment with variations on this technique. Instead of a high shelf, try boosting two peak bands and cutting two others on the mono track, then inverting the pattern on the wide track. With the mono track to anchor the sound, you can do almost anything you want with the wide track. Ditch the EQs entirely, route the original Arpeggio track back to the main stereo out, and fire up a send to the Wide aux. Ctrl+Start-click (Cmd+Ctrl-click) on the Short Delay plug-in to make it active, and set up a short de-correlated delay as you did in Chapter 3, "Time-Based Effects." (Be sure to mute the Middle aux.) Flip the polarity of one channel of the delay, and listen to how much wider the effect becomes. Because this is only an effect track, the effect will disappear in mono, but the dry track will not.

Mid-Side Processing

This next mix technique takes its cue from an ingenious recording technique. When you record in stereo, whether you're capturing drum overheads, a horn section, or a classical orchestra, there's a bit more to getting good results than simply setting up two mics. *How* you set up those two mics can make a big difference in the quality and character of the results.

Although most stereo techniques involve matching microphones, one imaginative method uses a cardioid microphone and a bidirectional (figure-eight) microphone. The two mics are placed as closely together as possible, with the cardioid mic facing the sound source and the bidirectional mic facing 90 degrees left from the sound source (shown in Figure 12.4). It may seem odd to place a microphone with its null facing the sound you're trying to capture, but as you'll see, it all adds up.

This is called *mid-side* (*M-S*, or sometimes *mono-stereo*) miking because the cardioid records a centered mono signal (Mid) while the figure-eight rejects the middle and records the sides. Significantly, the figure-eight records a polarity-inverted signal from the right, because all sound arriving from the right hits the back of the left-facing mic.

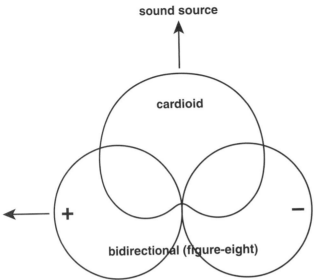

sound source

cardioid

+   **−**

bidirectional (figure-eight)

Figure 12.4 The Mid-Side (M-S) stereo microphone technique places a sideways bidirectional microphone together with a forward-facing cardioid microphone.

Through some clever math, these Mid and Side signals are turned into normal left and right channels. However, if you increase the level of the Mid channel, you narrow the stereo image, and if you increase the level of the Side channel, you widen the stereo image. With a bit of clever bussing, you're going to turn a stereo signal into Mid and Side channels, change their relative levels, and return the signal to stereo. Although this is a less dramatic effect than the polarity-inversion technique you just learned, it is more practical and less problematic when summed to mono.

Mid-Side Theory The key to mid-side processing is that the right side of the stereo image is actually captured in "negative" by the figure-eight mic. Because this mic faces left, everything that arrives from the right is moving the diaphragm from the back, creating a polarity-inverted right signal. Because the cardioid mic captures everything, including the left, right, and middle of the soundstage, deriving stereo left and right channels requires only a bit of arithmetic.

Because the Mid mic captures both sides, you can say mathematically that $Mid = L + R$. Because the figure-eight mic captures a positive left signal and a negative right signal, you can say mathematically that $Side = L - R$. Therefore, $M + S = (L + R) + (L - R) = (L + L) + (R - R)$. The two rights cancel each other, leaving nothing but left (2L, actually, which is why you will lower this signal by 6 dB). Adding the Mid and Side channels thus gives you the stereo left channel. Similarly, M − S = (L + R) − (L − R) = (L − L) + (R + R). (Adding negative R is the same as adding R.) The two lefts cancel each other, leaving nothing but right (2R, same deal). Subtracting Side from Mid thus gives you the stereo right channel. To be more technically accurate, adding a polarity-inverted copy of Side to normal Mid gives you stereo right.

If the math makes you scratch your head, just be sure to get your routing right and you will hear the desired effect. If you want to know more about M-S miking, consult any good recording text, such as *The Recording Engineer's Handbook* by Bobby Owsinski (Course Technology PTR, 2009) or *Professional Microphone Techniques* by David Miles-Huber and Philip Williams (Artistpro, 1999).

M-S Encoding

Your mission is to reverse-engineer a straightforward stereo signal into the Mid and Side signals from which it theoretically could have come. Your tools include a couple of tracks and buses and a Trim plug-in. It's time to put that math in motion.

1. Go to memory location 2, Stereo Width, and listen carefully to the excerpt. Get the sound of the stereo image clearly in your mind. Where are things located? What is the bass arpeggio doing? What's going on with the panning of the lead part? You're going to manipulate the soundstage with M-S processing, so you need to have a good solid grasp of where you started.

2. Assign the output of the stereo audio track to Bus 1-2.

3. Create a stereo aux input, and assign Bus 1-2 as its input.

4. Assign the aux track's output to Bus 3 (see Figure 12.5). The output of this aux track (Bus 3) now sums buses 1 and 2 together—in other words, you have just added the left and right signals of the stereo mix. This is equivalent to the cardioid mic in the M-S configuration, which picks up the left and right of the soundstage equally, so name this aux track Mid.

5. Because you are combining two channels into one, you are in danger of clipping Bus 3 whenever those channels approach full scale. To prevent this from happening, insert a multi-mono Trim plug-in on the last insert of the aux input, and reduce its Gain setting by 6 dB. You may need to hold Ctrl (Cmd) to make a precise adjustment (or simply type the value into the Gain field).

6. Duplicate this aux input by clicking its name and choosing Duplicate from the Track menu.

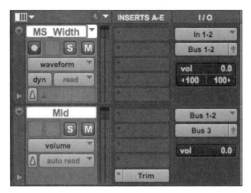

Figure 12.5 The Mid track combines the left and right channels of the original stereo image into a single mono channel.

7. Assign the output of the duplicate to Bus 4.

8. Open the Trim plug-in on the duplicate and click its Master Link button to unlink its left and right channels.

9. Click on the L button and choose Right to display the controls for the right channel, as shown in Figure 12.6.

Figure 12.6 Choosing to display the left or right channel of an unlinked multi-mono plug-in.

10. Click on the Phase Invert button to flip the polarity of the right channel. The output of this aux track (Bus 4) now adds the left signal to a "negative" of the right signal—in other words, you have just subtracted the right signal of the stereo mix from the left. In doing so, you have caused any elements that are common to the left and right channels to cancel themselves, leaving a hole in the center. This is equivalent to the bidirectional mic in the M-S configuration, which ignores the center of the soundstage and picks up the left and (inverted) right. Name this aux track Side.

M-S Decoding

You have successfully derived the Mid and Side signals that would have resulted if you had recorded this performance with an M-S microphone configuration. By changing the balance of the two channels, you can now change the stereo spread of the output.

However, you must decode Mid and Side into traditional left and right before you can hear the results.

1. Create two new stereo aux inputs, and assign Bus 3-4 as their inputs. Each is being fed by both Mid and Side.

2. Assign the output of the first aux to Bus 5, and you are adding Mid and Side together to create the left output channel.

3. Assign the output of the second aux to Bus 6, insert a Trim plug-in, and invert its right channel, and you are subtracting Side from Mid to create the right output channel. (Do not adjust the Gain of the Trim plug-in.)

4. Name these two aux tracks appropriately, and hide them, as you will never adjust them.

5. Create one more stereo aux input, and assign Bus 5-6 as its input. This last aux is the decoded stereo output of the entire M-S matrix, so name it M-S Stereo.

As you listen to this track, change the output levels of the Mid and Side auxes. You should hear the stereo image become wider as you decrease Mid and narrower as you decrease Side. With the two tracks at unity, you are hearing the original mix.

Note: If you increase the gain of either the Mid or Side track beyond 0.0 dB, you may clip Bus 5 or 6 if the source material is very hot. Watch for the clip indicators on the M-S Stereo track—you may find that you can only decrease Mid or Side. Apply make-up gain at the M-S Stereo track if necessary.

Although M-S processing is often applied to complete mixes—during mastering, for example—it can also be applied to any stereo element within a mix. Try the technique on drum overheads or room mics to make the kit sound bigger. Automate the levels of the Mid and Side aux inputs to make this happen only during the drum solo. Spread a stereo-miked acoustic piano a bit wider, or squeeze it into a smaller space. Since the Side component often corresponds to ambience to a large extent (think about where that mic is pointing!), narrowing the core of the piano with M-S processing would still leave some of the room sound spread out. By contrast, simply bringing the left and right pan sliders in would narrow the room along with the core sound.

Another popular M-S variation is to EQ either the Mid or the Side track. Consider the case where you wanted to accentuate the snare in a complete mix. You could simply apply a peak EQ to the entire mix, but that would affect every instrument that has any significant energy at that band. If the snare is panned center, however, EQing the Mid track would bring out the hat while leaving any instruments that are panned left or right alone.

The one down side to M-S processing, especially in a Pro Tools LE system, is that it takes six mono buses (see Figure 12.7). When you only have 32 buses to begin with, this is quite a big hit on your resources. You might need to print some effects returns to free up enough buses to construct the matrix. I'll discuss resource management in more detail in Chapter 14, "Managing Mix Resources."

Figure 12.7 M-S processing in Pro Tools requires six buses.

If you have a decent bidirectional mic available, try making some M-S recordings. You'll end up with two mono channels, and if you feed them to Bus 5 and Bus 6, you can use three aux tracks as you did in this section to decode Mid and Side into stereo left and right.

Note: In a Pro Tools HD system, M-S processing creates some delays between tracks due to processing. Be sure either to use Time Adjuster to compensate or to enable Automatic Delay Compensation. Pro Tools LE and M-Powered compensate for these delays automatically, so if you move a mix back and forth between home and studio you may need to adapt.

Checking Your Mix in Mono

There are two basic mixing functions that the Pro Tools mixer lacks. One, as you have discovered, is a Phase Invert button on each channel. The Phase Invert button is found only on plug-ins, so you must enable at least one plug-in on each channel whose polarity you wish to invert. Because most mixes involve at least one plug-in on each track, this is only a minor inconvenience. The second absent function is a Mono button on the main output. Even inexpensive mixers commonly sport a single button that combines the main left and right outputs so you can easily hear what your mix sounds like in mono. In Pro Tools, this used to take a bit of effort, along with three more of your oh-so-versatile buses. Pro Tools 8 includes a plug-in that simplifies the process, but I'll show you the long way first because it's a good exercise.

Old School Mono

1. Go to memory location 3, Mono Check, and take a quick listen to the excerpt. Sure, it sounds fine in stereo, but how will it sound when an FM broadcast sums it to mono?

2. To find out, start by creating one mono aux input, one stereo aux input, and one mono master fader. Name them Mono Mix, Stereo Mix, and Mono Bus, respectively.

3. Assign any unused mono bus to the input of the mono aux, and assign the mono master fader to the same bus.

4. Assign any unused stereo bus to the input of the stereo aux, and be sure both auxes are assigned to the main stereo output (see Figure 12.8).

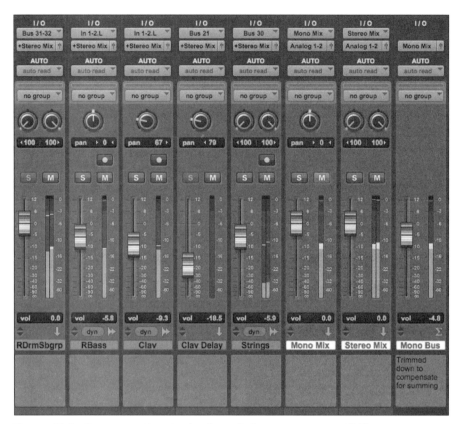

Figure 12.8 Proper routing to check a mix for mono compatibility.

5. Right-click on the input of each aux and rename the buses Mono Mix and Stereo Mix.

6. Although I have simplified things for this example, the next step takes some effort and care on a complex mix. You need to reassign the outputs of all audio, aux, and instrument tracks that are currently assigned to your main stereo outputs to the Stereo Mix bus. This simply routes them through the Stereo Mix aux so you can compare it to the mono mix. You'd like to use Alt (Opt) to apply this assignment to all tracks at once, but then you'd mess up any subgroups you've set up. Instead, you need to select groups of tracks and make efficient use of Shift+Alt (Shift+Opt) to reassign the outputs of all selected tracks.

7. After you have reassigned all relevant tracks to the Stereo Mix bus, repeat the process to make an additional output assignment to the Mono Mix bus. Remember that multiple output assignments are made by holding the Start (Ctrl) key while choosing the new output. Yes, you can Shift+Start+Alt-click

(Shift+Ctrl+Opt-click) to make an additional output assignment to all selected tracks. (Remembering what the various modifier keys do for you is an important step in becoming a Pro Tools power user!)

8. Press Mute on the Mono Mix track, and begin playback. What you hear through the Stereo Mix track should be identical to what you originally heard when the mix was routed directly to the main output. If it sounds different, review your output assignments to find what you missed. Mute the Stereo Mix track and un-mute the Mono Mix track. You are now hearing the left and right channels summed together as they would be in a mis-wired stereo system or a weak FM signal.

Note: Most MP3 encoders offer the option to sum the channels to mono. Doing so allows the codec to retain better frequency response at a given bit rate, offering you the choice of sacrificing stereo image for frequency response. If your mix dies in mono, this is not a useful option.

The mono mix most likely sounds noticeably louder than the stereo mix due to the summing. Trim the volume of the Mono Bus master fader down by 3 to 6 dB. This compensates for the volume boost. Some mixes will require a bit more or less volume reduction, but you should never have to trim more than 6 dB.

New School Mono

One of the interesting new AIR plug-ins included with all versions of Pro Tools 8 is the AIR Stereo Width processor (see Figure 12.9). Its intended purpose is to manipulate the stereo width of a track, subgroup, or mix as you've been doing throughout this chapter. You should go back to the first two memory locations and insert it as an insert effect on the Arpeggio and MS_Width tracks and compare its sound to what you've created already. In this case, however, you're going to set its width to zero and use it to create a mono version of the mix.

1. Use Revert to Saved to restore the session to its original state.

2. Go to memory location 3, Mono Check.

3. Create a stereo master fader assigned to the main stereo output.

4. Insert the AIR Stereo Width plug-in on the last insert of the master fader.

5. Set the plug-in's Width control to 0%. This effectively sums the mix to mono.

6. Use the plug-in's Bypass button to switch between mono and stereo.

Figure 12.9 The AIR Stereo Width plug-in can be used to widen or narrow the image of a track.

As you switch between the mono and stereo mixes, listen for any elements that get significantly stronger or weaker. What's up with those strings, anyway? Take a look at the mix, and you'll see that this is an example of the ultra-wide stereo you created earlier in this chapter. By itself, this effect would cancel completely in mono, but I used it after a short delay to keep it from disappearing. It was a calculated risk, and checking the mix in mono this way allows you to decide whether the benefit (how it sounds in stereo) outweighs the cost (how it sounds in mono).

Other effects may clash in mono. Short delays may simply sound "phasey" in mono. Phase-dependent effects such as chorus and flange may be more pronounced in mono. When you hear something that bothers you, tweak the effect while monitoring in mono to achieve the best of both worlds.

Once again, you've managed to apply some basic tools in creative ways to come up with interesting sounds. I hope you are seeing that the real "magic" in mixing is not a single button or trick but rather the imaginative application of some simple concepts. Every mix engineer knows what the buttons and knobs do—to be an outstanding mixer you need to integrate your ears, your knowledge, and your imagination.

13 External Effects

odern computers are insanely powerful, and the resources available for mixing within the computer seem virtually limitless. Nevertheless, there are times when you need to incorporate an outboard processor. Maybe you're fortunate enough to have access to a classic hardware compressor, or maybe you've got this sound in your head that only your favorite nasty-but-unique stomp box can provide. Either way, you need to get a signal out of Pro Tools, through that external processor, and back into Pro Tools.

If you've got a multichannel audio interface, such as the Digi 003, Mbox 2 Pro, or M-Audio ProFire 2626, you've got plenty of connections to accomplish this. If your interface provides only stereo output, like an Mbox 2 Mini, the process requires a bit more imagination and dedication, but it can be done. However, leaving the computer introduces a delay in the signal that must be dealt with. It may seem a bit daunting at first glance, but once you've got the hang of it you'll be able to integrate any external device you choose.

Making Connections

For this chapter, I assume you have some external effects processor through which you can run a signal from Pro Tools. Before making connections, you should have your gear nearby and powered up. Turn your monitors down so you don't abuse them or your ears with any abrupt pops or other ugly surprises when you plug and unplug cables.

Connect an audio cable with appropriate connectors (RCA, TRS, and so on) from an output of your audio interface to the input of the external device, and connect another cable from the device's output to an input on your audio interface. If you're going to use the device on a track insert, it's essential that you use the same-numbered output and input on your audio interface (for example, Output 3 and Input 3). If you're going to return the device on an aux input, as in traditional time-based effects routing, this is not necessary. If you don't have a hardware processor available right now, you can simply connect an appropriate cable directly from Output x to Input x and follow along.

> **Note:** It's important to be sure that the connected devices are using the same levels and/or impedances. Although complete coverage of level- and imped-ance-matching is beyond the scope of this book, most of what you need to know can be found in your device manuals. If the sound is distorted or unexpect-edly quiet, you probably have a mismatch. Depending on the circumstances, a direct box (DI), preamp, or impedance-matching transformer may be required. Most Pro Tools and M-Powered interfaces offer line-level connections.

Insert Effects

For a hardware compressor, EQ, or distortion effect, you would ordinarily insert the effect directly on the track to be processed, just as you did with dynamic plug-ins. There is then an additional procedure to compensate for the latency.

1. Open the session Chapter 13.ptf and go to memory location 1, Making Connections.

2. Listen to the sound of the unprocessed drum loop.

3. To apply the outboard effect, click on any insert of the audio track and choose the appropriate I/O pair (see Figure 13.1). It should be called Insert *x*, although this can be changed in your I/O settings.

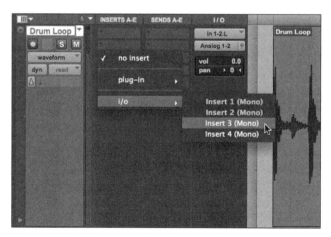

Figure 13.1 Choosing a hardware path as an insert.

4. Play the drum loop and adjust your hardware processor as desired. If you have made the correct connections, the entire drum loop signal is passing through the outboard box.

5.   When you have the external device's settings the way you want them, note them in the loop track's Comments field for future reference.

6.   If the processor supports it, you could save the settings as a MIDI SysEx dump in a Pro Tools MIDI track. Playing back the SysEx would then reset the processor to the current settings.

Note: If your external processor has digital I/O, such as S/PDIF or ADAT Optical, it's usually better to use this connection than it is to use an analog connection. Digital connections don't require any D/A or A/D conversions, and there is no problem with line noise, ground loops, or signal loss. It's imperative, however, that either Pro Tools or the device clocks to its external input so the two devices share the same clock. Set the device's clock to External or go into Pro Tools' Hardware Setup and set Clock Source to the appropriate digital input.

Latency Compensation

Although it may not be noticeable right now (because there are no other parts playing), the drum loop is now playing back at least slightly later than it did when it was not being processed. This is because Pro Tools LE, like all DAWs that depend on the computer's CPU for mixing, must pass the signal through a special RAM buffer as it leaves the computer to be processed and again as it re-enters the computer. In Pro Tools, this is called the *hardware buffer*, and its size is set in the Playback Engine dialog box (see Figure 13.2), accessible via the Setup menu.

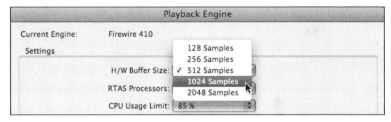

Figure 13.2   The hardware (H/W) buffer size is set in the Playback Engine dialog box.

To see the effect of this delay on the signal, do the following:

1.   Create a new mono audio track named Processed Loop.

2.   Set the input of the new audio track to a mono bus, and set the output of the drum loop track to the same bus.

3.   Arm the new audio track and record just a second or two of the processed loop.

Zoom way in on the drum loop and compare it to the processed loop. You will find that the first note of the processed loop happens many samples later than the first note of the original loop, as shown in Figure 13.3. If you select precisely from the original first note to the processed first note, you will have measured the exact round-trip delay of the processed signal. If you compare this to your hardware buffer size, you will find that the delay is equal to twice the buffer plus a few dozen samples for D/A and A/D conversion. (If you used a digital connection to your processor, the delay will be only a few samples larger than twice the buffer, because conversion isn't required.)

Figure 13.3   Measuring the delay of a hardware insert.

To compensate for the delay, all you need to do is shift the original audio earlier in the track by the same amount. However, you're going to do this on a copy of the original so you can always go back to the original if you decide to take a different approach.

1.   Click the loop track's Playlist selector (the small drop-down arrow to the right of the track name, as shown in Figure 13.4).

2.   In the menu that appears, click Duplicate to create a copy of the track's edit playlist.

Figure 13.4   Create a duplicate edit playlist.

3.   In the ensuing dialog box, name the track Shifted Loop.

Note: Pro Tools allows each audio and MIDI track to have multiple *edit playlists*. Edit playlists hold alternate versions of the audio (or MIDI) regions in a track, such as "clean" and "dirty" edits of a vocal track. All of a track's mix parameters (volume, pan, and so on) remain the same for all edit playlists.

---

4.   Triple-click with the Selector tool anywhere in the track to select all regions in the track.

5.   From the Edit menu, choose Shift.

6.   In the Shift dialog box, click the Earlier button and enter the appropriate number in the Samples field. This will cause the regions in the Shifted Loop playlist to move earlier by the amount you previously measured for the processing delay. By the time they are delayed by processing on their way to and from the external device, they will end up playing back at their original time.

7.   Click OK to close the dialog box. The processed track will now play back perfectly in time. Add a note about this in the track's Comments field for future reference.

Note: If you have the available inputs and outputs, you may choose to leave the outboard processor connected "live" like this, processing the track(s) in real time as you mix. Pro Tools allows such effects to be included when bouncing to disk. It may be wise, however, to record the processed track to make the effect permanent in case the processor is not available at mixdown. This procedure is outlined in Chapter 14, "Managing Mix Resources," in the section called "Printing Effects."

This same technique could be used to *re-amp* a guitar track. If you don't like the sound of a guitar part, you can run the guitar's direct signal out to a different amp and record the new sound long after the guitarist has left the building. Engineers often record both the amplified guitar and a direct signal from the guitar itself during tracking precisely for this purpose. The technique is the same as the one described previously, but you must be sure to match the signal going out of Pro Tools to the signal the guitar amp wants to see. Various "re-amping" gizmos are available to accomplish this.

Pro Tools does not give any indicator of the signal level leaving or returning to a hardware insert, so you could easily overdrive the processor or clip the Pro Tools input. However, if the audio region does not clip to begin with and no insert prior to the hardware insert clips, the signal going to the hardware processor will not be clipped. Use your ears and your common sense to keep levels sufficiently hot without distorting.

Send/Return Effects

If you choose to use a time-based hardware processor, you can run signal from individual tracks via hardware sends and return the signal from the processor on an aux input. In this case, the numbers of the send and return do not have to match. However, it's good practice to match the numbers for clarity, anyway.

1. Create a send from each track to which you want to add the time-based effect. Assign it to the output where the hardware processor is connected.

    Note: You can use either a mono or stereo send. It is in fact quite common to send mono signal into a reverb and return a stereo signal from the reverb. (Most hardware reverbs with stereo inputs will nevertheless accept a mono signal on the left input.) If you do so, however, you will lose the ability to pan the sends as they hit the reverb processor.

    ---

2. Adjust the send level from each track as desired. If you created stereo sends, remember that you can use Follow Main Pan (FMP) to apply the tracks' pan settings to the sends.

3. Create an aux track and assign as its input the interface connections to which you returned the signal from the processor. Solo-safe the aux.

4. Adjust the aux track's level to control the "wet" mix.

5. Watch the meter view on one of the sends to see if the sends' output is clipping. Create a master fader for that output to trim the level if it clips (see Figure 13.5).

Figure 13.5 Send/return routing for a hardware reverb.

6. Watch the external processor's meters (if it has any) to be sure it's not clipping, either.

7. Watch the aux track's meters with Pre-Fader Metering enabled to be sure the signal returning from the processor does not clip.

Delay compensation is easier to manage with send/return processing, as the delay can be considered part of the reverb's pre-delay or incorporated by ear as part of the overall delay time. As you did with time-based plug-ins, it's important to set the hardware processor's mix to 100 percent wet.

You can leave the processor "live" or record it to a track using the procedure in the next chapter. If you print it, you will be printing the aux track—the effects return—only. Keep in mind that any change you then make to the "dry" tracks may create a discrepancy with that track's wet signal.

14 Managing Mix Resources

N°o matter how much money you spend on a new CPU, lots of RAM, speedy hard drives, and so forth, you will someday create such a complex mix that you max out your system resources. Pro Tools will simply stop and display an error message that says you're running out of steam (see Figure 14.1). Don't fret—everyone must deal with this sooner or later.

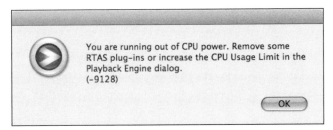

You are running out of CPU power. Remove some RTAS plug-ins or increase the CPU Usage Limit in the Playback Engine dialog.
(-9128)

OK

Figure 14.1 Sooner or later, you'll make Pro Tools cry "Uncle!"

You've spent 13 chapters learning new ways to spend your system resources, and in this final chapter you'll learn how to monitor, manage, and conserve those resources. You'll also learn a few tricks for staying productive when you've hit the wall.

System Settings

There are a handful of Pro Tools settings you can use to optimize your system's performance for mixing. I assume that you have already read the *Getting Started* guide that came with Pro Tools. This guide includes a variety of specific recommendations for optimizing your Mac or PC to run Pro Tools, from disabling energy saving features to enabling DMA on your PC's hard drives. If you have not already followed the advice contained in the *Getting Started* guide, please stop reading right now, break out the guide, and do everything it recommends. Pay special attention to ensuring that no other applications, virus checkers, or other complex background operations are keeping your computer from giving its full attention to Pro Tools.

Beyond what's covered in the *Getting Started* guide, doing the following will help give your computer sufficient processing time for complex mixing and reserve all available

CPU resources for the Pro Tools mixer. Note that these recommendations are valid for LE and M-Powered systems, and some would be different for HD systems.

1. Open the Setup menu and choose Playback Engine to open the Playback Engine dialog box.

2. Set the H/W Buffer Size setting to the highest value to maximize the hardware buffer. (Note that this will directly affect the delay involved in any outboard processing, so you may need to revisit the procedure called "Latency Compensation" from Chapter 13, "External Effects," to adjust your delay compensation on any such affected tracks.)

Note: Setting the buffer to its highest value would create great problems if you were to record any new tracks, as the monitoring latency would be quite high. (Of course, there are ways to deal with this, such as the zero-latency monitoring on an Mbox 2.) When you are mixing, however, signal flows only out of the computer, not through it, so latency is ordinarily not an issue (with the previously mentioned exception of external effects). If you are using a 003, CommandI8, or other control surface, you may find the controls to be a bit sluggish because of the large buffer. If this is problematic, lower the buffer size until you are done writing automation.

---

3. While you have the Playback Engine dialog box open, set the number of RTAS processors to the total number of CPUs and CPU cores in your system. For example, if you have a dual-processor system, set the RTAS Processors setting to 2. If you have a "quad-core" system with two dual-core processors, set this value to 4. (Ordinarily, the only time you would want to keep a processor from being used by Pro Tools is when you are making very heavy use of a ReWire application, such as Propellerhead's Reason or Ableton Live.)

4. Adjust the CPU Usage Limit setting to the highest value available. On a single-processor system, this will be 85% (see Figure 14.2), but on a multi-processor system it may go even higher.

5. Be sure that Ignore Errors During Playback/Record is *not* checked. During tracking and editing, this option might buy you a few extra CPU cycles, but mixing is your last chance to listen critically to your track. If you hear glitches that might be due to clipping or bad editing, you want to fix them, not ignore them!

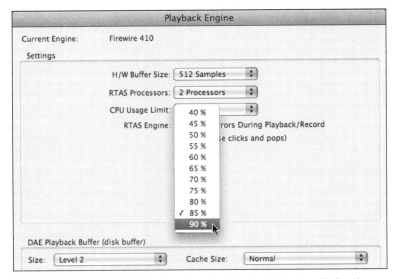

Figure 14.2 Adjust the options in the Playback Engine dialog box.

6.   Changing the DAE Playback Buffer value will not affect available mix resources. Leave this at the default setting of Level 2 unless you encounter a specific error message telling you otherwise. You can also ignore the Plug-In Streaming Buffer unless you are using a sampler plug-in such as Structure.

7.   Close the Playback Engine dialog box.

8.   Under the Options menu, you will find the Edit Window Scrolling options in a sub-menu (see Figure 14.3). During editing, it is common to use Page scroll, which shows the subsequent screen-full of your session's content each time the playback cursor runs off the right edge of the screen. This, of course, eats up CPU cycles while your system redraws the screen each time. For this reason, during mixing, you might choose the After Playback option or even No Scrolling to give your processor one less thing to worry about.

One other minor setting in the Preferences dialog box may help you squeeze out a last drop or two of CPU juice, at a price. It is Show Meters in Sends View, found in the Display tab. The two states of this option are shown in Figure 14.4. Although disabling this option certainly reduces the amount of graphic activity necessary, if you have enabled display for the controls of an individual send (for example, Send A), it also prevents you from seeing any level problems at your sends, so use this option with caution.

Figure 14.3 Set Scrolling options.

Figure 14.4 In Sends view, the onscreen meters (left) can be disabled (right) to minimize screen redraws.

AudioSuite Plug-Ins

It wasn't so long ago that computers weren't nearly fast enough to process complex effects such as reverb in real time. To apply reverb, one had to select an audio file and apply a *file-based* effect. This meant that a new file would be created, representing the sound of the original file plus reverberation. It was not uncommon to spend half an hour waiting for reverb to be applied to a three-minute vocal track.

File-based processors are still within Pro Tools in the form of AudioSuite plug-ins. For example, because certain effects, such as reversing an audio clip, are impossible to process in real time, there are AudioSuite plug-ins such as Reverse. There are also Audio-Suite versions of virtually all your real-time plug-ins (other than instruments and the AIR plug-ins) to help you manage your resources.

1. Open the session Chapter 14.ptf and go to memory location 1, AudioSuite.

2. Listen to the excerpt with the real-time Eleven Free, then bypass the Eleven Free by Ctrl-clicking (Cmd-clicking) on its insert, and listen to it dry.

3. As you did in Chapter 13, click the EPiano track's Playlist selector (see Figure 14.5) and create a duplicate edit playlist so you can always go back to the original version.

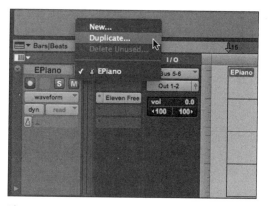

Figure 14.5 Creating a duplicate edit playlist.

4. Select the EPiano region and then extend the selection by two seconds so the reverb tail will not be cut off.

5. From the AudioSuite, Harmonic menu, choose Eleven Free.

6. Click the real-time Eleven Free's insert so you can see the real-time and AudioSuite versions of Eleven Free side by side.

7. From the real-time Eleven Free's Librarian menu, choose Copy Settings (see Figure 14.6).

8. From the AudioSuite Eleven Free's Librarian menu, choose Paste Settings. Note that all the controls on the AudioSuite plug-in now match the corresponding controls on the real-time plug-in.

9. Set the AudioSuite plug-in's parameters as shown in Figure 14.7:
    - Selection Reference: Playlist
    - Use in Playlist: on (selected)
    - File Mode: Create Continuous File
    - Process Mode: Entire Selection

Figure 14.6 Copy settings from a real-time plug-in.

Figure 14.7 The proper AudioSuite settings to replace the dry region with the processed region.

10. Click Process. The plug-in will process the audio region and replace it with a new region that includes the reverb effect.

11. Close the AudioSuite plug-in window.

12. The real-time Eleven Free is no longer needed, so Ctrl+Start-click (Cmd+Ctrl-click) its insert to make it inactive. Making the plug-in inactive removes it from the CPU's to-do list, so it no longer eats up processor cycles. However, it also retains all the plug-in's settings so you could come back to it later, tweak the sound a bit, and re-print the effect.

> **Note:** If you look at your System Usage window and observe the CPU gauge before and after the preceding section, you will notice that some of the CPU's resources have been freed up. Many of Pro Tools' included plug-ins don't use nearly enough system resources to show a dramatic change when you print an effect and make the plug-in inactive as you have just done. Rest assured, however, that there are plenty of third-party plug-ins that would demonstrate a big difference. The worst CPU hogs are things like guitar amp simulators (such as Eleven Free) and convolution reverbs.

Printing Effects and Submixes

This last technique for recovering system resources draws heavily on earlier topics. You will record one or more tracks *with their effects* to new audio tracks and then make the source plug-ins and tracks inactive in order to free up voices and CPU resources. Pro Tools LE provides for as many as 128 audio tracks, but only 48 of them can be active at once. Each active stereo audio track counts as two tracks, so if all of your tracks were stereo you could have only 24 of them active at once.

An inactive audio track retains all its original settings, including input and output assignments, plug-in assignments, plug-in settings, automation, audio regions and edits, and so forth. It is removed from the playback queue, so you will not hear it at all. It does not take up any of your system's disk or processor resources.

Inactive tracks make it very practical to move a session back and forth between a Pro Tools LE system and a Pro Tools HD system. You might choose to start a session in a big studio, tracking live drums, guitars, bass, keyboards, vocals, and horns to a Pro Tools HD system. You could easily end up with many more than 48 audio tracks. You could then move the session to a smaller, less-expensive room equipped with Pro Tools LE and do your edits and overdubs without sweating the cost so much. When you open the session, the first 48 tracks would be active, and the rest would be inactive. You can choose which 48 tracks are active by selecting tracks and making them active or inactive from the Track menu (see Figure 14.8) or by right-clicking on a selected track's name.

> **Note:** Pro Tools HD allows up to 256 audio tracks, so it's possible to create an HD session that can't be opened properly in LE. If your HD session exceeds 128 audio tracks, you must break the session up into two smaller sessions to work on it in LE without losing tracks.

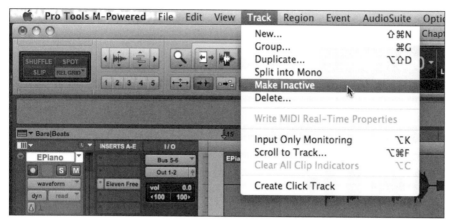

Figure 14.8 Making a track inactive.

Printing Effects

If, as with the AIR plug-ins, a processor-hogging plug-in has no AudioSuite equivalent, or if the effect is being automated, you can simply record the processed track to a new audio track in real time. This technique follows the same procedure as printing synthesizer tracks in Chapter 8, "Bouncing Your Mix."

1. Go to memory location 2, Printing Effects. This drum loop is being processed by several plug-ins, one of which (the EQ) is being automated. By printing the loop to a new audio track, you can achieve exactly the same sound with much less effort on the part of your CPU.

2. Select the Loop track and create a new stereo audio track. Selecting the track forces Pro Tools to create the new track immediately below the selected track.

3. Name the new track Loop FX.

4. Assign the output of the Loop track and the input of the Loop FX track to an available stereo bus (see Figure 14.9).

5. With the Selector, triple-click in the Loop track to select all regions in the track. In this case, that's only one region, but you want to be sure you print the entire contents of the track. If the source track were to include any reverb or delay plug-ins, you would want to extend the selection to be sure the effect's decay didn't get cut off, just as you did in the previous section on AudioSuite processing.

Next, you're going to set the Loop track's volume to unity (0.0 dB) so it records at full volume to the Loop FX track. If you've been paying close attention throughout the preceding chapters, you can do these three steps with one click each by using modifier keys. I'll list them in a note at the end of this section.

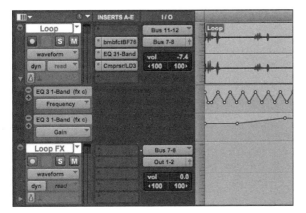

Figure 14.9 The original track is bused to the new track, ready to be printed.

6.   Note the Loop track's volume, and then set it to 0.0.

7.   Display the Loop track's Volume playlist.

8.   Suspend Volume automation on the Loop track.

9.   Now set the Loop FX track's volume to what the Loop track had been so it will play back at the original volume.

10.   Record-arm the FX track and press 3 on the numeric keypad to start recording.

11.   When recording is done, make the Loop track inactive and hide it from the track name right-click menu.

Your session sounds the same as it did before, but your CPU has less on its mind. If you decide later that the loop doesn't sound quite right, you can always make the original Loop track active again, tweak its effects or automation, and re-print it to the FX track. If you had several CPU-intensive tracks, you could print them simultaneously, each to its own audio track.

Note: Those three clicks are as follows, in order:

■   Alt-click (Opt-click) on a parameter to set it to nominal (in this case unity).

■   Ctrl+Start-click (Cmd+Ctrl-click) on a parameter's control to display its playlist.

■   Ctrl-click (Cmd-click) on the track view selector to suspend automation for the displayed parameter.

How many did you remember?

Printing Submixes

To both liberate CPU cycles and increase effective track count, you can record multiple tracks to a single track and then make the original tracks inactive. This technique is identical to the process of printing submixes in Chapter 10, "Stems and Submixes." Our focus in that chapter was organization and flexibility, but the same procedure can also help you manage your resources.

The classic scenario is taking a dozen drum tracks and bouncing them through a stereo bus to a stereo audio track. The stereo audio track incorporates all the individual and group EQ and compression from the drum tracks. If you have applied any short delays to individual parts, you could include those delay auxes in the submix as well. Once you have recorded the submix, make the drum tracks (including delay auxes if you printed them) inactive.

A quick way to make several tracks inactive is to select the tracks in the Mix view and Shift+Alt+Ctrl+Start-click (Shift+Opt+Cmd+Ctrl-click) the track type icon of a selected track (see Figure 14.10). This is the four-modifier shortcut to which I referred

Figure 14.10   Shift+Alt+Ctrl+Start-clicking (Shift+Opt+Cmd+Ctrl-clicking) on the track type icon of a selected track makes all selected active tracks (left) inactive. The same procedure makes all selected inactive tracks (right) active.

back in Chapter 6, "Advanced Signal Flow." Ctrl+Start-clicking (Cmd+Ctrl-clicking) a track type icon makes a track inactive, and adding the Shift+Alt (Shift+Opt) modifier keys applies an action to all currently selected tracks. Together they make all selected tracks inactive.

Because you have reduced 12 audio tracks to one stereo track, you now have the ability to create 10 new audio tracks for overdubbing background vocals, horns, strings, or whatever suits your fancy. If you are working on a high-track-count session that originated on a Pro Tools HD system, you can now select any 10 inactive tracks and Shift+Alt+Ctrl+Start-click (Shift+Opt+Cmd+Ctrl-click) any one of their track type icons to make them active so you can edit and mix them. Working this way, submixing and selectively making tracks active, you can get an enormous amount of work done on a Pro Tools LE system even though you can't play back the entire session at once. For reasons of creativity, convenience, and cost, this is a valuable technique to know.

Everyone hits the performance "wall" eventually—it's part of the creative urge always to want more. If you understand your system's limitations and know how to deal with them or work around them, you can keep the creativity flowing. Never let an over-worked CPU stand between you and your ideal mix!

Epilogue—Final Mix

Some 240 pages ago, we set out together to dig more deeply into the craft of mixing in Pro Tools. Using the sample sessions on the CD-ROM, you have reshaped sounds with EQ, massaged them with compression, given them space and life with time-based effects, and decorated them with special effects. You have organized them, balanced them, rearranged them on the virtual stage, and animated them with mix automation. Finally, you took it all to the next level by messing with timbre, stereo image, and other advanced techniques.

You now have a solid understanding of the Pro Tools mix environment. Honestly, there's not a whole lot more to know about it from a technical level, even if you were to read the manual from cover to cover. However, there's always more to know about mixing. Every engineer listens constantly to new (and old!) music to figure out how great sounds are created. With the fundamental tools under your belt, you will find yourself recognizing mix techniques in your favorite recordings. Try re-creating them; the worst that can happen is that you fail to re-create the sound perfectly but end up creating some different sound instead. Keep listening, keep using your imagination, and keep experimenting.

I hope these pages have helped you gain a deeper understanding of mixing in Pro Tools. I doubt I have answered all your questions. In fact, I hope you're now inspired to ask some questions that hadn't occurred to you previously! That's the nature of any creative endeavor. On the path to enlightenment, as you approach each destination, you become aware of how many more destinations are available to you. May all your creative journeys be filled with inspiration!

Index